T0369451

THE PRE-ATOMIC AGE

Leslie Eugene Fooks

Order this book online at www.trafford.com
or email orders@trafford.com

Most Trafford titles are also available at major online book retailers.

Print information available on the last page.

ISBN: 978-1-4120-9153-4 (sc)

Trafford rev. 07/06/2018

www.trafford.com
North America & international
toll-free: 1 888 232 4444 (USA & Canada)
fax: 812 355 4082

CONTENTS

TO MY PARENTS,
Mack & Katy Fooks,
Who raised five sons that
served their country in air battles over
Europe, in sea battles in the South Pacific
and in the Korean conflict.

Mack and Katy Fooks

Family reunion after World War II

FORWARD

This is the story of the first twenty-four years of my life. The related events always present a problem. How accurate are the stories that occurred 60, 70 and 80 year ago? I cannot declare 100% accuracy in every detail. I can, however, say definitely that the stories themselves are correct. Some of the details in the events are not as accurate as when they first took place, and the wording is not as pure in the dialogues as when first spoken.

When my two older sisters, Etta and Jessie, and I have visited the many times through the years, we spent much of the time rehashing and rehashing the events of our childhood. Mostly we agreed. When we disagreed, I had to rely on my own recollection, and information received from old timers and stories handed down to their children and grandchildren. I've made numerous returns to the valley and spent hours talking with the natives.

Newspaper accounts and other documents, about the 1920s and 1930s, have been available for my perusal.

As for dialogue, which is not completely accurate as worded. In my multiple visits to the valley, and when I lay in bed at night, I have visualized these dear people, their habitat and mannerisms recalling their speech.

In Ponca City, Oklahoma, I've recalled with my dear friend Roy Essary and my cousin Chloe the times of our high school years.

My wife, Dorothy, and I have often talked about our years together.

Records left behind in the annals of the Army Air Corps speak for themselves. What is missing in the Army records, I've talked over with former Sgt Howard Dull and former Lt. Frank Hoch, two men who were very close to me in THE PRE-ATOMIC AGE.

If some friends are surprised or embarrassed by some of the language I used in a few places in the book, please try to understand. I have not used such language in over half a century. I put the language in the book because I wished to draw a contrast between then and now. I also wished to make my story as truthful and authentic as possible.

Leslie Eugene Fooks

PREFACE

After visiting with many "baby boomers" and their children and grandchildren, I learned they know and understand very little about how different life was in America during the 1920s, 1930s and the war years of the 1940s...

Most of us lived on farms without indoor plumbing or air conditioning. The average income for a family was only a few hundred dollars a year. There were only a few paved roads. Automobiles rattled and often had trouble while traveling.

Some families had radios that produced about as much static as talk or music. Television was non-existent. Buggies were often seen on the roads. We experienced the Stock Market crash in 1929, closing of banks in 1933, the Great Depression across the land and Dust Bowl in the prairie states.

Many of us went to one room schools in the country. After school, we walked home, milked the cows by hand, slopped the hogs, fed the horses and gathered the eggs. Sometime we didn't start to school until after Thanksgiving for we helped gather the crop. Most of us had one change of good clothes we wore to church on Sunday. The rest of the time we donned patched clothes and went barefoot. We made our own toys and planned the games we played.

The generation, that grew up during this period, fought battles on land, sea and in the air in World War II. We defeated two determined enemies: one in Europe and another in Asia and the South Pacific Good American citizens, not on the battle fields, were diligently working in factories on the home front making weapons for servicemen to use in combat.

This was the most devastating and most widespread war the world has ever known. After the war, those of us still alive returned home and built an economy that gave citizens the conveniences and the luxuries we have today.

This story, **THE PRE-ATOMIC AGE,** is the story of my life from the time I was born in 1921 to the detonation of the first atomic bomb in the desert of New Mexico on the White Sands Missile Range, July 16, 1945.

My story is unique in many ways. But every American that grew up during The Pre-Atomic Age has a unique story to tell. Most of their interesting stories are yet to be written.

Leslie Eugene Fooks

ACKNOWLEDGMENTS

Since I first made my appearance on planet Earth in 1921, good, honorable citizens in New Mexico, Arkansas, Oklahoma, Kansas and Texas have helped me grow physically, mentally and spiritually They have been my parents, brothers and sisters, daughters, grandchildren, school teachers, Sunday School teachers, Christian ministers, friends in the Army Air Force, comrades in the American Legion, the Veteran of Foreign Wars, lawyers, judges, reporters, publishers, writers, politicians, farmers, craftsmen, aunts and cousins, many good friends and slight acquaintances. All together, they do not equal the providential care, protection and counsel received from the Godhead.

I must mention two more friends who wrote in letters such nice things about the book. My dear friend, Larry E. Henderson, retired Superintendent of Guadalupe Mountains National Park and ex-City Councilman wrote: "Leslie Eugene Fooks, (Gene to most of us) has taken us on a journey through his life experiences, in times that would be difficult for most of us to imagine today. Through his recollection, I was able to vicariously experience the harshness, deprivation, love and pain of a family growing up in eastern New Mexico during the Dust Bowl times, while at the same time enjoying the natural beauty, the subtle interaction between the land, man and the wildlife. He grew with the spiritual enhancements that accompanied this.

"From the harsh dry lands and poverty of his boyhood, though the challenges of growing up, and the lucid, detailed accounts of his Army Air Corps training and flying a B-17 in WW II, we are led by word picture and personal experience down the path from boyhood to manhood by the author. Gene has given us a chance to look into the love, fear, thoughts and life-changing experiences that made him the man he is today.

"This interesting, sensitive and often gripping account will serve as painful reminiscence to some and a window opening on a past that many did not have to endure.

"Hats off to author, Gene Fooks, for his unvarnished look at growing up in "The Pre-Atomic Age.""

John Clay, a writer and poet in his own right, is another good friend who read the manuscript and wrote: "Gene Fooks tells a remarkable story of a barefoot boy dodging rattlesnakes on a hardscrabble New Mexico farm to flying combat missions through the skies of Europe, a tense escape from captivity and a challenging return to a new age.

"This page-turner of two decades of a life in another, different America, is a must-read, for those under sixty, to understand and appreciate the nation we live in today."

In addition to the above, I wish to mention specifically dear friends who have labored over the first drafts of a poorly written manuscript and dared to write letters giving their encouraging critiques of my writing. Other friends have inspired me, in so many different ways, to continue writing.

Jerry Remler and Helen Rowen have honored me with a luncheon each year when each of us have a birthday. These are times of good conversation and laughter. The visits with these ladies have inspired me onward.

Dorothy Orrell and the Wordsmith group have given me a boost through the years.

Commander Earl Diggs and the comrades of the VFW, Post 3277 gave me encouragement that I appreciate.

Dr. Charles Beeson, and his wife Jeanne, was a course of delight and joy.

Leland Leak and his wife, Ann, with hearts as big as Eddy County, have always been near by to spur me on. Thanks, you big tough guy with the tender soul of a child.

Fay Gibson has always cordially invited me into her home when I knock. We have had many enjoyable visits. Fay is 96.

Clarence and Carolyn Olson have been my next-door neighbors for 35 years. Few men have had better neighbors. Ollie and I have solved the world's problems while chatting over the fence.

Rudy Matney read a part of the first draft of the book. I was encouraged by the nice things she said.

I always wondered where my daughter, Jackie, got her intelligence and varied abilities. It had to be from her mother. I've tried in vain to equal her. Always fell short.

My daughter, Kathy, who is an excellent writer, read the first draft at night after working all day in public. Her editing and comments were most helpful.

Talks, about the book, with Don Kidd, Bank President and former State Senator, have been very enlightening.

I appreciate Dr. Kate Asbill taking the time from her busy schedule to read the manuscript. The Sunday lunch with her and her husband, State Senator Vernon Asbill was most delightful.

My good friend, Manny Anaya, City Councilman, has been a constant sourse of encouragement through the years.

I think I shall forever remember the intelligent, entertaining, lovably guys I've eaten lunch with on Thursday for the past several years. Thanks boys (You were boys 30 or 40 years ago) for your friendship, and for letting me win so many arguments.

The Fellowship of Believers group meets on Sunday afternoons to learn from one another, encourage each other in spiritual growth and study the Scriptures together. This has been an uplifting experience.

I would be remiss if I failed to mention my friend Lewis Diggs who has been so diligent to come by and help me with my computer that I know so little about. I'm grateful also to Frank Nymeyer, instructor at NMSU-Carlsbad, for helping me with the intimidating contraption.

The good works of guys and gals in the Lions Club have inspired me. I even slipped in the back door, and was president one year.

In any list, somebody has to be last - but never least by any means. This time, it happened to be my long-time friend, Dr. Bill Harris. Dr. Bill was born just a hoop & a holler from where I was born, in the same year. He always takes time, whatever he is doing, to chat and say, "Good job." The doctor is an honest man, but I sometime wonder, *Is he kidding me?*

I am very grateful to each and every one of you. May our sovereign God continue to bless you all.

Leslie Eugene Fooks

VISITING THE PRE-ATOMIC AGE

I'm tethered to the dry, deserted valley by an invisible tough, rubbery band that can stretch just so far in distance and time. After awhile, I feel myself pulled by the strong elastic force of this umbilical cord from which I have never been severed completely. The sinewy band stretched to its limit, draws me irresistibly back to the land of my childhood.

In late spring, while it was still cool and the morning sun was advancing slowly toward its zenith, I left my home in Carlsbad, New Mexico and traveled seventy miles eastward on four-lane US Highway 62/180. Within an hour I rolled into Hobbs, one of several 'Oil Capitals.' Then I turned north toward Lovington about twenty miles away. At this county seat of Lea County, I hit State 206, a highway running parallel to the Texas line. I passed through the small cowtown of Tatum, and drove another eighty miles passing through the farming community of Dora. About noon I drove into Portales, the peanut capital of the southwest and the home of Eastern New Mexico University. There I stopped for a mid-day snack.

Leaving the small café, I noticed the sign on the bank showed the temperature had climbed to eighty-five degrees. This indicated it would be really hot by mid-afternoon. I found US 70. This highway took me past Black Water Museum that contains artifacts from the Clovis Man era, reported to be 10,000 years ago and the oldest inhabitants in North America. In Clovis my thoughts turned ten miles eastward to Texaco, New Mexico, a small town on the Texas border where I was born more than 80 years ago. Since I left home early in the morning, I had traveled almost two hundred miles across a small northern portion of the Great Chihuahuan Desert. The early Spaniards called this track of savanna the Llano Estacado, which means Staked Plains.

During the morning, rabbits and roadrunners had scurried across my path. Herds of antelope and cattle grazed on the rangelands. Buzzards, searching for carcasses of dead animals, circled high above me silhouetted against the blue sky.

As I drove down the highway, fresh, clean air flowed in through the open window bringing with it the smell of new plants and fresh soil turned over by the farmer's plow. I heard hungry baby calves, with empty stomachs, bawling for warm milk from their mothers. Busy men in farm and ranch pickups whizzed past me. Vehicles of all sizes, with distinguishing logos sped by going in both directions rushing to make a living in the oil fields. All along the way, pumps with their huge beams sat over oil wells sucking up black gold from deep within mother earth.

I left the modern, up-to-date prairie city of Clovis, with Cannon Air Base nearby stocked with the latest combat jet planes. The pilots of the planes are poised ready to scramble or fly to some distant land across the sea the moment the president gives the order.

After traveling another twenty-five miles, I came to Broadview with its two churches, a service station, a closed implement store and a small but interesting antique and art gallery. The wheat fields that surround Broadview furnish bread for the world and stretch out as far as the eye can see in all directions. The fields are watered from wells that go far below the surface into aquifers. Dry playa lakes dot the flat, treeless plains.

As I left the small community, the gentle breeze caused American flags, in yards and attached to houses, to wave a friendly good-bye. I became aware that a thin layer of clouds covered the land, shielding it from the extreme heat of the afternoon sun. Far in the distance to the west, heavier clouds were peppering spots of dry land with rain.

After about two miles, I left the blacktop and traveled down a dry, dusty, dirt road. When I saw a piece of land to the right, my memory went back more than seventy years. Before farmers had fences around their property, somebody had to guard the milk cows as they grazed on the spring wheat so they wouldn't wander over onto the neighbor's fields.

It was my job, as a boy of eight or nine, to make sure the cows stayed where they belonged. Dressed in patched overalls, no shoes and no hat, I sat all day long on the bare back of old Mose, a black plow horse with a sway back, droopy eyes, and a white spot in the middle of his forehead. When a cow began to trot toward a neighbor's field, Mose and I had to bring her back. But Mose didn't like to move faster than a slow walk. To get him to move fast enough to head off the cow, I took the bridle reins and hit him back and forth across the ears. This was the only way I knew to get the old nag to move fast enough to bring the wandering cow back to the herd I was to guard. Dad saw me mistreating the horse and said, "Young man, if I ever see you treat a horse like that again, I'll use the reins on you." He would, and I didn't.

The hot sun seemed to focus on my nose. It caused blisters. The blisters would burst. In a few days a dark brown scab covered that part of my face. I lived with it, in spite of the jokes my brothers and sisters directed at me.

My air-conditioned car, with all the amenities of home, brought me suddenly to the caprock. There I parked on the edge of the rugged escarpment. I looked down the old unpaved, rocky road that I had traveled so many times by wagon and car. With deep emotions, I stared for a long time across the dry ageless hills and arroyos onto the floor of the valley eight hundred feet below. I had landed, once again, smack-dab in the middle of *THE PRE-ATOMIC AGE.*

TO ARKANSAS AND BACK

My friends, Larry, Robert, Dick, Gary, Rob, Richard and I were sitting at a round table in a cafe owned and operated by brothers Milton and George. It was a Thursday afternoon when we usually got together to eat and agree or disagree on our ideas about local, state, national and international affairs. The lively discussion came to a moment of silence. With a group of active, intelligent men with quick tongues, it couldn't last.

All minds were focused when someone said, "Question! What man in the past would you most like to talk to?" Several men were mentioned. Lincoln, Churchill, Teddy Roosevelt, Carver, Hitler, Hamilton, Franklin, Washington, and Stalin. I had not spoken, so they all looked at me and asked, "Whom would you like to talk to?" All the time my mind was going back to my childhood. With a nostalgic look in my eyes, I replied, "Men, I'd like to talk to my Dad. Because when I was a boy, I never listened when he tried to talk about our family roots. Dad has been dead for more than fifty years. Facts that I dearly want to know today about my background are lost forever."

As a small boy, I had the privilege of knowing my Dad's two brothers Ed and Jay. I remember, for some reason, that their mother's maiden name was Ward. Beyond that, nothing comes to mind. My mother's family called themselves 'black Dutch'. I knew all members of her family except her mother. Grandmother died during the flu epidemic of 1918 before I was born.

The first immigrant by the name of Fooks (A Dutch name pronounced Folks). came to America from England in 1740.

5

His name was Mathis, age twenty-five. He made his home in Pennsylvania. Others followed. Even today there are only 214 families in the United States who bear the name. Looking in history books searching for the Fooks name is a futile exercise. I've found no politicians, military heroes, writers or public enemies in the annals of history. There's one exception: Robert Fooks, a butcher, who was used as a guinea pig for Dr. Downe of Bridgeport, England, in 1771. Robert volunteered to be vaccinated in the smallpox experiment.

Though none by our family name is listed in Who's Who in America, the factory workers, farm laborers, land and slave owners have fought in all of our nation's wars from the Revolution to the present. We've paid taxes, contributed to our communities and exercised solid citizenship while keeping the name from scandal and the police blotters (There are a few exceptions).

I have no way of telling how or why my progenitors ended up in the wooded hills of northeast Arkansas near Jonesboro. But my Dad, who was named Mack, left the swamplands for the high plains of the desert Southwest in 1906. The twenty-four-year-old husky heard that a young man could come to New Mexico territory, file on one hundred sixty acres, improve it and after living on it five years claim it as his own with a clear title. With hopes of a new, exciting life and owning land, he made the long trek alone in a wagon drawn by two horses to a place near the foothills of the Rocky Mountains. He got his acreage about thirty miles northwest of Clovis in a community called Wheatland only a few miles from the caprock. The small trading town of Grady nearby was beginning to thrive.

Charles Miller, with his wife and seven children, left a farm near Springfield, Missouri about the same time. This family of three boys and four girls filed on land near Grady. My mother, Rosie Katoria, known as Katy, was one of the teenage girls in that family. They came by train to the Territory that was opening up to eager, hopeful settlers from many points back East.

These eager singles and families failed to consider there was a great deal of difference in one hundred and sixty acres in Arkansas and Missouri and an equal number of acres in the arid desert on the high plains of the West. Rainfall was three or four times more each year in their former homes than in New Mexico. Frequent rains that brought plenty of water for gardens and grass for cattle and crops for market made it possible to make a decent living back home. It was altogether different here in the desert Southwest before irrigation was developed. Here enough rain fell only every three to five years to produce a profitable crop. What grain, beef, eggs and cream they did produce had to be hauled great distances to market in a wagon. It took enduring patience to tend a few cattle, plow the fields with their crude implements and sell their produce in those days. All this for a few dollars to buy the bare necessities such as clothing and food they couldn't raise on the farm.

These farm families made do with what they brought with them, and what little they could purchase from Grady or Clovis if they had the time to make that journey of several days by buggy or wagon. They took their wheat to a neighbor who had a grinder. For pay, the man who ground the wheat got a fourth of the produce. After the wheat was ground, it was made into gram bread for the family table. (Today we call it whole wheat bread.) It also could be made into mush for breakfast. Sometime the grinder was set for the wheat not to be ground so fine. This larger mesh could be put into a wood stove oven, heated, put in a bowl, and covered with whole milk for morning cereal. All farmers raised their own hogs to butcher for ham, bacon, hogshead cheese, sausage and pickled pigs feet. Cracklings were made from the skin of hogs. (Such is sold today as pork rinds in grocery stores across the land.) Each family raised its own chickens for eggs and Sunday dinner.

Some families didn't have a dime to buy a can of lye to make soap for washing and bathing. So to make lye which was necessary, they would put ashes from the wood stove in a metal container and let water drip through the ashes into a glass jar below, for as long as necessary. The residue in the lower vessel became strong lye water. Parts of the slaughtered hog that couldn't be eaten, with sufficient water and lye, were put in the iron kettle out in the yard. A wood fire was built under the kettle. The contents were brought to a boil, than cooled. When the concoction cooled to atmospheric temperature, a layer of lye soap formed on top. This strong soap was used for washing and bathing.

Since money was often more scarce then hen's teeth, the barter system was used almost exclusively. If one farmer had a blacksmith shop and his neighbor raised more hogs than needed, the man with the hogs would go to the blacksmith and say, "I need my plowshares sharpened before I prepare my land for planting. If you can see fit to sharpen them, I'll give you a couple of pigs when my old sow delivers." The deal was struck, they shook hands, and that was all that was necessary.

A mother with several children may go to a neighbor who had a sewing machine and say, "My family needs more quilts for this coming winter. I have a bunch of scraps left over from making the girls dresses and cutting out the good parts of worn-out britches. If you could see fit to sew the scraps together for quilt tops, I can give you the scraps you need." The deal was made, the exchange was done, and everybody was pleased.

By this method of helping and being helped by neighbors, most families were able to hang on to their 160 acres until the required five years were up. Then some sold or bartered their claim to neighbors and went looking for greener and more productive land. So, the remaining family now owned 320 acres and could make a better living for members of his household.

During these difficult times, the settlers built schools, churches and had social activities such as dances and community picnics. In every gathering, there were one or two people who played the guitar or violin brought with them when they came west. If they couldn't sing the tunes of the day, there were other pioneers who could. These activities were a pleasant respite from laboring in the hot, dusty fields.

In the midst of all this, my Dad must have had his eye focused on one of the growing Miller girls they called Katy. I know nothing of their courtin' or their marriage except, in later years, when their children asked to see their marriage license they replied with a disdainful look, "We don't have a license."

A chorus of great surprise went up from their children asking, "How come?" They told us the inept frontier minister who performed their wedding ceremony messed up the legal document. It was so smeared with ink from the fountain pen with a rubber bladder, they refused to accept it, and never got another one. Being their children, we accepted this explanation without question.

But I do know Dad was a hard worker and good talker. He taught singing schools back in Arkansas. He had a clear tenor voice that is remembered by church members to this day. It was a voice that most professionals would have envied.

Dad weighed about 225 pounds with a five-foot-eight-inch frame. He was quicker than the strike of a rattlesnake. As I look back and see the many failures in his life, I think he was not cut out to be a farmer, a laborer or a businessman. He was born one hundred years too soon. With his build, strength and quickness he would have made a great lineman on anybody's professional football team. With his distinctive tenor voice, with the proper training, he could have drawn standing-room-only audiences around the world. But his times were not right. Dad never got to develop the potential he certainly had.

If it is true that opposites attract each other, this must have been one reason Mack and Katy got together. Mother never weighed more than 110 pounds unless she was with child. She was a quiet lady, speaking only when necessary. She wore a pleasant smile; her black hair was twisted into a bun worn on the back of her head. She sang in her heart for she couldn't carry a tune with her voice.

Twenty-seven-year-old Mack and eighteen-year-old Katy were married by a country preacher in the year of our Lord 1909. Dad, with the help of neighbors, dug a rectangular hole in the ground, probably eight-by-twelve-feet, on his farm. He went to the breaks under the caprock where he cut cedar poles that he laid across the eight-foot span of the hole. Then he laid boards on the poles. To cap off the dwelling and to seal it, sod from the prairie was shoveled on the boards until it formed a rounded mound. Being underground, it was pretty nice in one respect. In winter it was warm; in summer it was cool. Steps were fashioned down into the dugout. This opening was covered with a slanting, hinged door.

My father brought his recent bride, my mother–to-be, Katy, to their new windowless home. For a newly wed couple this type of dwelling was not unusual in New Mexico when the 20th century was new. Even if they had the money, it was difficult to get lumber and nails from distant places like Clovis, Tucumcari and Amarillo. Therefore, so many newly married couples made do with what the plains had to offer.

The first two children of Mack and Katy were born in the home below ground level. The first, a boy, was born in 1911. They named him Churchell. The second child was a girl born in 1913. Her name was Annabelle.

Life was exceedingly simple and slow compared with ours nearly one hundred years later. Cooking was done on a wood stove with its stovepipe running through the sod roof. Their toilet was a bucket, called a slopjar, used at night and emptied outside each morning. For light, they used a coal oil lamp, or they may have used candles made from tallow gleaned from butchered steers.

After the Territory met all the requirements set by the United States, New Mexico became the 47th state in the Union in 1912. Arizona followed as the 48th state the same year. New Mexico had tried to become a state for many years, but was denied by the U.S. Congress because of political quarrels, fights and killings in the territory. Citizen Albert Fall became the first United States Senator from the new state. He pulled the proper strings and became Secretary of the Interior. His dealings in the Teapot Dome scandal caused his downhill slide. Despite all the squabbles between the Republicans and Democrats, people in the new state from Jal to Farmington, from Lordsburg to Raton, celebrated the birth of the state with grand exuberance.

The farm that Dad owned and worked for several years was sold to a neighbor who wished to expand his holdings. This was happening more frequently as settlers gave up on making a living on farms where rain was so unpredictable. There were fewer and fewer settlers, and the remaining farms grew larger and larger.

The money Dad received from the sale of the family farm was invested in a new automobile tire manufacturing plant in Texico, New Mexico. The growing family moved there and Dad started working in the new plant making tires for the thousands of automobiles coming off the assembly lines in Detroit. Dad had great hopes in the future of the plant and wrote a letter in 1917 urging his brother Ed in Arkansas to sell out and come to New Mexico to work with him.

In the meantime, two daughters were added to the young, growing family. Etta Mae was born in 1916. Jessie Jane was born in 1919.

The Fooks Family was well established in their new home in Texico. With the investment in the tire plant and regular work, Mack was making more money than he had ever made. Just inside New Mexico, near the Texas border, on November 22, 1921, I, Leslie Eugene Fooks, was born as the fifth child of Mack and Katy. The name Leslie came from the doctor who was present at my birth. Eugene came from Eugene Debs who was known across the land for his campaign oratory. He formed the Social Democratic Party and ran for president of the United States five times under that banner. This powerful political figure led the Chicago Pullman strike in 1894. He was put in prison for his activities. I was never told, but I'm almost sure Dad voted for him.

Shortly after I was born, it was rumored that some of the executives in the tire establishment embezzled the company's earnings. True or not, the plant closed. Dad lost all his money and his job. Along with many others, the head of our growing family was hopelessly broke. The desert Southwest had not been kind to Dad.

Disappointed in business dealings and tired of hard work on the farm with little to show for it, Dad decided to take us all back to his old home in Arkansas. With his strong and agile body, he knew he could provide for us by cutting down trees, hewing them into ties and selling them to the railroads that were expanding rapidly.

I was only eight months old, but as I remember the family stories handed down, Dad made a deal with Mother's single brother, Lee Miller, to take us to Arkansas where his two brothers still lived. The eight of us were crammed into Uncle Lee's two-seated, convertible Model T. A bedroll was tied on the back of the car.

We began our journey from the high, dry plains down unpaved dusty roads that were sometimes muddy. We made our way across the plains and caprock of west Texas on roads that were not much more than wagon trails made by early pioneers going to and from the West. We traveled at speeds of twenty to thirty miles per hour dodging rocks and high bumps in the road.

Flat tires were common. But Dad and Uncle Lee had prepared for that taking along tire tools and patches and glue to repair damaged innertubes.

Service stations were few and far between, and most had no restrooms. When one member of the travelers felt the need for a rest room, the car was stopped and relief was had behind a bush or tree. Motels were unheard of on the trail. Such conveniences came much later. The carbide-powered headlights on the car may or may not provide light for night driving. When night fell, the bedroll on the back of the car was unrolled and placed on the ground for sleeping. Still some family members had to sleep in the car.

We came to the rolling waters of the Red River that separated Texas from Oklahoma. No bridge had been built. No problem. For a price, men stationed on the riverbank made their living by ferrying cars and cargo across. With the family inside the car, we made it to the Oklahoma side with ease. The men on the ferry started back toward the Texas bank. The driver of our automobile, Dad or Uncle Lee, gunned the Model T Ford in order to make it up the steep bank. With its heavy load, the ancient car stalled and began rolling back toward the deep water. With mere manpower, the men on the ferry used their long pole, to steer the ferry, rushing back to rescue us from drowning. The combined power of the car's motor and the strength of the husky men saved our family from being swallowed by the swirling waters. Had they not done some quick thinking to save us, that may well have been the end of the Fooks family story, and I may never have seen my first birthday.

With poor maps to direct us, and poor roads to travel, it took us about three weeks to cross Oklahoma and to arrive in northeast Arkansas. We settled close to the heel of Missouri on the north and the mighty Mississippi to the east.

Dad was in familiar territory, and among the family with whom he spent his early years. But it was all new and unfamiliar to Mother and her brood. The family was broke and Dad had no time to waste. He had to get to work to build a house and put food on the table. After food was supplied, he went into the forests that surrounded the cotton fields, cut logs and before long he had built, our new two room house made of logs. It stood on the edge of a field of cotton with a thick stand of tall, stately trees behind.

I was past two years old when the first memory in my life occurred in the yard of our cabin. A giant tree had been cut down, by two men with a crosscut saw, leaving a stump protruding about a foot above the ground. It was early morning, the sky was clear and the sunshine was filtering through the tall pines. A heavy frost covered the ground with an extra portion atop the stump. My older sisters, Etta and Jessie, were in the yard, and I followed after them with the drop seat of my coveralls unbuttoned and flapping against my heels. They dared me to sit my bare bottom on the frosty stump. I accepted their challenge, and the shock caused my memory to record events since.

Twin boys were born while we lived in the log cabin on the edge of the cotton patch. Dad teased Mother saying the boys should be named Pete and Re-pete. Mother, who was serious much of the time, said, "Now, Mack, you know that wouldn't be right." The boys were named Ray and Raymond with no middle name. This proved confusing when the boys started to school and later when they joined the Navy in World War II. After the War, Ray drew disability pay from the government. Raymond did not. Thinking they were the same person, the officials were about to throw the book at Ray until they learned they were twin brothers.

In the mid 1920s, Dad was making pretty good money cutting down trees, hewing them into ties and selling them to the railroads. The log house was far too crowded for the family.

Dad, with the help of neighbors, built a real house for us with unseasoned lumber cut from large trees and shaped at the sawmill When the twins were about two years old, we moved into our new home with a fireplace. Dad was home relaxing and pulled a five dollar bill from his pocket.

(It was equal to fifty dollars or more in today's currency.) He was telling us how hard he worked for the money, saying, "I bet my twin sons know the value of this bill." Dad gave the bill to Raymond who was enamored by the flickering flames. Without hesitation his young son threw the bill into the fire. Dad's quickness saved the money that was slightly singed around the edges.

Near our new house was the fenced lot where Dad kept his two horses. Inside the lot stood a big, ancient oak tree. In early morning I'd watch Dad harness the horses, hitch a doubletree to the chain traces that ran alone the sides of the horses. Then he'd fasten huge tongs to the doubletree. After he felled trees to make railroad ties, the sharp points on the tongs pierced the logs to drag them to a clearing to be hewn into proper shape. All this fascinated me. I was even more fascinated when I saw two black snakes, each longer than I was tall, climbing among branches of the tree. As I stood watching from the shade of the tree I wondered how the snakes could climb the tree and play among the branches when they had no arms and legs like mine?

It was here that I watched, for the first time, a small, single engine airplane sputtering overhead. This was a great wonderment to me.

In Arkansas, I learned the power of swirling winds in a tornado. Dad took a load of chickens to Hoxie to sell. While he was gone, the heavens turned black with threatening, ominous clouds. I stood in our yard watching one of nature's dynamic powers as funnels danced and swerved among the distant tree tops. This spectacle was indelibly etched in my mind. When Dad returned home, he reported that nine members of one family had been wiped out when the tornado hit their farm home.

I'd kept the image of an incident in my memory since I was five years old, but was never sure if it was real or a figment of my imagination. In later years I asked Etta, my sister who is six years older than me, if it was true or just an imagination hidden in the back of my mind through the decades. "Etta," I said, "please tell me if this story is true or something I dreamed up. It is an incident that has drifted through my mind many times through the years."

It was dusk and darkness was gathering rapidly under the mammoth trees on the edge of the forest. Etta and I were standing beneath a large oak tree with our teenage cousin who was fat, with breasts larger than most women had. Suddenly an owl high in the branches of the tree we stood under began hooting: who-o-o-o, who-o-o-o, who-o-o-o. We looked up and spotted the owl camouflaged among the leaves. We immediately began throwing small stones and twigs at one of nature's most interesting creatures. The owl didn't appreciate our trespassing on his territory. The big brown fowl with his huge eyes turned his head from side to side apparently looking for a place in the tree to hide from the missiles we threw. We kept up our barrage of stones and twigs. With no place to hide in his chosen tree, he finally became irritated. Spreading his wings with one swooping dive, talons on both feet wide open, the owl grabbed both breasts of our cousin. We fought the owl off, it returned to his roosting branches, and we scampered to our respective homes. Etta assured me that the incident actually happened.

I learned at an early age that horses have minds of their own. Exactly how this happened has faded from my memory. But after more than seventy-five years, this part is still fresh. It was early morning, the sun was shining bright, a grown-up was riding his horse, and I was on the bare back of another nag. We were riding down a country lane side by side. The horse I was riding was aware that I, a five-year-old, could not control its wants. When we got about a mile from our destination, my horse suddenly turned, and despite all I could do, hit a dead run going back to its home. There was no way I could control the animal that had a mind of its own. I held onto its mane with all my might screaming and crying. The adult on the other horse, turned his mount and tried to catch my horse to rescue me, but to no avail. When it got home, my horse stopped at the gate. My adult companion lifted me from the runaway steed, and, while I whimpered, he tried to comfort me.

Dad brought home a baby goat, thinking the twins, Ray and Raymond, who were getting close to three, and I needed a pet to play with. The goat was a lively, rambunctious little critter that soon learned he could have the run of the house and the entire yard. Our windows, without screens, were always open to capture any breeze in the sweltering heat and high humidity. Much to Mother's dismay our pet soon learned to run and leap through the open windows into the house wreaking havoc with the beds and the whole house, before rushing out the back door.

Ray and Raymond had picked up on Dad's sense of humor. They learned that if they would bend over, with their little buttocks in the air, the goat would run and butt them, giving them a tumble in the grass. This was great fun. My sister Jessie took a liking to the playful pet goat. She spent her spare time grooming and keeping our pet clean. One night while the family was asleep, the young goat got into the pantry, opened a bucket of lard and ate much of the contents. Next morning, we found our pet lying on its side outside the back door so sick it couldn't stand. Jessie made it her job to care for our pet we all had learned to love. In spite of all she could do, the little rascal died within a day or two. Regret and sorrow filled our household.

It was in the mid-1920s that I was playing in the yard in the shade of a tree while the sun was shining in all its glory. Suddenly the sun was not so bright. No clouds were above. It grew darker. Hens began to cluck, cluck, cluck, for their babies. When they gathered around, the mothers took their young to the chicken house as they usually did when the sun went down. Soon it was twilight. Frightened, I ran in the house. Mother told me and her other children that she had seen such an event before, and soon it would be light again. An eclipse of the sun had occurred.

These and many other events and associations taught me something in my young life about people, animals and strange happenings in the natural order of things. In our home we never talked about science, so when an event as the eclipse occurred, we called it funny, meaning it was strange or different.

There was no music in our home except when Dad tried to teach his sons and daughters to sing church hymns. This proved an impossible task since all his children took after Mother who couldn't possibly carry a tune. The only paintings we had were those in the great out-of-doors done by the invisible hand of 'nature's God.' Our priceless paintings were the sunrise and the sunset, the hills covered with trees and flowers with real live bees, birds, squirrels and other animals playing in the midst of all our surroundings. All of these and many other things gave my curious and imaginative mind things to ponder when I was alone.

For the mid-1920s Dad was doing well financially making ties and selling them to the railroad and his farming operation He had provided the family with a new house and managed to buy a new Model T Ford. But misfortune loomed on the horizon. Mother was pregnant again with her eighth child. She spent most of her time in bed while the older girls did the housework. I could see that Mother was getting bigger around the middle, and was told that the stork was coming to bring another baby girl or boy. I wasn't fooled, for I had seen animals breed, grow big around the middle and deliver their young. Though I didn't understand, it didn't take much brainpower for me to figure out the same thing could happen in the case of humans.

In the afternoon when Mother began to have contractions, Dad hustled about, taking his offspring to uncle Ed's house and making sure a midwife was present to assist in the delivery. The next day, we were told our new brother had made his presence known in the world at about four o'clock in the morning by kicking and crying. This showed he was active with plenty of lungpower. They named him Jay Bertie, probably after Dad's brother.

This was the eighth birth from Mother, who was never very strong. The hot climate, with high humidity, surrounded by swamps infested with mosquitoes, added to her misery. It was more than Mother could stand. She couldn't recover from the ordeal. She grew weaker.

The doctor finally told Dad, "If you don't get your wife out of this environment into a high, dry climate, she's going to die." The physician also told Dad that Mother would perhaps die on the way if he tried to take her out of Arkansas by automobile. The doctor couldn't be sure, but "The safest way to take her to a dryer climate was by railroad in a Pullman car."

Dad communicated with Mother's father, Charles Miller, telling him the condition of his next to youngest daughter. Whether Grandpa was in New Mexico of in Ponca City, Oklahoma where some of his children had moved with their families, I cannot say. But I do know he rushed to Arkansas to do all he could for his daughter.

Though I never heard Dad complain, he must have been chagrined, knowing he must give up his business that had put him in the best economic condition in his life. He decided to take his family back to New Mexico that he had left five years before. This would meet the doctor's requirements for Mother, and he would be among old friends and acquaintances. While Dad was accumulating property and other holdings, he had nothing long enough to build up much equity. Nevertheless, he busied himself making plans to leave. Mother, Grandpa and baby Jay were put on a train to stop in Oklahoma to visit her siblings.

My older brother and sisters did what they could to prepare to go back west. Churchell was about 16, Annabelle was approximately 14, Etta was around 11, Jessie was about nine and I was getting close to six. The twins were somewhere close to three. Dad had his hands full taking care of business and tending to his children who did our share of fussing and fighting.

When all was ready, the eight of us piled in the Model T with our meager belongings and headed for Ponca City where Mother and Grandpa were waiting for us. About the only thing I remember about this leg of our trip was the terrible thunderstorm that hit us, soaking all of us to the bone. We stayed with relatives for a few days visiting cousins I'd never seen or forgotten. We took pictures of our kinsmen and visited the 101 Ranch owned by Zack Miller (no relation) and his brothers. We saw bears and a host of other animals they used in their circus that traveled widely in the summer.

Leaving our relatives behind, we traveled to New Mexico where we settled temporarily on the high plains only a few miles from the place Dad filed on as a young, unmarried man. He was starting again at square one, for his pocketbook was nearly empty after he sold his new holdings in Arkansas and the expenses of moving.

Our next home was a rented dwelling, on the corner of a wheat field. It was in poor condition even by 1927 standards. Across the street lived a farm family whom we considered rich because they had a lug wheel tractor, an automobile and could eat three square meals a day. Their son Ralph, who was also about six years old, often came over to play with me in the yard. He brought his little pot metal cars colored black, red, green and blue. They were about the size of a man's thumb. While pushing the tiny cars over roads and bridges we built, we'd make noises like a Model T racing down the road.

Ralph was a kind child. He knew I had no cars, so when his mother called him home for lunch, he give me one of his. I held the gift gently in my hand as he ran home crying out, "I'm comin'." The little car was my most precious possession, a treasure that caused my eyes to bug out, and my heart to pound with joy. Jewels and gold could not have meant as much nor made me happier. I was walking on air as I ran into our house to show Mother my treasure.

But Mother was not convinced I had acquired the car as a gift. After all my crying and trying to persuade her otherwise, she still thought I'd picked up the toy car without my playmate's knowledge. I knew I hadn't, but it was no use. Mother insisted that I take my precious gift back and give it to its rightful owner.

I knew Mother was teaching me honesty and integrity. In that, she succeeded. But at the time, I just couldn't understand, since I knew in my own tender soul, that I had not stolen the toy car.

My youthful heart was breaking, my body shook with grief and tears rolled down my freckled cheeks as I carried the little car back across the dusty road. I dropped it in his yard and ran back home to hide in shame and disappointment. Shortly after this incident, Dad announced he had made a deal to move the family down into the valley. He had rented the old Gibbs place that gave him access to the farm and the grasslands. For rent, he agreed to give the owner a percentage of the proceeds from the crop each year.

Leslie Eugene Fooks

THE SEVENTH GENERATION
by Leslie Eugene Fooks

It's disconcerting to be told
Our Generation has grown old.

Born early in the twentieth century
In cities, towns and open country.

Groomed by the Great Depression,
We kept freedom alive in our nation.

We worked the ranch, farm and shop;
Backs to the wall; no time to stop.

The work was hard with little pay,
Often as small as a dollar a day.

Some of our peers stayed in school;
Soon we'd need this learn-ed pool.

Strong and agile from hard work,
Resolved never a tough job shirk.

Dark clouds formed over the earth;
And the lovely land of our birth.

To armed forces came the clarion call;
Millions signed for the world-wide brawl.

We left homes and sweethearts far behind
To serve the world for all mankind.

Looking invincible in their awful sin,
Some thought the Axis were sure to win.

We fought with ships, planes and tanks,
Never concerned who got the "thanks."

Battles intense and most horrific
In Africa, Europe and the wide Pacific.

We won't forget the workers at home
Who made the weapons that freed Rome.

Nor forget our mothers who prayed
To our Father above who gave us aid

Young men from our streets and farms
Battled professionals with mighty arms.

It took four years to whip those guys
Who fought to control earth and skies.

Collapse of Axis came like thunder
With "Unconditional Surrender."

We'll long remember those who died;
Now at rest in graves side by side.

Boys returned home as seasoned men;
Cockiness gone with ranks now thin.

Victory parades gave great relief;
We'd won the war for our belief.

No time to rest; loomed another hill.
We trained for it with the GI Bill..

Marriage and baby boomers came.
We set to work and staked our claim.

In the beginning it was very slow.
Soon the economy began to grow.

We put our shoulders to the wheel;
Learned to make the sweetest deal.

Children and grands now are free
To grow into whom they want to be.

Our generation paid an awful price;
Yet this old world is no paradise.

There are more battles to be fought;
Fight with grit as you've been taught.

THE POCKET OF PERPETUAL POVERTY

Standing on the caprock, I looked down the same lonely, deserted road I've seen many times since I first saw it nearly eighty years ago. The unpaved road, that leads down on to the valley floor eight hundred feet below, is still steep and winding. The ancient hills and canyons are still as forbidding as ever. Each hill is surrounded in mystery and each scrub cedar and pine tree, that I have observed since I was six, speaks of ancient times before red man, brown and white discovered them. This must be the reason the umbilical cord, from which I have never been severed, keeps drawing me back to this forsaken place.

I stood on the top looking down the bumpy passageway that winds through the breaks and across the ravines, I thought of the days long past. I'm no longer the co-pilot who flew combat missions over Europe in World War II. Nor am I the retired minister, the writer, and the husband of a former intelligent businesswoman. I wasn't thinking of my highly educated daughters who have traveled the world and succeeded in their chosen professions. Even my three handsome grandchildren who are working on advanced university degrees in different disciplines had vanished from my mind. I was completely focused on this forgotten valley and the activities of the ten families that lived here during the Great Depression. I remember their faces, their names, the names of their children and many of their mannerism that made each different. The peculiarities that made each family stand out from the rest came to mind.

23

They are all gone now, scattered to the wind. The adults of that time are all dead, and two of the boys were killed in the Great War.

Why is this small part of the extended valley so deserted and desolate when all around it is vibrant with activity. Seven miles north the busy four-lane Interstate Highway 40 runs along side old Highway 66. Sixteen thousand automobiles travel each day east and west on this modern thoroughfare. In addition, thousands of eighteen-wheelers from the West Coast filled with cargo speed daily toward Amarillo, Oklahoma City, Chicago and New York. More thousands of heavy trucks race from the metropolitan centers of the east toward Albuquerque, Phoenix and Los Angeles. Twenty thousand vehicles travel the highway each day.

Just north of I-40, two large lakes lie nestled in canyons of the Canadian River. Each lake, the Conches and the Ute, is a paradise for fishermen and vacationers.

Behind me, where I stand on the plains, the blacktop roads are busy with farm trucks filled with cattle or produce rushing past one another for world markets. To the east just across the Texas state line, the irrigated farms and the many feedlots surrounding the Hereford community are going night and day to supply the public demand for their products. All around, the world is working, changing, and alive with commercial enterprises, vacationers and beautiful homes. But the valley, the lonely, desolate valley of my youth, surrounded by a world of activity, is deserted and forgotten by all but a few. The Pre-Atomic Age has been preserved. I had come to think of this six-square-mile-township as the *pocket of perpetual poverty.*

There are no farms left. A few cattle graze on the sparse grass collected around mesquite bushes. Come noon, the bovines gather around the windmill for a mid-day drink, lie down, chew their cuds and sleep through the heat of the day. Not one soul lives in this portion of the valley. The houses we lived in seventy years ago have tumbled down. Only coyotes, rattlesnakes and other varmints remain in the land I once called home.

It was time for me to get in my late-model automobile with air conditioning and drive comfortably down the same twisting, dirt road for the umpteenth time. My family drove for the first time in the Model-T in 1927 down this same old road.

Though I am eighty-four-years-old, my heart feels the same sensation I felt as we drove through the escarpment in the clattering 'tin lizzy' when I was six. The hills and the canyons I've seen so many times before still intrigue me. I want to climb each peak and explore each ravine. I stopped the car several times, got out and walked on weakened legs to the base of the hills and peer upward wondering as I gaze on the ancient formations. If I could climb a little higher, perhaps I could see a mother deer with her fawn, or perchance a mountain lion or a herd of antelope.

Slow and careful not to stumble and fall over a ledge, I walked to the precipice of a canyon and peered over the edge. All the time I was vigilant, looking for rattlesnakes that might be lurking under a rock or in the shade of a bush.

This is a far cry from the way I viewed these breaks when I was growing up. It was then that I ran barefoot, wild and free as the animals that made their home in this rugged landscape. Instead of my legs growing weaker, they grew stronger. To run up the hills and down into the canyons was nothing. Rattlesnakes were no problem for I learned these gentle creatures most of the time hissed and rattled their tails before striking. They only wanted to be left alone and would give warning when disturbed or threatened.

I felt compelled to examine once again the peculiar rocks that are a conglomeration of thousand of smaller stones of all colors and chemical composition. These small stones are welded so tightly together only the powerful stroke of a hammer can separate the smaller pieces. Many of these rock conglomerates are larger then my car. Since I first saw them, I've been fascinated by their appearance and I wondered about their origin. I thought perhaps, they were meteorites that had fallen from the sky in the distant past.

In the nineteen-sixties, when we lived at Hereford, Texas, I found one of the conglomerates that I could heave into the trunk of my car and took it to a geologist at a University. I told the professor what I thought it might be. He disagreed, saying, "As you see it shows these stones are welded together by tremendous heat. The intense temperature near the center of the earth caused this. As the earth made its slight movements over millions of years, these stones worked their way to the surface." I didn't tell him, but I left thinking my theory was as feasible as his.

I've spent much time in the deserts of the Southwest, the Rocky Mountains, the colorful mountains and flatlands of Utah, along the West Coast from San Diego to Seattle and the East Coast from New York to Georgia, but I have never seen stones as big, colorful and mixed as these. There are many things found in nature that cannot be explained to everyone's satisfaction.

The styrofoam cups and plastic bottles found in the hidden canyons and caves of the escarpment inform me lovers and picnickers still return occasionally to get away from the hectic, fast-moving world they live in.

The car took me down through the enchanting breaks on to the flat valley floor. There I stopped and surveyed the township my family and nine other families called home in the late nineteen-twenties and the nineteen-thirties. Most of the land is now overgrown with giant mesquites and cacti with their beautiful red, yellow and purple blooms.

Only one house is standing erect in our part of the lonely valley. It belongs To Elmer Boney and his schoolteacher daughter, Kelly. Elmer and I competed in marble games when we were boys. I got acquainted with Kelly on my previous visits when she was a girl. That was in the days when her hero, Johnny Bench, played baseball for the Cincinnati Reds. Before they had to move because of Elmer's health, I drove down the lane to their house and Kelly met me in the yard. After we exchanged greetings, she called her father. This World War II veteran was not well and had difficulty walking to where we stood talking. This gentleman, in his eighty-second year, told me his wife of many years died a few months before.

It was soon time to move on to reminisce in the vicinity where I spent many formative years of my youth. As I drove down the rutted roads observing the broken-down houses my family and our neighbors lived in, my mind became more engrossed in thoughts of another time. I left Elmer still talking about the need for precious rain.

In my mind, I was transported back to Calvin Coolidge's days in the White House. Mr. Coolidge is the first president I remember. The radio and the airplane were coming into common use. Charles Lindbergh had just flown across the Atlantic alone. Coolidge declared, "I do not choose to run again." This announcement catapulted Herbert Hoover into the Oval Office. The population of the United States was a whopping 125,000,000. The stock market was about to crash. I only heard adults talk about these things, and they were of little concern to me, being a child.

It must have been the rich soil that brought the first settlers to the valley around the turn of the twentieth century. I imagined the excitement of those pioneers as they harnessed their mules, hitched them to wagons and spent days going to the nearest railroad junction to buy lumber and nails to build their homes. Dreams of prosperity must have danced in their heads with hopes of passing on to their children a better life than they had inherited.

Uncle Sam gave the land to each family for a simple filing fee. These hearty souls were deceived by their own eagerness. They apparently thought they were getting something for nothing. The haunting beauty of the rugged breaks that formed the southern end of our valley drew them, perhaps. The lush grass in the early spring rising from the fertile soil watered by the bitter snows of winter made the attraction more hopeful. The clean air and the lovely blue skies must have played a part.

There was a constant wood supply for cooking and heating from the dead and dying cacti, cedar and pine trees in the hills. This was a rare commodity, indeed, in the desert Southwest. But the determined early settlers overlooked one very important ingredient in their plans to make their dreams a reality.

All the pluses they added up still came to zero without water. In these parts. a sufficient water supply was almost as scarce and the dollars they labored for. These settlers had to dig by muscle power at least ninety feet to reach water. Even then there was barely enough for family use, a small garden and a few livestock. There was no water for irrigating the crops to make them grow and produce for market.

The rains were marginal at best. Often when they did come, the rains attacked the valley, coming down with violent winds in lashing torrents. These drenching downpours caused the dry arroyos to suddenly become raging rivers washing over their banks onto farms and ranches, destroying crops and drowning calves and aging cattle.

The gentle rains came every three to five years blessing the farmers with crops for the markets and the ranchers with fattened yearlings for the butcher shops of the great cities. Three to five years was too long to go without money for clothes and food.

To pioneers before us, disappointment was learned the hard way. The suffocating heat in the valley from the boiling sun in summer, the chilling, freezing winds of winter, the long hours of toil and heartbreaking uncertainties, took a devastating toll on the men and women, causing them to grow old in body and mind before their time. Dreams for their children were dashed, and the settlers, who didn't die, began to move from the valley one by one. The young people escape, by way of resolute determination, from the dreadful pocket of perpetual poverty for more favorable clime.

When I go back for a solitary visit, I can bring my family and our old neighbors back to life in my mind. I can reconstruct the scenes, as they do in producing motion pictures, and reunite the settlers. The Pre-Atomic Age comes to life and the good folk are walking, talking, laughing and toiling once again.

My Dad, Mack, was nearing fifty when the family moved into the valley to farm. He was still robust, agile and strong. I don't remember ever seeing him sick, but I have seen him worried and depressed. He wasn't afraid of hard work for he fought it from daylight to "dark-thirty" almost every day. He just didn't seem to get into the economic flow of things. Money and worldly possessions seemed to evade him. He was an idealist cast in the world of material things where he didn't fit.

On the other hand, Katy, our mother was weak and sick much of the time, yet prepared to follow her husband, as much as health permitted, in all his decisions.

Our family was among the second generation of unsuspecting settlers to move into the uncompromising environment. Since the original group had already died or moved away, nobody was left to warn us of the disappointments the future held for us. So, we settled in with the same hope and exuberance that filled the hearts of the first farmers twenty-five years earlier.

The Gibbs house we moved into must have been built around nineteen hundred. It was a wood frame structure with three rooms, high ceiling and tall narrow windows. The outside paint, was so old and bleached by the western sun, it was difficult to determine the original color.

The house formed an "L", and outside the overall structure was a porch that faced east. On the north side, attached to the house, was a lean-to, and under it we parked our Ford car. A fireplace was in the middle room that served as a combination living room and bedroom. The room next to the porch was the kitchen where we cooked and ate. This room also served as a bedroom. As a result of the cramped quarters for ten people, we often jokingly sang the ditty, "I've got a gal. She's six feet tall. She sleeps in the kitchen with her feet in the hall."

The floor of our new home was covered with soft pine lumber filled with splinters. It wasn't unusual to spend much time picking pieces of wood from each other's bare feet with a needle from Mother's sewing bag.

On the floor of the middle room, a red substance had been spilled over a large area. Whatever it was had soaked into the soft pine and was impossible to remove. It didn't take my sister Jessie and me long to imagine and to whisper to each other the possibility of it being blood for some victim of a fight among cowboys in the past. We entertained ourselves by telling scary stories about the big red blotch.

The packed soil that, formed the knoll on which the house stood, was almost as hard as concrete from the long years of trampling by domestic beasts and people. Not a blade of grass grew on the naked yard, not a flower, or a tree. The rock-hard dirt was bleached nearly white from the intensity of the relentless sun. This barren piece of ground was a portent of the desolation that was about to over come our family's hopes and hard work.

About twenty steps from the southwest corner of the house, previous dwellers had dug a storm cellar we referred to as our 'fraidy hole.' We ran to the cellar when a tornado threatened. It also served as a storage place for home canned fruit, vegetables and meat we butchered.

Milking cows by hand was a chore accomplished morning and late afternoon. After the last of milk was stripped from the mixed breed cows, we'd pour the milk in the bowl that set atop the separator and turn the handle by muscle power. The multiple thin disks in the housing of the separator caused the cream to come out one spout and the skimmed milk out the other. This precious cream, what little there was, was deposited in a large can and later hauled to town and traded for sugar, salt or spices. The skimmed milk was poured into a container, taken to the cellar, placed in a pan of cold water with rags wrapped around the container to keep the milk from turning sour. We drank the milk we called 'blue john' and cooked with it.

One of the most disliked shores on the farm was breaking down the separator afterwards and thoroughly washing the parts and the forty thin disks.

Our place was as primitive as any farm in the days when Billy the Kid shot his way to fame in the early days of the Anglo in New Mexico. It would have been no different for us had electricity never been harnessed, plumbing never been invented, radio station not broadcast nor newspapers never been printed, for we had none of these amenities.

The lots for the horses, cows and hogs, and the cribs for their feed were perhaps one hundred steps east of the house. This was wise planning on the part others. The lots were on a gentle slope that led down to a dry creek. When the scarce rains came, the animal refuse was washed away. The prevailing southwest winds blew the odor from the lots and carried it to the east of the house.

Nearly half mile to the south of our home was a prairie dog town that covered perhaps ten acres. The area was as bare of vegetations as the palm of our hand. The roly-poly little rodents ate all the grass, weeds and their roots leaving the appearance of a moonscape. They rendered the land absolutely useless for farming or grazing. These cute little critters, with their destructive eating habits, proved only one of the many enemies we faced.

Mr. Stomple, his wife and two daughters lived in a pretty, new house about a mile southwest of us. Another house, old and dilapidated a mile further toward the hills and gullies in the escarpment served as a temporary home for many families passing through our valley in wagons or buggies or on horseback.

To the east of our rented farm was a dry, dusty country road that weaved down from the plains, through our community, northward past ranches, windmills and watering tanks and cattle guards until it reached U S Highway 66. At this juncture stood the: Heckendorne general store and the U S Post Office named Bard.

This road passed by Charley White's farmhouse that was within hollering distance of our place when the wind was blowing from the right direction. The World War I veteran lived with his wife, his son Willie and two young daughters. He operated a blacksmith shop that was built in the side of a rocky cliff.

Northeast of White's place, a mile or so, was the Clark ranch. The Clarks lived in Amarillo while the Tuckers lived on and operate their holdings. The Tucker's daughter, Billie Sue, later became my first 'girlfriend', though she was oblivious of it. The Fred Kerr family lived in a half-dugout farther north a couple of miles off the road. They kept busy trying to make a living on a dry land farm. They had a son named W. S and, as I remember, two small daughters.

Mr. Aston, a rancher who had little to do with farm families, lived across the road from the Kerr family to the west. I never saw any women around his place. Several cowboys, with boots and broad brimmed hats drifted in and out of his place waiting to be hired if needed. His farming was a precautionary measure in case the livestock couldn't forage grass and mesquite beans during the howling winds and deep snows of winter.

Travelers who traveled northward on the lonely road toward Bard could look to the east and see a graveyard as they topped a hill with deep washes. White tombstones within a wire fence were visible from half a mile away. On the lone prairie, in nineteen- hundred-three, a family of several members, as the story was told, lived in a dugout covered with a mound of dirt. During the night while they slept, the poles across the top that held tons of dirt, gave way and buried the entire family alive. Neighbors left them in the dugout where they died and placed stones to mark their home and burial place.

Running north a couple hundred yards from our rented home were two ruts that formed a road. This exit from our dwelling was lined on both sides with mulberry trees that bore fruit every summer. At the end of this short lane ran a dirt road hemmed in by a barbed wire fence on either side. Not far down this road to the west was a small three-room house sitting on half a section of land. This property belonged to Mrs. Albert Leach who lived on the plains with her family. The house, abandoned long ago, leaned precariously form the weight of many years and the harsh weather.

Going west past this pitiful old dwelling was a wire gate that had to be opened by leaning a shoulder heavily against a perpendicular pole at the end of the gate. With the gate opened wide, a team of horses could proceed through it. They pulled the wagon down the crooked road that meandered through a pasture. This land was covered with a type yucca we called beargrass. Scattered tuffs of grass on sandy knolls covered the roadside. A deep, dry arroyo cut through the land. A wooden bridge, without banisters, afforded passage over the wash.

Mr. Johnson, a rancher and friend of Mr. Aston, lived in a small, white house beside the road. He always had a horse or two saddled and hitched to a cedar rail in front of his bungalow.

A few miles down the winding country road lived the Massey family. They farmed and ranched. There were several children in this family. I remember most of all Lorene who was about my age, but much smarter than me.

On the left bank of a dry creek was a clump of giant cottonwood trees. Vultures, crows, hawks and smaller birds made their home in the branches of these trees. Badgers, raccoons, porcupines and pack rats dug their burrows at the base of the magnificent trees among huge boulders.

No bridge crossed this arroyo. It was wide and flat. The road was in its bed. If there were heavy clouds over the breaks to the south, the origin of the arroyo, a sudden down pour of rain was a distinct possibility. In this case, torrents of water could come rushing down the wash in a flash, carrying small trees and all kinds of debris. If passengers going over the road were caught in the flood, they were swept along and perhaps drowned. When a flood was a possibility, we waited awhile, and before long. the bed of the arroyo was dry as ever.

Traveling on this road in a general northwesterly direction about fourteen miles from our house, we came to the village of San Jon with its three hundred residents. These good folk managed to subsist by serving travelers on Highway 66 and caring for the needs of area ranchers and farmers.

Other families drifted in and out of our valley because they had no other place to go. They'd stay a few weeks or months, then hitch up their wagons, go to another settlement seeking means to keep body and soul together. They also sought another precious need, though intangible – human companionship.

A one-room schoolhouse built by the first group of valley people sat at the foot of the escarpment of hills and canyons. Much of the white paint on the building was curled or missing. Like the tattered garments of a homeless man, the paint was torn and ragged from the long exposure to the blistering summer sun and the freezing winter winds. The school was about two miles from our place. It stood alone and vacant for years since the first settlers moved away. Now that Mack and Katy moved into the neighborhood with their eight children, there was exciting talk about opening the humble house of learning once again.

At the Quay County courthouse in Tucumcari, the name of the district was listed officially as Fairview. This sounded like a misnomer to most citizens outside our community, and they laughed when they heard the name. These people just couldn't conceive of our dry valley of hard knocks having a Fairview of any kind.

Despite the many jokes that circulated among the more prosperous plains dwellers and in other outlying areas, the school was in a lovely setting. The rocky hills and ravines covered with dwarf evergreen trees and the mysterious tales of outlaws, cattle rustlers and lovers' quarrels that circulated made the location both a fair and enchanting.

Only a few citizens used the official name of the school. Most folk called the district Punkin Center. Nobody seemed to know how the derogatory name originated or why. But it stuck, and stuck good. Though the school has been dead for seventy years. Old timers, living in the twenty-first-century still call the entire community Punkin Center. The younger generation knows the area only by the uncomplimentary name.

The farmers in our part of the valley did raise pumpkins for their own use. But many farmers all over the eastern part of the state grew pumpkins. I suspect our school was called the name because the more affluent neighbors with more modern schools thought of us as a bunch of pumpkin headed country hicks. If this were the case, they may not be far from right, because ignorance reigned concerning many worldly things beyond our community.

I think it was the year I started to school that Dad introduced me the godevil. This small plow was used to cultivate the long rows of corn, Sudan grass, and maize. The godevil had two basic two-by-six foot wooden runners about eight inches apart with metal strips on the ground edge so they would last longer. Up front on the runners, stubby wings were bolted on each side. In the rear on each side were three disks designed to be adjusted to ride the ridge, made by the lister/planter, and roll moist soil into the furrows around the young plants. There was a seat on top for the plowman to sit. Up front was a hitch attached to the doubletree to which singletrees were secured. Two harnessed horses were hitched to the singletrees. They pulled the plow down the long rows killing weeds and breaking up the surface crust on the soil so the moisture would last longer.

In the spring of twenty-eight, I was six. and Dad thought I was old enough to earn my keep over the protest of Mother. He lifted me upon the seat of the plow. I rode to get the feel while Dad walked along side guiding the horses with long leather lines that ran from his massive hands through the harness to the bridle bits in the horses' mouths. Dad assured me by saying, "Son, you're big enough to ride this thing while your brother and me do heavier work."

I felt important and plenty big. As the sun climbed higher and higher into the clear morning sky, Dad positioned the horses to walk on the ridges so the godevil could run down the furrows and do its work The horses walked down the half-mile rows and Dad walked alongside instructing me in the art of plowing.

We soon discovered I was not heavy enough to make the disks on the plow bite deep enough into the soil. We stopped, found a heavy stone, tied it to the plow and proceeded with our task. When Dad thought I had enough instructions, he warned me, "Son, remember this plow ain't got no wheels. It just scoots around corners when you have to turn into the next row. If you ain't careful, the plow will flop over on you. So, whatcha gotta do is stop the horses at the end of each row, get off the plow and stand on the left wing if you're turning right. Be careful or the plow might flop over and kill you."

The pride and excitement of doing a man's work wore off after a few days. Plowing became a tiresome and boring job. When the morning sun warmed the atmosphere, I'd get drowsy riding the plow and almost fall off. If that happened, the disk would run over me. Fortunately, when I'd nod and begin to fall, the old horses were walking so slow I could catch myself avoiding disaster.

Our first home in Arkansas – Circa 1923
Front Row (L to R): Etta, Jessie, Annabelle,
(Anna died in 1936) and Leslie Eugene
Back Roe: (L to Right): Churchill, Mother and Dad.

Graduation from High School in 1940

After graduating form Army Photo School
Aug. 15, 1941

With my wife, Dorothy, after graduating
from Abilene Christian University
August, 1948

Our daughters Jackie and Kathy
Circa, 1955

*Enjoying an outing at Living Desert State Park (Circa 1988)
with our son-in law, Dr. Larry Gage and our daughter, Kathy Gage
(valedictorian),and their children (From left to Right) Derek
(an attorney today).I'm lifting Leslie D'Ann (who has a
Masters Degree in architecture today), and) Brian (who
is an Aeronautical Engineer today).*

Our daughter, Dr. Jackie, in our back yard.

*Me, Dorothy, and Ruth, who is the wife of T. E. Baxter,
my good friend since our college days.*

Dorothy Hendrix and I were married
Aug. 17, 1943

The
Last Flight of Holey Joe

Kneeling (L to R): Pilot Robert W. Kaub, Co-Pilot Leslie Eugene Fooks,
Navigator Thomas F. Cavanaugh, Bombadier Charles D. Grover,
Engineer Richard O. Wright.
Standing (L to R): Radio Operator Frank Howell, Armament Raley,
Gunner Roscoe L. Overton, Ball Turret Gunner Roy G. Munsey,
Tail Gunner Robert M. Lee.

Leslie Eugene Fooks

Fl. Ep. 13 Lagekroki von23. 9. 44

I'm most grateful to Stefan Naef, a European writer, I met at a convention in San Antonio, Texas 1995. Stefan searched the archives in his home country and found pictures of the B-17 airplane, named **Holey Joe**, we landed after the electricity and oxygen were shot out by enemy fire. Below is the image taken by radar as we made the approach for landing. Date 9-23-44.

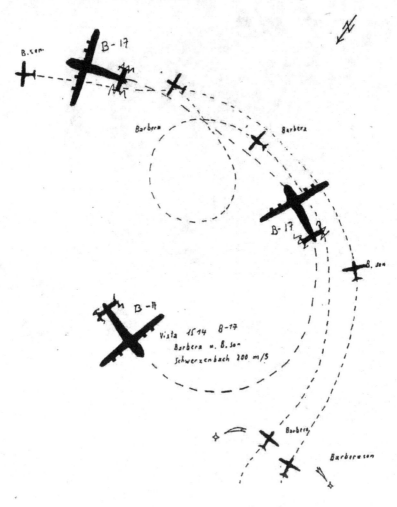

WORK, DANGER, MYSTERY

"Heave! Everybody's gotta heave! And give it everything you've got. This thing's heavy. When we get ready to lift, remember to look out for rattlesnakes, for those slimy critters like to bed up under places like this for the winter," Dad was reminding the working crew.

It was the busy spring of 1928. The men in the valley and few from the plains had gathered to move the Fairview one-room school house from its old location to a more central place on the corner of the half section owned by Mrs. Albert (Mary) Leach. (The tools they had for the job were crude and ancient by today's standards.) Two flatbed wagons, with small steel wheels below the wagon beds, stood ready to haul the schoolhouse to its new location. With cedar poles cut from trees in the breaks, several men got on each pry-pole to lift the house off its foundation. When it was high enough, the wagons were rolled underneath. Two horses were hitched to each wagon. When all was ready, they began to pull the load slowly down the mile-and-a-half bumpy road to the new spot where a foundation of stones was waiting

Sure enough, when the building was lifted and sunshine flooded the ground that had been dark for years, a nest of rattlers, coiled around one another, began to move slowly, drowsily from their winter's hibernation. In this condition the snakes did not hiss or rattle. The men had a job to do, and left the 'slimy critters' to their own purpose. Some of the men, who hated rattlers, wished to return and exterminate the entire lot.

With plowing, planting and the many other chores to do on each farm, it would take the better part of a year for the men to prepare the school for students. In the meantime Dad was set on his children "gettin' some learnin'," even though we'd have to go to some distant school while doing work each of us was suited for at home and in the field. Seldom did we start school when it opened around the first of September. For there was canning of vegetables and fruits, hogs to butcher and crops to gather, all of which came before school.

I didn't know how it came about, but we were sent to the New Hope school on the plains in Curry County while we lived in Quay County. In the fall when most of the crops were laid by, Churchell, who was going on seventeen, was allowed to drive our touring Ford from the valley up through the breaks on to the plains where we attended school.

Our older brother was slender and a few inches taller than Dad. He was strong, agile and intelligent. Sometimes I thought he was meaner than a hungry coyote. There was conflict between him and me, for he often tried to make me do things I did want to do. Even in those days, we had different outlooks on life. Churchell was leaning toward the wild side by rebelling against our parents' wishes. He began to run with the wrong crowd, stayed out late some nights, and used words intentionally to embarrassed Mother, and made his younger siblings wonder, for we never heard Dad use such words. Mother would reprehend him by simply saying, "Son, you ought to be ashamed of yourself." He made it worse my laughing at her rebuke.

I was accused of being Mothers pet for I was content to obey her, and take up for her when the rest of the family teased her because of her old fashion ways.

When work on the farm was nearly complete in the fall, Dad thought it was time for his older children to start school on the plains. Leaving the younger boys, Ray and Raymond and Jay in the care of Mother, Anne, Etta and Jessie got in the back seat of the Model T while I sat in the drivers seat to manipulate the controls while Churchell cranked to get the motor started.

My big brother put the crank in the hole under the radiator and began to twist the crank using only muscle power. My job was to adjust the "ears," one on each side of the column, just below the steering wheel. The "ears" were handles sitting on a sliding scale, one controlled the amount of gasoline entering the motor, the other controlled the magneto or spark. If I didn't give it enough gas or spark, the motor would never turn over to start. If I pulled the handles down too far giving the temperamental "beast" more gas and spark than needed, the motor would "kick" by twirling the crank by such force and speed that it could break Churchell's arm or "kick" him to kingdom come. Adjusting the "ears" was a tricky job with little margin for error that a six-year-old had no business working unless it was an emergency.

When I didn't give it enough "juice" to start the motor, Churchell would stand up straight and tall in his overalls, call me uncomplimentary names and order me to give it more. If I gave it more gas or spark than needed, the crank would begin to twirl. Churchell would release his grip on the crank before it hit his arm, rise to his full height and tell me in plane language what he thought of his young helper.

Finally the motor started. Big brother pushed me aside and jumped into the drivers seat and we were off for school in our patched and faded clothes. For lunch, we carried a large bucket that contained lard spread on cold biscuits, a jar of home canned fruit or vegetables and some boiled eggs.

As Churchell gave the automobile full throttle, dust from the country road rose high in the air, and neighbors in our valley knew the Fooks kids were off to school. As we passed the prairie dog town, the chubby little rascals chirped a warning to their colony, wiggled their tails and made a beeline for their burrows. The wheels of the car, with their wooden spokes, jumped in and out of the ruts in the awful road. Sometimes we had to hold on with both hands or be bounced out of the automobile.

While driving through the breaks, I wondered about the mysteries held by the hills and canyons. It was rumored that whiskey stills, operated by some of our neighbors and the plains people, were hidden in the ravines far from the roads. Occasionally, on a calm day, we could see the telltale columns of smoke ascending toward the sky. This made us think there might be some validity to the rumors.

If we got a good run up the caliche road, we could top out on the caprock making it onto the plains without a mishap. Because the 'tin lizzy' had no fuel pump, gasoline was gravity fed to the motor, Churchell turned the car around, pushed the reverse pedal to the floorboard and shot up the hill backwards. All the time the girls in the back seat were shouting, "Don't go so fast. You're going to kill us all!" Big brother only laughed with a smirk on his face.

We got to the New Hope school in Curry County in nothing flat, parked the car, and got out frightened half to death because all those "rich" (at least in our minds) children were having fun playing in the yard. Anna, our oldest sister, carried the lunch bucket that all five of us had to share at the proper time. As we approached the two-room brick building that sat near the middle of the township, one of the two women teachers met us and asked politely, "May I help you?"

I gawked about as the teacher led us into the school building. There were two large rooms divided by a folding partition that could be opened up by sliding it on a long rail. One room was for youngsters in first grade through fourth, the other was for youth from fifth grade through eighth. A teacher's desk was at the front of each room. If a special assembly was called for, the separating wall was pulled back. When the entire school was together, the children faced a western pioneer painting that served as a backdrop to the rear of the stage.

We were enrolled, but there was a question if we would be permitted to stay in the school since we lived in Quay County. They allowed us to remain until the school board answered the uncertainty. The inquiry took a few weeks and we stayed for the rest of school the year.

Churchell was a real daredevil behind the wheel. One afternoon school let out while the sun hung high in the sky. The five of us took our place in the Model-T and big brother wanted to have his kind of fun by traveling lickety-split in the dusty, country roads on the plains. A sheriff's deputy spotted us racing recklessly and began to chase us. Our wiry, daredevil big brother out-maneuvered and out-ran the deputy until we lost him. We ended up on the lip of the caprock among a field of cacti, commonly called prickly pear, which had produced an abundant harvest of bright red fruit.

Our wild driver was wise regarding natural surroundings, and since all of us were tired and hungry, he encouraged us to eat the fruit of the cacti. He warned us not to eat without first cleaning them because each pear was covered with stiff, hair-like needles that could hardly be seen. If these needles got in one's mouth and on the tongue, they would cause misery for months. So we cleaned the pears by rolling them in the dirt, and wiped the dirt off by rubbing them on our clothes. We got home that day in time to do the night chores.

As far as I know, Dad was never told the truth why we were so late. But Churchell wasn't so fortunate in his next wild episode. Coming home from school one afternoon, Churchell stopped the car on the edge of the caprock just before we started down the rocky, winding road through the escarpment into the valley. With his strength, he easily pulled me out of the automobile and deposited me hard on the car's black hood stating, "If you want to ride, you can ride down this hill sitting on the hood."

While the three girls cried for him not to make me stay on the hood, he got in the drivers seat and started driving down the curving, humpy passageway. I screamed to the top of my voice. When I tried to grab the top of the windshield with my hands to keep from falling off, Churchell hit them with a ruler. While I was slipping and sliding from one side of the hot metal hood to the other on the sunny afternoon with temperature close to one hundred, my sisters were screaming for our big brother to stop and let me back in the car. My screams echoed off the hills and canyons bouncing back to us giving an ominous, mysterious warning of disaster.

While I cried, Churchell was having the time of his life laughing every time I slid across the hood. Before we got in sight of home, I was allowed to get back in the car. Big brother scolded me for "acting like a baby," and he warned us all not to tell Dad about the episode.

Jessie was more than two years older then me, but I had grown to be near her size. We had become the best of friends. She always wore her black hair in two long pigtails that fascinated me. If Mother was partial to me, Dad was partial to Jessie and she knew he would stand by her. With the evening chores complete, after the ride down the caprock road, warning or no warning, Jessie told Dad what Churchell had done. All his explaining about "just having fun" and "made sure he didn't get hurt" did not satisfy Dad. The argument that ensued upset the entire family. Finally Dad had enough of crying, screaming and yelling. He reached for his old fashion leather strap, he used to sharpen his straight razor, and ordered his oldest son to bend over and gave him a whipping that none who witnessed it will ever forget.

Churchell was tough and refused to cry. As dusk enveloped our valley, this family drama was played for real on the front porch. Big brother, nearing seventeen and feeling sure and confident declared several times, "I'm going to leave home, and I'm not coming back!"

Mother was sobbing nearly out of control pleading with her son not to say things like that. She was stating her heartfelt desire that he stay home for she loved him very much. Mother, the girls and I were crying. Dad was angry.

Dad got tired of arguing with his oldest son, and called his bluff. "All right, young man, if you want to leave, I'll take you over to Highway 66 in the morning and you can hitchhike anywhere you want to go." This challenge caused an uneasy calm to hover over the scene.

The next morning before the sun peeped over the horizon, all of us, who were old enough, were out of our beds ready to do our morning chores. The cows had to be milked, the hogs slopped and the horses fed. Churchell was calm and subdued. Not a soul said a word to him about leaving. The long restless night brought cooler heads and more reasonable hearts. The family was staying together for a while longer.

It was one of those glorious mornings when the early New Mexico sunshine was chasing away the chill on the high plains. While Mother tended to the younger boys, the girls filled the big iron wash pot with water. It set on flat stones in the front yard. Under the pot they built a roaring fire, for they needed boiling water to do the family wash. In his rush, Dad stopped to check the ashes in the hopper to make sure water continued to trickle through them into the glass jar below that collected lie water for future soap-making. Churchell and I were in the lot harnessing the horses to hitch them to a wagon for this also was wood-gathering day. The twins, Ray and Raymond, wanting to learn, were underfoot and at the same time getting a good scolding for being in our way.

While the early morning air was fresh, Dad drove the team of horses, George and Mose, as they pulled the wagon across the dry prairie toward the breaks. I stood beside Dad watching the buzzards soar in circles high above in the cloudless, blue sky. I heard the birds singing their melodious songs. As we passed the prairie dog town, I was amused watching the antics of the pesky little rodents eating their breakfast on the outer perimeter of their town. When they heard the squeaky, rumbling wagon, dozens of the fat, brown butterballs stopped their eating, sat up and took notice of the passing monster. In unison they chatted loudly to warn their brothers and sisters.

Each of the many burrows in the dog town had a mound of dirt that looked like a huge chocolate donut, piled around it. The furry little animals sat on the mounds chatting mockingly at us. When we got closer they wiggled their tails and disappeared in a flash into the protection of their diggings. I laughed at the activities of God's creatures.

Before the sun had risen to a forty-five degree angle in the eastern sky, we had gathered half a load of wood. My assignment was to drive the team pulling the wagon as Dad and Churchell directed while they walked looking for wood.

Dad carried a long crowbar for prying up roots and stumps, and my brother carried an ax on his shoulder to cut wood down to size for loading. A variety of woods were thrown into the wagon along with a number of dried cow chips for good measure. Dead, dry cacti, from which lamp stands are made sometime, were plentiful and good for a quick, hot fire for they burned fast. Dead pine, with plenty of resin, also burned rapidly and was found in abundance in the breaks. Scrubby cedar could be found in great variety in the rocky hills, and it was choice fuel for it burned more slowly and had a lovely aroma as it blazed.

Dad also wanted to haul in a good supply of mesquite wood even if getting it took a lot of sweat and sore muscles. Dry mesquite roots are about as tough and hard as iron rails. If the ax was dull, and if the root wasn't hit square, the ax would just bounce off like striking a block of granite. But when the hard, dense mesquite was finally cut down to size, it made a roaring fire that lasted a long time.

We worked hard to get home shortly after noon for there was plenty of work on the farm to keep us busy until dark. We had no timepiece, but we knew it was mid-day when the sun reached its zenith and began its decent toward the western horizon. When we got home, the wood was stacked in piles according to the kind it was. Dirty and sweaty, we went to the house, washed our hands and faces in a blue galvanized pan filled with water and ate the victuals the girls had prepared. Dad took a nap on the floor with his muscular right arm crooked under his head. After a half hour of rest, he was ready to mend a broken down fence, walk over the field to check on the crop, inspect the condition of the two brood sows that were about to deliver pigs and settle arguments among his children. Looking back over a day well spent in behalf of the household, Dad, along with his family, was ready to bed down after the night chores were done.

Before many days had past, the two sows, each weighing about 350 pounds, gave birth to thirty-four piglets. One of the sows had a litter of eighteen and the other produced sixteen babies. Dad thought this was a record production for two female swine, for he had never heard of so many offspring being born to only two mother sows at one time. Without the record book, he could not prove his assumption.

But Dad was happy telling the family that if we raised the pigs until they were ready for market, we could have enough money to buy needed things for the farm and extra cash to buy new clothes for school. Beside that, he hoped he could buy Mother a store-bought dress, and she wouldn't have to wear one she made herself or some hand-me-down.

But Dad's happiness was diminished somewhat when he went out one early morning to check on the sows and their broods. He found the heavy mothers had rolled over on the piglets during the night and killed several of them. Yet Dad reasoned that it was not so bad for the sows had too many offspring to suckle, and the ones left could have more mothers' milk and be healthier. But the mother swine continued to smash their babies during the following nights. When only fourteen piglets were left out of the entire two litters, we separated the babies from their mothers at night and let them return to nurse several times during the day. Within a few weeks the remaining pigs had grown to be about forty-five pounds each.

It was spring, and all around our place grass, weeds and the seeds in the long rows in the field were sprouting and coming forth in beautiful greenery. The nights were cool, and the daytime temperature was low. Hopes were high with the pigs maturing so well, and the winter snows had left moisture deep in the soil-making prospect for a good crop come fall.

While things had settled down and guarded hopes were better than usual, Mother and Dad decided to take the weekend off and visit old friends on the plains. Churchell had hiked up through the breaks to the plains to be with his friends. Anna was dreaming of her boyfriend who lived on a farm close to San Jon. Etta, Jessie and I, were left to do the farm chores, and baby-sit our younger brothers.

I invited W. S. Kerr and Billy White, who were about my age, to come play on the Sunday afternoon. We had heard the cowboys in the area talk about broncobuster rodeos, and we had seen a few of the local bigger boys ride yearling calves for fun. With these ides floating in our heads, we decided to do some calf riding. We herded a five-month-old calf into the lot where milk cows dropped the waste from their bodies on the ground. While W. S. and Billy held the animal secure, I tied a rope around its chest just like we'd seen the big boys do. Then I climbed on the calf, clutched the rope tightly with my left hand, threw my right hand in the air and yelled, "Let her rip," like a real cowboy. My "bronco" jumped as high as he could, twisted his rear end and came back down to earth. As I leaned forward, trying desperately to stay astride the calf, the agile little beast jerked his head upward hitting my nose with one of his tiny horns that was just beginning to emerge from his head. I fell off the little steer into a fresh cow-pie with my nose bleeding and big tears rolling down my cheeks. That ended our rodeo.

Somehow the fourteen pigs broke out of their pen where we fed them corn from the crib and weeds we pulled from the surrounding area. It was impossible for my siblings and me to chase the pigs down and herd them back where they belonged Had Dad been there, he could have found a way to catch them and herd them back to their pen.

The sun was sinking in the west, and it was time to milk the cows and feed the livestock. Jessie was mad, for some forgotten reason, and refused to leave the house and help with the chores. As Etta and I left the house, we noticed the pigs lying still in open areas as the long shadows disappeared in the early evening. We tried to wake them, but it was no use for they were dead. We could not understand this mysterious turn of events. What would Dad and Mother think? What would Dad do? His hopes of selling the hogs for money to buy needed supplies for the farm and clothes for school will be shattered, I thought.

The darkening shadows of twilight moved slowly across our valley. Etta and I continued with the chores while Jessie lay on her back on the porch throwing a rubber ball against a wall. Before we finished with our work, Jessie came running to the animal lots. Before she got halfway down the slopping ground that led to the lots, Jessie was screaming, "I'm scared! There's something strange going on in the house" She was almost out of breath when she reached us, but managed to say, "While I was throwing a ball against the wall, there was another sound. It was louder than the noise made by the ball." Recalling the bloody appearing blotch on living room floor, she blurted out, "I think it might be a ghost!"

While Etta tried to calm Jessie down, I was thinking about the red stain on the living room floor wondering if that had anything to do with ghost like noises she heard. Did the fourteen dead hogs lying around the house have anything to do with the strange noise that frightened her?

After we talked it over, we decided not to go back to the house. We left the buckets of milk in the lot, and got the younger boys together, then the six children of Mack and Katy's made haste stumbling through the darkness over the fields and pastures and through barbed-wire fences to the safety of Charlie White's house.

The light from the coal oil lamp, shinning dimly through the window of our neighbor's home was our beacon. Etta knocked, and before Mrs. White had opened the door completely, Jessie asked breathlessly, "Can we come in?" Inside, Etta, with Jessie and me interrupting, told why we had come so late in the evening. While we told our story, Charley White sat in a cane-bottom chair chuckling because he didn't believe in ghosts and thought every event had a logical explanation. This old World War I veteran, who had crawled half way across enemy territory dodging German bullets, while many of his buddies died, wasn't about to be taken in by our fantastic tale.

Near ten that evening, Dad and Mother came home from the plains. They drove down the rutted road lined with mulberry trees. As they came close to the house, the dim headlights from the "tin lizzie" shined on a few of the hogs lying near the yard. There was no light in the house, and not one child could be found. Mother, her big hat still on her head, with more emphasis than usual, exclaimed in her soft voice, "This has me worried sick! Mack, where can all the children be?"

Dad was at a loss, for he knew nothing of what went on in the early evening. He didn't answer Mother's question; rather he scurried about the yard trying to learn the answer to her question. He went into the darkened house; struck a match and lit a lamp with a blackened chimney. He just couldn't understand what had happened. He was worried also and muttered, "Something terrible has happened. But what can it be?"

With an old flashlight, he searched every corner of the house again but found nothing to unravel the mystery that confronted him. Leaving the house he looked over the yard and beyond and saw not a single thing unusual except the dead hogs scattered around the place. A search of the cow lots and the pigpens gave him no clue. But when he found the milk buckets sitting half full on the ground of the lot, his worries deepened.

Dad went back to the car where Mother was still seated. She was crying. Dad had to tell her the children had simply disappeared, vanished. They were nowhere to be found. While trying to console Mother, he looked to the northeast and through the darkness saw a dim light in the home of Charlie White. "That is unusual, for Charlie goes to bed long before this time of the night," he thought. In a flash, a second thought occurred to him, "The children must be over there waiting for us to pick them up."

He jumped in the driver's seat of the car with its motor still running, turned it around and started down the rutted road lined with mulberry trees. Coming to the country lane, Dad turned to the right giving the motor full throttle. While driving, he told Mother of his hunch. She was most hopeful and her crying stopped. Only sobs remained. Dad stopped in front of Charlie's house, jumped out of the Model T, rushed to the door and knocked. All of us made a mad rush for the door, opened it, and smothered him with hugs. We chatted like a bunch of blackbirds, attempting to tell him what happened.

All of us children piled into the "tin lizzie," with Mother and Dad, and the car clattered all the way home over the dusty, bumpy, country road. Thinking of the mysterious events of the day and wondering what would happen next, there wasn't much sleep that night for any of us. But as dawn broke the next morning, Dad was up investigating. He was anxious to learn why all his young hogs had died, and what caused that unusual sound Jessie heard that frightened us so much that we left everything behind and ran through the darkness to our neighbor's house.

First, Dad looked carefully at the vomit some of the hogs had spewed out on the ground as they were dying. All hogs liked weeds that they were fed regularly along with corn and other grains. (The weeds were to them what vegetables are to humans.) As Dad, using a small stick, moved small bits of the vomit about, he found some suspicious morsels. Though these morsels had been partly digested, they still made him think the mystery was closer to being solved. He put a few of the pieces in his hand, and then walked around the farm, checking young plants that were just coming up. He knew that under certain condition some sprouts, when eaten, are poison to hogs. Among these poisonous plants are cocklebur sprouts when they first appear out of the ground bent in the shape of a jackknife. Dad compared the morsels he had in his hand with the thousands of sprouts found among the larger weeds. After making a comparison, he concluded they were the same and regretfully surmised the hogs had eaten the poisonous cockleburs while gorging on weeds.

The mystery of the dead hogs had been solved, but he was determined to learn about the strange noise Jessie heard that scared us half to death, causing us to leave everything behind and the entire farm deserted. Dad checked inside the house hitting the walls with his fist, trying to find boards that might be loose. He crawled up into the attic inspecting the dark place with the shine from the flashlight. There was nothing.

Next, he went outside looking for loose boards that might flap against the house with the slightest breeze. Dad found a perpendicular board on the northwest corner of the house that was not nailed down securely. Dad called for Jessie. When she arrived, he pulled on the board and released it so it hit the house. Then asked his youngest daughter, "Is this what you heard?" She replied, "That sure sounds like it." Finally the mystery of the frightening noise was solved.

Our Father seemed to take every disappointment with stride - without much fanfare. Though he must have been devastated, he showed little outward emotion over the great loss of his cash crop - the hogs. He prepared for breakfast by taking water from a galvanized bucket with a dipper, pouring it into a pan and washed his face and hands. He dried off with the same towel the whole family used and sat down to eat.

When we were all seated at the long table to eat red-eye gravy, slices of ham from last year's butchered hogs, eggs and homemade biscuits, Dad led us in prayer of thanksgiving. Before we tasted the first bite of food, Dad said, "Unless the row crop comes in better than I expect since rains have been scarce, we can't get the needed things for the farm, and we can't buy the new school clothes for you kids." All eyes were focused on Dad as he spoke in earnest. For the first time ever, we witnessed tears roll down his heavy cheeks and his large, rough hands wipe them away. Jessie was moved, jumped up, ran outside crying out, "I'm not hungry!"

NEW HOME – NEW SCHOOL – NEW RESPONSIBILITY

Mother got up early December 24th, 1928, arousing her sleepy children with her mild voice calling out, "Christmas Eve Gift." She was carrying on the tradition her childhood family brought to New Mexico from Missouri. As I recall, the first to repeat the tradition was supposed to get a gift from all the rest. Since money was so scarce, the dear lady knew there would be no gifts from her children. But Mother did manage to hide enough eggs gathered from the hen's nest to sell for a dime a dozen when she went to town. With the money, she bought each member of our family an orange as a present to be given on Christmas Day.

When the evening chores were done on the day we celebrated the Birth of our Lord, Churchell played the part of Santa Claus. He dressed in a long, black overcoat, work gloves and boots and hid in the attic. When Mother gave the signal, he came out of the opening in the ceiling, dropped to the floor and shouted, "Merry Christmas!" At this point, Mother gave each member of her family an orange, wishing all a happy holiday. Her warm smile and joyful attitude warmed the hearts of us all.

The year ending had been busy and eventful, but 1929 promised to be busier and more eventful. Dad told us we were moving again. Herbert Gibbs, whose parents owned the farm we rented, wanted to move back to the old home place.

Dad assured us everything was all right, for he had made a deal with Mrs. Albert (Mary) Leach to rent her half section by giving her part of the proceeds from the farm. The old house that sat on the land hadn't been occupied for years and was in great need of repair. Dad had to help renovate the schoolhouse, repair the house, we hoped to move into, and dig a water well at our new place while keeping the Gibbs farm operating until the crops were laid-by in the fall.

I had turned seven and was becoming more adventuresome. So, when Dad told us we planned to move to the place less than a mile to the northwest, curiosity forced me to hike across the plowed field and grassland through two barbed wire fences and check it out. Reaching the old house, I found the front door off its hinges and reluctantly stepped inside only to discover a big hole in the rotted, wood floor. When I looked through the hole, a large, but harmless king snake, green in color, was peering up at me. I never knew why, but when the snake's eyes met mine, I was "charmed," and I couldn't move until finally the snake wiggled away among the stones collected under the house.

Dad had built a barbed wire fence around the yard of the Gibbs house to keep livestock away. For a gate, he dug two holes about three feet apart with a muscle-powered post-hole-diggers. He put a pine pole in each hole, tamped dirt around each post that stood about six-and-a-half feet high. To make the post steadier, Dad put a double strand of barbed wire at the top of the posts. Then he put a stick between the strands, twisting the wires into one strand. The high wire was a challenge for me. So one morning coming to breakfast after feeding the hogs, I stopped between the posts, jumped as high as I could and missed touching the high barbed wire. Tried again and missed. I mustered all the strength in my legs and jumping higher than before, slapped one of the barbs on the wire with the middle finger on my right hand and was suspended in mid-air for a fraction of a second. When the flesh ripped from my finger, I dropped to the ground. Blood gushed from the wound.

When Dad was called, he ordered one of the girls to bring some coal oil. He thrust my wounded finger into the liquid that immediately turned red with my blood. Next he called for a clean rag, took a wad of tobacco he was chewing from his mouth, placed it on my finger, tied the rag around to hold the chew, then said with whimsical assurance, "Now get out of here, and get ready for breakfast."

In a few days, the wound was healed, but from that day until now, I've worn a scar that reaches almost around my middle finger.

Dad was busy helping neighbors renovate the schoolhouse and working with Albert Leach to repair our future dwelling. Mr. Leach bought supplies from Clovis hauling them in his truck to the valley making the place livable for the ten of us. Churchell and I were left to care for the farm, Anna, Etta and Jessie milked the cows, fed the livestock operated the separator. They put the milk and cream in the cellar so these items wouldn't sour. The twins, Ray and Raymond, had their lesser chores to do, and Mother took care of baby Jay who was nearing two. We continued to fire up the Model T and go to school on the plains when time permitted.

The atmosphere had felt strange since early morning. Big brother had gone to help work on the house we hoped to move into in late fall. By noon, the whirling winds on the ground kicked up dust devils that danced crazily across the open fields. The cows and horses acted as if something mysterious was about to happen. Strong winds aloft churned up the darkening clouds that constantly changed their threatening shapes and colors.

Not long after the pair ate their sack lunch, Dad said, "Son, I think we'd better get home for something awful seems to be brewing in the clouds."

When they got home, they found Ray and Raymond, using a choice marble attempting to shoot other marbles out of a ring they had drawn in the yard. The boys were oblivious of the threatening storm. Jessie and I were in the living room throwing round rubber fruit jar sealers at the nails driven into each number of the large calendar we got at the grocery store. If a sealer looped a nail by a number, we put that number down on paper. At the end of a certain time, we each added up our numbers and the person with the highest number won. The evil winds and clouds meant nothing to us at the time.

Churchell rushed into the house making an ugly remark about the hard rains in the breaks. Mother thinking his speech was vulgar, said, "Son, you ought to be ashamed of yourself." He laughed and went on unconcerned.

Dad took a position on the edge of the porch to watch the storm as it continued to form. Knowing that I enjoyed watching weather and its fury, Dad called for me to join him. I found him leaning on the corner post completely enamored by the spectacle in the sky. We watched the ever-changing, evil-looking clouds that were churned by tempestuous winds. The lightning and thunder were getting closer.

Without warning, a mighty crack of lightning hit the house and followed the metal drain gutter along the edge of the roof. A splinter of electricity bounced off Dad's balding head, and he staggered backwards. The whole family gathered around him frightened and excited beyond belief. When he gained his composure, Dad said, "I'm all right. Mother nature is just playing a little game with me." He rubbed his head and continued, "You know she did get a little rough. That felt just like I was hit in the head with a ballpeen hammer."

Mother pleaded with Dad to come into the house, but he refused, exercising the theory that lightning never strikes twice in the same place. He loved to watch the great natural drama being played all around us by the powerful forces of nature overhead. The drum-rolls of thunder and the spectacular streaks of lightning were to Dad the same as a grand Broadway production, the Boston Symphony and a Hollywood extravaganza rolled into one.

Pointing to the southwest, Dad said to me with exuberance in his voice, "See that funnel cloud on the caprock. That's a real tornado, and it's coming down through the breaks!" His excitement grew, "It's coming down onto the valley floor!" Then he cried out so all the family could hear, "A twister's comin' off the cap, headin' our way. We all better make a run for the cellar!"

Dad gathered his smaller children into his powerful arms and herded the older ones while leading mother. Within a minute or two, he had all ten of us safely underground with the cellar door only partially closed. The door was left ajar for light and air. But there was another reason: Dad wanted to continue watching the changing formation of the clouds and the tornado as it danced a zigzag path across the valley floor. My interest was also piqued, and I nestled close to him taking it all in. Dad gave a blow-by-blow account of the approaching storm as if he were broadcasting a football game. He wanted to keep the family informed and perhaps give the benefit of his wisdom about storms accumulated over the years.

Calmly he reported, "Well, looks like the twister is headed straight as an arrow toward the Stemple's house. As powerful as this thing is, if it hits, you can kiss the house and the family good-bye. They'll never live through this storm, and they don't have a cellar to scamper into."

We watched as the tornado made a beeline toward their house. When it hit, the dwelling exploded as the roof lifted. It was torn into a million pieces. Splintered boards did crazy antics in the air. Mattresses, bedsteads, stoves and furniture floated hundreds of feet above the ground in the strong, twisting winds. The storm passed one-half mile south of us over the prairie dog town carrying its cargo of destruction.

When the tornado was beyond us to the east, Dad, Churchell and I ran the mile across the treeless pasture to investigate the damages. We expected the worst for Mr. Stemple, his wife and their two teenage daughters.

While we were a considerable distance from the place where their house had stood, to our great surprise and delight, we saw the four of them walking around checking on what was left.

Dad yelled, "Anybody hurt?"

"No more than a scratch," Mr. Stemple responded.

As we approached the four, Dad asked eagerly, "How in the world did you get out of this alive?" Noticing a basement below the kitchen, Dad continued, "Ya'll went into the basement?"

"No," Mr. Stemple answered with a calmness and assurance that only a man with deep convictions and superior faith could muster, "If we had gone down there all may have been killed. You see that hole in the floor over the basement? Well, the storm threw the sewing machine through the floor. If we had been in the basement, the thing might have killed us all."

"We watched the twister take your house. I don't see how you came out alive," Dad spoke incredulously.

Mr. Stemple explained, "When we saw the tornado coming, I called the family together. We kneeled and prayed for the Lord to take care of us. He has seen us through, and we are safe. We are most thankful."

The Stemple family was more educated than ours was, and I took note of their better English and pronunciation.

"Your house and furniture are all gone," Churchell spoke with a trace of doubt in his voice. "I'd recommend gettin' a cellar."

"That's right, young man," Mr. Stemple responded with unbelievable stability in his voice after the shocking experience. "I don't know why the Lord allowed it to happen. But He did spare us to be His witnesses, and we accept His will."

I think Dad was a little skeptical about the direct intervention of the Lord, but the whole incident left a lasting impression on my seven-year-old mind.

The Stemple family was in a long line of victims of the harsh environment, uncertainties and dreadful realities of life in our valley - the pocket of perpetual poverty. They moved away after the storm, and we never saw them again.

(In later years, I was chaplain at Lakeview Christian Home, a nursing and retirement firm, in Carlsbad for eighteen years. During my tenure there, I tried to learn something about each resident. I saw a lady sitting alone at a table. After introducing myself, she told me her name was Mrs. Miller. Since the 400 residents in the Home came from many points of the United States, I ask Mrs. Miller, who was well into her seventies, "Where did you grow up?" She replied, "I'm not an import, I'm a rarity, for I was raised in New Mexico" "Me to," I said. Then asked, "Where in New Mexico? "North of Clovis." I responded with excitement, "So was I, and where did your family live?" "Under the caprock in the valley." With much more excitement I said, "That's where my family settled, but I don't remember you." She said, "We lived the old Gibbs house." "This is unbelievable, we also lived on the Gibbs' farm. Whom did you know in the valley?" She told me she knew the Stemples and that their daughters were her best friends. I told Mrs. Miller about the tornado blowing their home away and that none of them was hurt. She didn't know about the storm or perhaps she had forgotten.)

In the late spring, a younger sow delivered a litter of pigs. Our family's hopes were brightened. On a lazy afternoon while Dad and Churchell worked on our future home, I was restless and walked down to the cow lot in the hot sunshine for no particular reason. When I got there, I was surprised to find a three-week-old pig lying still in the sun. This was unusual for even a baby pig has enough sense to sleep in the shade. I tried to wake the little fellow, but he didn't move. Running back to the house, I told Mother and the girls about my find. Anna, Etta, Jessie, Ray and Raymond followed me down to the stock pen.

As we ran, we wondered if this was a repeat of the fourteen shoats dying only a few months before. It wasn't, for all the other pigs were in the shade sucking at their mother's breasts.

Supposing this lone little fellow was dead for some mysterious reason, unanimously we agreed that we should have a funeral for it. Jessie was chosen to preach the ceremony, and at the appropriate time, the rest of us joined in singing hymns from memory - off key of course. When the exercise ended, Jessie and I picked the pig up and tossed it over the fence, expecting to take it to the nearby creek in the cool of the late afternoon so its decaying body wouldn't stink up the place.

To our great surprise, when the pig hit the ground, it gave a big belch and whatever it was that put it to sleep came from its mouth. The little fellow jumped to its feet and ran across the plowed field. We stood in complete amazement.

The summer of 1929 was a busy one. Dad worked with different crews on both the schoolhouse and the dwelling we prepared to move into after the crops on the Gibbs place were gathered. Churchell worked hard dividing his time between helping Dad and caring for the fields and livestock with my help, and the girls did many of the chores and the housework. Yet, the school would not be ready for ready for some time.

There was a lull in activities on the Gibbs place while waiting for the fields to ripen for harvest. It was a quiet Sunday afternoon at our house. Churchell had hiked up through the breaks to the plains to be with friends. Anna had gone horseback riding in a sidesaddle with her beau from the San Jon area. The rest of our family, except Jessie and me, were asleep with windows and doors wide open to catch the slightest breeze. These openings with no screens allowed flies from the pigpens and cow lots to enter and crawl over the faces of sleeping victims.

The two of us, with our vivid imaginations, embellished stories about the big red blotch on the living room floor. We told of a villain disguised as a barber who was shaving his enemy with a straight razor, and at the proper time slit his throat causing the blood to gush out onto the floor. Or perhaps the stories of Billy the Kid being shot in Fort Sumner were wrong, and maybe it was in this very house that Pat Garrett shot the youthful outlaw. Or, could this be the room where the famous outlaw Black Dart shot one of his victims leaving his blood splattered over our floor. As the stories continued the more gruesome they became, and fearful shivers began to race up and down my spine for Jessie was an exciting storyteller.

As our new home was nearing completion, I had to run over there several times to see how the work was progressing. The outside diminution of the house was 12 steps by 12 steps. It faced east, and the foundation held the structure about two feet above the ground. There were two doors, one on each side of the east wall Tarpaper was secured over each of the outside walls. The workers stretched chicken wire over the tarpaper. And over the wire, the workers smeared a thin layer of cement. Boards with knotholes covered the sloping roof, and the boards were covered with galvanized sheets of corrugated iron. A large, flat, limestone rock that served as a step-up, was placed in front of the door that led into the kitchen This room ran the full length of the house with a bed at the far west end. Windows with wooden frames were on the north side.

I remember well the wood cook stove with its stovepipe that ran up through the roof, its warming oven and the other oven where cornbread and other eatables were cooked. Different woods and dried cow chips were put inside and fired up for heat. A long table was in place between the stove and the bed. A long bench was placed on either side of the table where us kids sat while eating. Mother and Dad sat in cane bottom chairs at the ends of the table.

The rest of the house was divided into two rooms. The first was a combination living room and bedroom. The back room was for sleeping with two or three beds. In the middle of living room was a heating stove with a stovepipe that ran up through the roof with its damper to regulate the heat in winter. No one had ever seen before or after a stove like this one. It was a unique original in every way. Dad took a fifty five-gallon oil barrel and cut a ten-inch square hole in the top. Then he made a metal door on hinges to cover the opening. He made a grate and put it inside. He followed that by bending two inch-and-a-half steel pipes that were fashioned in such a way to form a cradle for the barrel to lay in horizontally, and at the same time have four legs to keep it about eight inches off the floor. He flattened a place out between the two ribs on the barrel so we could boil lima beans in winter, or, if beans were not cooking, a pan of water was placed on the flat surface to boil moistening the exceedingly dry air. It was our humidifier. In many things Dad did, he showed a strange sense of humor that others wouldn't dare show. Above the door of his homemade stove, he painted two eyes and beneath them, he painted a smiling mouth. With a roaring fire blazing inside, when the door was opened, it made a spectacular sight.

When he had time, Dad, with Churchell's help, dug a large hole about fifty steps west of the house. Over the hole, they built a two-hole outhouse from rusty metal sheets with many nail holes scattered on the sheets.

Sixty steps downhill from the house a tripod of cedar poles from the breaks were put in place where a water witch determined we could find the precious liquid. At the apex of the tripod, a pulley was fastened with a rope running through it. A heavy bucket, with sharp points for digging, was tied to the end of the rope. At the other end of the rope men pulled up and down, day after day for weeks, lifting the bucket up and letting it fall to bite into the rocky soil to bring up a few handfuls of dirt at a time. By sheer manpower, since there was no machinery to do the job, the hole got deeper by a few feet each day. Finally, they reached a depth of ninety feet, and there they found water.

Next, the men built a windmill tower with fourteen-foot four-by-fours over the well, and on top of the tower, they put the store-bought windmill, made all the connections and when the wind blew, water began to flow from the well

After the windmill was working satisfactorily, horse corrals, cow lots and hog pens had to be built. A brand new, shining water tank for the farm animals was put in place. Land for a garden was measured off near the windmill A smokehouse was built for processing meat when we slaughtered hogs and beef for family use. By the time the crop was gathered on the Gibbs place, we were ready to move into the renovated house.

I can't remember what happened to our Model T. The last time I remember seeing it, the old car was sheltered under the lean-to on the north side of the Gibbs house. I remember seeing chickens on the car where they found shade on hot summer afternoons. After a while their droppings just about covered the old jalopy. My guess is that twelve-cent-per-gallon gasoline and the cost of parts and repairs that were needed were more than our pocketbook could stand.

Since the one room schoolhouse was not ready for the fall of 1929, the authorities in Tucumcari, our county seat, made arrangements for a bus to transport the children in our end of the valley to the San Jon school about fourteen miles away. The rickety, rattling old bus must have had something wrong with the motor for every day some of us got sick from breathing the awful smelling fumes produced. There were no windows in the back of the bus where the children sat. To keep hot sunshine or freezing winds in the winter out, we could roll down a canvas. If the weather were mild, we could roll the canvas up.

There was no such thing as air conditioning, as we know it today, so when the winters were exceedingly cold, Dad put a fifty-pound rock on the flat place of the homemade stove. With a fire burning all night in the stove, the rock was hot the next morning. He wrapped the hot rock in gunnysacks and put it on the floor of the old bus. While shivering, we could put our feet on the rock to keep them from freezing. Even then, some of my toes were frost bitten.

When we reached San Jon, we found a large brick schoolhouse divided into rooms, one for each grade with a teacher for that grade. With more than one hundred students in the school, we felt intimated and very much out of place. I was assigned to the second grade and finally found its room location. In the early fall when watermelons got ripe, we took one to school for lunch. This gave the other children opportunity to laugh at us since they had lunch boxes that contained sandwiches and fruit. This experience lasted for only one school year.

When the 1930 school year started our one room school was ready, and Mrs. White was chosen to be our teacher. She lived on a ranch in the San Jon area. Each school day she drove her car to our school accompanied by her son Eugene who was about my age. Mrs. White was a kind lady, very intelligent and highly motivated to teach the students in the Fairview - alias Punkin Center - school.

We had to have a certain enrollment in school to keep it open. But, with Etta, Jessie, me Ray and Raymond, Dad and neighbors had to beat the bushes to find enough students. In addition to the five in our family, there were Charley White's two children, Fred Kerr's two, the Tucker's daughter, the three Massey children and Leon and his brother from a transit family who lived in a cabin in the breaks. With fifteen students the authorities allowed the school to open.

The outside of the schoolhouse had changed little except for its new location. The workmen had not painted it. The old white paint was still curled in places because of the blistering heat in summer and the cold, freezing winds of winter. There was a large bin behind the school mostly for wood, but sometime it contained coal that was brought in. On the north of the building, the men had built two outhouses, one for the girls and one for the boys.

There was a single door in and out of the building on the east side. A large potbelly stove in the center dominated the entire room. Desks were given to our school by some district that didn't need them. These desks, with iron sides and sloping wood tops with an inkwells in the upper right hand corner, had a place under the top for books. The desks were neatly arranged in rows on either side of the large stove. The teacher's desk was in front. Someone had donated an ancient pump organ with pull out stops that sat in a corner.

Mrs. White did her best to drill into the heads of us Punkin Center kids the value of an education. She arranged for knowledgeable people to come to the school and give us extra instructions on the natural phenomena that existed all around us. One time a lady came from Santa Fe and led the whole school on a field trip down a nearby arroyo encouraging each of us to find different kinds of rocks, and she identified them for us. I found a human tooth that had turned brown by age and the blazing sun. The vivid imagination of the students thought it might be a tooth from an Indian who fought with a white man long ago. Geologists tell us this entire valley was a salty sea in ancient times. When we found sea shells embedded in stones, it indicated they might have been right.

Mrs. White ran an orderly school. The only time she had to punish any of us was when her son Eugene and I chose up sides to play war like men did in World War I. During the noon hour, we dug trenches. The boys and girls he chose were in his trench and the ones I chose were with me. The trenches were only about ten yards apart. The rocks we used for ammunition could easily be thrown to the "enemy." Sometimes the rocks hit a member of the "enemy," and the child began to cry. That was when Mrs. White came out of the schoolhouse to learn what was going on. Our "war" was over when she made her appearance. When she learned that I was the one that cooked up this "war," she led me to her desk, pulled from it a thick foot ruler, took my right hand, bent it back with the palm facing up and proceeded to blister my hand with the ruler. "Now," she said, "that should teach you not to throw rocks at other people."

When Dad found out about the punishment, he laughed and said, "I hope you've learned your lesson."

At recess, the girls often played jacks, and boys played marbles with the winner of the game leaving with the loser's marbles. Sometime at recess, the entire student body would chose sides and play anteover. One side would be stationed on the north side of the schoolhouse, and the other group would be on the south side. One group would throw a rubber ball over the house, and if someone in the opposing group caught the ball before it hit the ground, that student would run around the house and throw the ball at the opponents. The student "hit" had to drop out of the game. While this game continued, there was more hollering and squealing than one can imagine.

Mrs. White directed us in plays at school and invited parents to see the productions. I remember one in particular, but have no recollection of the play's name or who wrote it. My one line in the play was, "Down, down, into the dark dungeon from whence thou hast come!" Or something like that.

What I learned the few years Mrs. White taught in the little one room country school formed the foundation for all I have learned since. My grades were not very good. In fact, they were bad. Many years later, I visited with Clark White, the oldest son of our teacher. As we talked about the Depression years, he said, "By the way, when Mother died she left me the records of her students that attended Fairview School." Clark rummaged through a chest, found my grades and handed the paper to me. It was an uncomfortable revelation.

There was no water well on the school grounds. We lived less than a quarter of a mile away, so the school board made a verbal contract with me to carry drinking water each day to the school for one dollar a month. To carry two galvanized buckets of water that distance was quite a chore for a youngster. In spring and fall, it wasn't so bad, for I could stop and rest when tired or the wire handles on the buckets dug into my hands. In winter, it was a different story. Often I had to scramble out of the way of an approaching wagon or a cowboy passing on a horse. The icy water would splash on my hands and freeze. Dried by the dry, desert air, without a lotion of any kind, open, bleeding cracks formed on my hands. Mother rubbed hog lard into the cracks hoping this would assist the healing process.

When the students went to the buckets to get a drink of water, Billie Sue Tucker pulled from her dress pocket a collapsible aluminum cup and drank from it. All the rest drank from the same dipper

Sometime after March 3, 1931 Mrs. White read to the student body a paper from the United States Congress: "After 150 years Americans finally have a song that they can call their own, officially. Congress today sent President Hoover a bill designating *The Star Spangled Banner* as our national anthem." Though we didn't understand much about this legislation, we stood and clapped.

Everything was changing rapidly. Mother saw her children leaving the nest one by one for various reasons. Churchell never went to Fairview School after the men moved the building, and he was gone more and more of the time. Anna had married Varlo Mitchell who got a job as janitor for the Wheatland School on the plains. They had a salary with living quarters thrown in. Etta had dropped out of school to pick cotton so she could buy a new dress and other things she wanted.

Dad allowed Jessie to transfer to the Wheatland School where she stayed with our married sister. All this change left me as the oldest child at home most of the time

Mother was expecting her ninth child.

73

LIFE OF A SHARECROPPER'S FAMILY

Albert and Mary Leach, who owned the farm we rented, drove down from the plains early on a Sunday morning to go to church with us. They brought their three younger sons: Kenneth, about my age, and Wallace, about the age of the twins, Ray and Raymond, and Earnest, who was closer to Jay's age.

Mrs. Leach, who was a strong Roman Catholic, brought her family to attend church in the schoolhouse with the valley Protestants. As I recall, no two families in this pocket of perpetual poverty were of the same denominational persuasion. The lack of people and money made it impossible for us to meet separately. The dire circumstances forced all the different brands in the Christian community to meet together as one body. This was common in the Depression days where the population was thin, and there were little or no enforced denominational ordinances from higher Ecclesiastical authorities. Each family in our valley read the Bible and determined, after laying all our differences aside, the most important action of all was to worship the Creator as best we could under the circumstances.

When Sunday morning rolled around, after a hard week's work in the fields, each family who wished got up early. We ate breakfast, did the necessary chores in the house and on the farm, ate lunch and took a nap. When we awoke, a week's collection of dirt was washed from the ears of the squirming, crying children, best clothes were donned and each family piled into the old car or wagon or on horseback going to the assembly that started some time in the middle of the afternoon. The schoolhouse was never locked, so the first ones there opened all windows if it were warm or built a fire in the potbellied stove if it were cold.

On this Sunday, with the Leach family as our guest, it was my job to chase down a couple of fryers and wring the chickens' heads off and stay with them while they flopped all over the yard squirting blood everywhere until they died. Dad took the fryers, plunged them neck first into hot water and proceeded to pluck all the feathers off preparing them for the frying pan.

In *The Pre-Atomic Age*, adults always ate first, while the children's mouths watered, as they smelled the fried chicken, hot biscuits, corn-on-the-cob and fresh vegetables from the garden. While the older people ate, Dad began to tease me saying that I was "sweet" on Billie Sue Tucker who was perhaps a year or two younger than me. This made me uncomfortable and caused me to squirm and blush. My actions brought both families in on the teasing.

The banter toward me continued while we of the younger generation ate. Finally Dad, with his offbeat sense of humor, dared me to get on a horse and go get Billie Sue and bring her to church. Even at the tender age, I wasn't one to let a dare go unchallenged. So I went to the horse corral, bridled old Mose and began the two-mile trek riding bareback. By this time Mose had lost a lot of weight. His hipbones stuck out like giant doorknobs, and his backbone where I sat had the shape of a two-by-four. I remember shifting from side to side because it was so uncomfortable riding on that "rail."

Mose walked all the way. Not knowing what to do when I got to the ranch house where Billie Sue lived, I parked the old nag outside the fence still shifting about with the hot sun beaming down. When Mr. Tucker saw me sitting on Mose, he came to learn what I wanted. Stuttering, I told him I came to take Billie Sue to church. The father took off his ten-gallon hat, kicked the dirt with his cowboy boots searching for an answer to my request. He took a good look at my transportation. Not wanting to embarrass me further, the kind man said, "Billie Sue isn't ready just yet, but I think it best if she goes with us in the car."

I turned Mose around and he walked back home where I was greeted by hilarious laughter.

My family, with the Leach family, was the last to reach the schoolhouse. Horses that pulled the wagons and saddle horses were tied to the barbed wire fence that ran along the south and west of the building. Children were playing in the yard. Inside the big stove dominated the scene. Adults crammed themselves into seats of the student's desks, discussed the drought and possibilities of the coming crop while fanning themselves with paper fans contributed by some funeral home. When all was ready to begin the worship period, the children, with sweat rolling down their faces, were called in, and the ancient organ was pulled from the corner where it waited to be used. Dad stood before the congregation in his freshly washed overalls and asked, "Is everybody ready to begin?" When all nodded in the affirmative, Mrs. Kerr rose from her desk wearing her Sunday bonnet with strings tied snugly under her chin and approached the organ ready to play at the proper time.

After someone led the assembly in prayer, Dad asked all to turn to page 176 in the hymnals. The shuffling of pages was heard. Mrs. Kerr played a few notes as she pulled the proper stops and pumped air into the ancient instrument with her feet. In a loud voice, Dad led the worshippers in singing, "Onward Christian soldiers, marching as to war....."

With the singing complete, Dad, with his fourth grade education, invited all to open their Bibles and read together a few chosen verses. Then he encouraged all to respect the Creator and one another. His was a simple lesson uncomplicated by others by theological jargon.

When the last "amen" was uttered, the children jumped from their sitting positions on the floor and raced outside to play. The adults lingered talking, fanning themselves with the gift from the funeral home with advertisement printed in bold black letters.

Knowledge of my plowing ability had spread throughout the neighborhood. Mr. Aston, the rancher, had a field of maize that was about to be overrun by weeds that stole the moisture from his tender plants. He hired me for a dollar a day to plow his field. I also got my noonday meal. I rode the godevil up and down the rows to cut the weeds on the ridges and put fresh soil around the baby plants. One day when the sun had reached its height, I unhitched the horses from the plow and led them to the watering tank. When I went into the ranch house, I saw a number of cowboys sitting around in dirty Levis and sweaty hats smoking roll-your-own cigarettes and drinking something. One of them called out to Mr. Aston, "Hey, boss, why didn't you hire one of us to plow your field instead of this kid?"

I've never forgotten Mr. Aston's reply, "Because you old cowboys will smoke all of cigarettes and drink up all my booze, and this kid won't."

Sometime later Mr. Charley White asked me to plow his field with no agreement what he would pay. He and Dad had become good friends, and since Charley was busy sharpening plow shares in his blacksmith shop for area farmers, I was told to go help our neighbor out. After several days of labor under the boiling sun, I went to his blacksmith shop to learn what my pay was. Mr. White paid me no mind as I watched him work with the red hot coals in the open hopper. He put a dull plowshare on the hot coals, and with manual force he pumped air through a hose in the bottom of the hopper to keep the coals as hot as possible. When the plowshare was hot as the coals, it was removed with tongs, put on an anvil, and he proceeded to beat the metal share until the leadng edge was sharp. When the sharpened share was attached to the plow properly it would glide under the surface busting up the soil making the field ready for planting.

Mr. White took time out from his backbreaking labor to notice me. I said to the World War I veteran, "Sir, I've finished plowin'."

He stopped his work and said, "Yeah, I noticed. For a kid, ya did a pretty good job. Now, son, ya know I ain't got no money to give ya. But I still want to pay ya something. My old sow had pigs a few weeks ago, and I'm gonna give ya the pick of the litter. And I'm gonna give ya pair of my boots. Ya can take them home, throw 'em in the water tank for a week, and they'll draw up to fit your feet so you will have somethan' to wear to school this winter. And I'm gonna throw in my .22 rifle I've had since the War."

With the pig, a pair of boots and a rifle, I thought I'd come out pretty well. So I carried the boots, the rifle and the kicking, squealing pig a mile down the country lane to our house When I got home, I put the boots in the water tank expecting them to shrink to fit my feet in a week as Mr. White said. I put the pig in the pen with our hogs. When I told Mother about my treasure, she was skeptical about the boots and the gun but thought the pig might be a good thing.

The rifle was an old single shot. In order to shoot it, the trigger had to be pulled back with the thumb to put a bullet in the barrel. My imagination was in high gear dreaming of hunting rabbits, coyotes and other animals that roamed the prairie and the breaks. I was thinking of raising the pig until it weighed 250 pounds and selling it to buy something that I really wanted. When Dad came in from the field tired, sweaty and dirty, I ran to meet him with gun in hand breathlessly talking a blue streak about what I'd earned working for Mr. White.

"Dad said, "Hold it, son. Not so fast." When told about the boots and what I did with them, he laughed. He looked the gun over and was even more skeptical than Mother. The pig, he agreed with Mother was a pretty good deal.

"Go back to the house," Dad said, "and when I get the harness off the horses and feed them and make sure they have water, I'll be right up."

After supper I was anxious for Dad to make a closer inspection of my prize possession. He took the rifle in his huge hands feeling it and looking it over carefully. "It's real dirty and has to be cleaned up. I bet it hasn't been fired in years. Go get the ramrod and put a small rag in the slit at the end. We've gotta clean out the inside of this barrel."

He put the rod in the barrel and began to laugh real loud, saying, "Son, you got gypped. This gun's got a crooked barrel." He held it up before the light of the coal oil lamp, "See there's a slight curve in the barrel. Any body that shoots this gun is gonna have to aim slightly to the right if he wants to hit something directly in front of him."

My countenance fell to the floor. When Dad saw my great disappointment, he said, "Tell ya what we'll do. Tomar, before I go to the fields, we'll take the gun out a ways from the house and see if it will shoot at all."

About sunup the next morning after eating a breakfast of hot biscuits, red eye gravy and a slice of ham, Dad and I went a piece from the house to check out the gun. It worked perfectly if it was aimed just a little right of the object we wished to hit. After making sure I could handle the gun safely, Dad gave me permission to take it to hunt for rabbits. But he warned me never to carry the loaded gun while it was cocked.

A week later I fished the boots out of the water tank. To my great dismay, instead of them drawing up to fit me, they were warped all out of shape. When I showed them to Dad, he laughed heartily, and said, "Son, even in a trade, ya gotta look a gift horse in the mouth."

It was a slack time on the farm. When Jessie was home from school at Wheatland, she went rabbit hunting with me. After a while we scared up a cottontail that scampered fast as it could to the nearest clump of beargrass and hid. At first sight of the rabbit I cocked my gun pointing it down toward the ground. I circled the rabbit's hideaway thinking all was safe as Jessie followed behind. The rabbit got away, but when we got home I got a good scolding for my sister told Dad that I carried the loaded gun with the trigger cocked.

When time was nearing for Mother to deliver her ninth baby, she stayed in bed much of the time. Neighbor women aware of the approaching birth made many visits to our house bringing little blankets, clothes and booties they made with their own hands. There was no thought of going to the hospital or calling a doctor in preparation of the new arrival. But when labor pains began, two women from the neighborhood were called to assist. There was no way to tell if the child would be a boy or a girl so preparation was made for either. Mother's first baby was a boy born eighteen years before when she was a young bride living in the dugout on the plains.

A string of three girls followed. Four boys in a row were born next. This time she was so in hopes of a girl.

After the delivery and the pain of childbirth subsided, she was told the child was a precious little girl. Our dear Mother, who had known severe pain and heartache though the years, smiled and expressed her thankfulness.

Without consulting any member of the family, the proud mother named the new baby girl Alta Maria. But something was wrong. The baby was not breathing as she should. With no life support equipment available, there was nothing to be done. On the third day of life tiny Alta Maria died. Sorrow with tears filled our home.

I can see Dad, as if it were this very moment, at a table building a wee little casket out of sun-baked lumber found on the farm. As tears rolled down his heavy cheeks, he nailed the boards together making a box slightly longer than it was wide. A lid was made for covering the box. But he was not finished. Then Dad covered the lid with a soft, colorful blanket that was given to comfort Alta Maria. After this blanket was tacked down securely over the lid, Father covered the entire box with blankets and put a small pillow in the bottom of the little casket. I looked at this loving work of art and thought it was the most beautiful thing I'd ever seen.

Dad took the small coffin into the darkened room where the baby girl lay close to Mother's side. With massive hands that had felled trees, handled horses that pulled the plow, dug water wells, slaughtered hogs and gathered crops, Dad tenderly and compassionately lifted his little daughter and placed the body with great care into the coffin he had fashioned for her. Before covering the remains with the lid, he took the baby to Mother for her to view her baby daughter for the last time. Mother wept and Dad's great body shook with grief.

Dad knew what he had to do. He went to the lot and harnessed two of our youngest horses, Fox and Lake, hitched them to the wagon and drove them to the house. Without saying a word to anyone, he picked up the tiny casket, carried it out and put it in the wagon. All alone, without another soul to accompany him, Dad made his way up into the springseat of the wagon and drove off down the country lane toward the schoolhouse and beyond to bury his baby daughter.

I stood and watched as the lonely funeral procession slowly moved away. The picture that was etched on my memory in those few moments has hung on the gallery wall of my mind until this day. Often I go back to view the scene that still brings tears to my eyes. I saw the great hulk of a man, my Dad, sitting slumped over with the massive weight of grief on his shoulders, sitting in that old squeaky springseat contemplating the job he was forced to do. He had the lines to guide the horses in his rough hands. I saw plainly the soft, pretty little coffin sitting in the bed of the wagon. I watched until Dad opened the gate at the schoolhouse and made the bend in the road disappearing out of sight.

As far as I know, nobody ever knew where Dad buried his new born. Nor did we ever learn how he felt or what he said when he lowered the baby into the ground and covered the grave with the dry, dusty soil of mother earth.

Mother bounced back pretty fast from the ordeal, and within two months she was ready and able to ride in the springseat of the wagon with Dad. News came to us, by word of mouth, that a revival was in progress at the New Hope School on the plains. It was in the fall when we waited for the crop to ripen before the gathering began. Churchell never wanted to go to such meetings, so when he was home to do the evening chores, Dad hitched the freshest horses to the wagon and put quilts in the bed to make it more comfortable for his younger children. With Dad and Mother up front riding in the springseat of the wagon and four rowdy boys on the quilts in the back, we left home as the sun was sinking behind the Rocky Mountains. Our parents wished to travel the seven miles in order to be at the meeting place before the preaching started.

I got in a wrestling match with the twins, Ray and Raymond, who were about seven years old. I was strong from working on the farm. My strength made it relatively easy for me to handle the both of them. As they kicked and giggled, I'd grab one of them with my right hand, hold him down, then take the left hand grabbing the other and force him on top of the first. With this method I could lay on top of them until they cried 'calf-rope.' While this was going on, three-year-old Jay B. was quietly observing everything.

Eventually Mother got nervous with all this activity in the bed of the wagon, and said to Dad, "Can't you make those boys settle down for awhile?" Dad, wishing to accommodate her wishes, turned his head toward us and said, "All right boys, that's enough. If ya don't settle down, I might have to take my belt off and use it on each of ya."

In the silence nothing was heard except the squeak of the wagon wheels and the groan of the horses as they pulled their load up the dusty road through the breaks. I watched the sinking sun paint the clouds with gold and crimson as it slowly disappeared below the western horizon. In the dusk we saw a whippoorwill grab an insect in its bill as it flew through the air. A deer that had settled down for the night under a bush, beside the road, was frightened by the oncoming wagon and jumped from its bed startling the horses. In their fright the horses began to bolt, but Dad's firm hand on the reins settled them down.

We arrived at New Hope School as darkness enveloped the countryside. Children were playing, chasing one another and laughing. In the cool of the evening, men leaning on wagons were talking, discussing problems and hopes. Soon the preacher came to the front door calling everyone inside by announcing, "Brethren, it's about time to begin our services."

While still talking about the weather, crops and family problems the adults sauntered through the door taking seats in the student's desks. I was pushed aside by youngsters rushing to get preferred places on the floor. In the building, I noticed the partition that divided the room had been folded back. The white oil lamps hanging from the ceiling were bright with the gauze-like mantles glowing and spreading plenty of light for all to read the hymnals and Bibles if they wished.

I looked at Mother sitting silently wearing her church-going dress and hat that was fashionable at the time. Dad sat beside her in his clean overalls looking around to see old friends who were present and perhaps looking for something that needed to be done.

When all had settled down the imported preacher, dressed in black, mounted the stage telling us how glad he was to meet with us, and how thankful he was to be invited in to homes where food was plentiful. Soon he was wound up and began to shout saying all of us sinners needed the Lord. He went on until many of the children on the floor were asleep and some of the adults were nodding. He brought his presentation to a close by imploring all to come to the altar.

I was very observant taking it all in wondering to myself if the shouting was necessary. Why couldn't the man speak in a pleasant voice like Mrs. White did in our Fairview school. In my own heart, without telling anyone else, I determined that I certainly wouldn't want to holler like that before a bunch of people.

After we were dismissed and the people finished visiting among themselves, each family got into their ancient automobiles or wagons to go home. Mother took her station in the spring- seat beside Dad. He gave the horses a gentle slap on the rear with the reins, and we were homeward bound. My younger brothers were soon asleep on the quilts in the bed of the wagon. But I was awake lying on my back looking up into a clear sky trying to count the stars – wondering, wondering about many things. Before long, I was asleep.

At a time when Etta and Jessie were home, Mother told them about Mrs. Kerr's new sewing machine with a newly designed bobbin. They talked about it with excitement and were anxious to see how it worked. Now in those days when you went to visit a neighbor, it was an all day affair. One Sunday at church Mrs. Kerr invited Mother and the girls over for a visit and to see her new machine. We were allowed to hitch the horses to the wagon and trot the couple of miles to Kerr's home. They lived in a half-dugout. Dad did not go for he was working.

Still the small living space was limited for the two families. So the kids stayed outside most of the time before lunch. I was still curious about that bobbin Mother and the girls had talked so much about. But I misunderstood all the while, how they pronounced it. I slipped back into the house, and while the mothers stood at a counter cutting up vegetables for lunch, I went up behind Mrs. Kerr and punched her on the back with my finger. She turned and asked, "What do you want?"

The excitement of the ladies in my family had rubbed off on me, and I exclaimed in a loud voice filled with urgency, "Mrs. Kerr, I want to see your bottom." Roaring laughter from the women was spontaneous.

It was understood before the visit began that we would pick green beans from their bean field to can for the winter. Shortly after lunch the women wearing, faded dresses and bonnets that shaded their faces completely, each totting a gunnysack headed for the field. The children with smaller sacks followed. It really wasn't all that bad for the ladies visited and the youngsters played about as much as they worked. Each bean picker chose a long row, and we began to fill the sacks. The Kerr's little brown and white dog accompanied the crew. The little canine ran in front of us sniffing for some small creature to chase. After a while he stirred up a rattlesnake in Mother's row. Mother believed these snakes often had a mate close by. She chose to move to another row and continue picking green beans.

While she was busy picking and talking, the little dog continued his activities and found another rattlesnake in Mother's new row. After the second snake was killed, she decided to go to another row to continue picking beans. The third snake began to rattle and hiss as its two buddies had. After we killed the third snake, Mother, taking this as some sort of sign of bad things to come, threw up her hands and exclaimed, "I quit." By this time, we had picked enough green beans to last our family through the coming winter.

We went back to the Kerr's half-dugout where Mose and George were waiting patiently still hitched to the wagon after spending much of the day in the sun. We threw the bags of beans into the wagon, and after bidding the Kerr family farewell, we loaded up. I drove the members of my family back to our place.

Upon arriving home, we dumped the beans into two large washtubs. Then I drove the horses, still hitched to the wagon, down to the lot that was near the windmill, unhitched Mose and George and took their harnesses off. Free from their burdens, the horses shook the sweat from their bodies and went to the tank for a fresh drink of water. I hustled an arm full of hay for each horse and went back to the house.

After a restful nap, Mother told me to go to the cornfield and get fresh roasting ears so we could have corn-on-the-cob to go with the green beans she planned to cook for the meals to come.

With one of the emptied gunnysacks over my shoulder, I went to gather newly formed ears of corn. When the sack was full, I brought it home and dumped the corn on top of the green beans that were in the washtubs.

Immediately before sunset and as twilight crept over our valley several actions usually took place. We milked the cows, slopped the hogs and fed the horses. When Dad came in from the fields, he washed the dirty sweat from his face and got ready to sit at table and eat the victuals his daughters prepared for him. We saw Herbert Gibbs leave his house. We watched as he rode his bay horse across his pasture heading in a northwesterly direction. Mr. Charley White left his family and came riding toward our house. When he arrived at our place, he tied his horse up to the barbed wire fence, come in and told stories about that great war of 1917 and 1918.

Having come into contact with mustard gas in 'The war to end all wars.' Charley stuttered making it hard for him to speak a complete sentence that could be easily understood. This neighbor of ours had not been able to stop using some of the curse words he picked up during his time in the service of our country. Since we had no newspaper, magazines or radio, Mr. White was always welcome for he was our entertainment and news source.

After Charley left to return to his family that night, our family gathered around the washtubs to shuck the corn and snap the beans preparing them for canning. Tired from all the long day's activities, Dad and Mother went to their bed in the far end of the kitchen. Their children went to the back bedroom where two or three or four of us piled into each bed.

JOY AND SORROW

The next morning, the dawn's light began to brighten the eastern sky. It was telegraphing the message to our valley that the sun would soon be rising giving us light to do our work for the coming day. Dad stuck his head into our bedroom and announced in a strong voice, "Wake up sleepy heads, we've all got work to do."

With drowsy, grudging voices, each of us rolled from crowded beds snapping at one another. Etta shook her head vigorously to shake the 'cobwebs' from her mind. She walked slowly over the splintery floor to the kitchen to help Mother prepare breakfast for the family. Jessie was griping because she had to make the beds. But before the beds were made, she must pour a little bit of coal oil in a tin can, pick bed bugs off the mattresses and drop each pest into the can where they met their death.

Ray and Raymond, who were growing up, were told to make sure the livestock had plenty of hay and water. I was told to go to the back pasture and bring the cows in so we could milk them. I ran the quarter of a mile and found the cows lying down. Each was chewing a cud. They seemed to dislike being aroused from their beds as much as we did. I began driving the bovines homeward, but their walk was far to slow for me. So I picked up a stick, grabbed one of their tails, and began beating the cow into a run. It was almost like flying while holding the tail of the racing animal. Running alone my stride was only three or four feet. Having a firm grip on the tail, my stride would stretch to ten or twelve feet. I was having great fun until....

Dad saw me abusing the source of our family's milk supply. He scolded me good and proper, and warned me if he ever caught me forcing any animal to run while I held the tail, he'd use the stick on me. Past experience with Dad caused me to believe him, and that was the end of my "flying."

While I milked the cows, the women worked in the house. Dad worked in the yard putting the four legs of the black wash pot on flat stones. Then he filled it with water and built a fire under the pot, for this was washday. By this time breakfast was ready and the warming sun was shining through the screenless east door that led into the kitchen. Etta had swept dust from the floor that had blown in during the night Countless dust particles could be seen floating in the air in the sunlight.

One more chore had to be done before breakfast. A multiple number of flies had found their way from the stock pens down by the windmill into the kitchen through the open windows and door. Some members of the family grabbed rags to shoo the flies outside where we hoped most would stay while we ate.

This was a routine washday and each of us knew the work we had to perform. Etta stayed in the house to wash the dishes, sweep all the floors and clean the rest of the house. Mother was expecting her tenth child and she went back to bed to rest for she didn't want to loose this one as she had lost Alta Maria.

Thirteen-year-old Jessie carried an arm load of dirty clothes into the yard where she deposited them in the wash pot containing water that was near the boiling point. She stood there patiently poking up and down on the clothes with an old broom handle to get as much dirt and sweat out as possible before putting them in a tub of water for washing on the rub board.

After she had poked the clothes sufficiently, she got one of the tubs that were filled with green beans and roasting ears the night before. She put the tub on a stand beside the pot of hot water and walked down the hill with a galvanized bucket in each hand to the windmill for water to fill the washtub. When it contained enough water, she used the broomstick to carefully transfer the clothes from the pot into the tub. Next she retrieved the washboard from its resting place and began the rubby-dub-dub, up and down motion pressing each piece against the board until all the dirt and sweat was extracted from each garment. After each piece was clean, she rinsed it in clear water in another tub. By this time, most of the morning had vanished, but there was one more step to be taken. She took each individual garment and hung it to dry on the barbed wire fence that separated the dusty lane from our yard.

Etta and Jessie were both tired from the morning's work, but there was still plenty for them to do. They made sure Mother was comfortable, and had everything she needed, while babysitting Jay who walked around in the house crying for his wants. They had to prepare lunch for Dad and me who would soon be coming in from the fields where we had been since early morning. The twins, Ray and Raymond, were hungry from pulling weeds to feed the hogs supplementing their diet of various grains and slop.

But when the morning was cool and fresh, Dad and I went down to the lot to harness the horses for the day's plowing. First we put the harness on the older and gentler horses Mose and George that would be hitched to the plow I would ride. Then we harnessed the younger and more spirited horses Lake and Fox. Lake was a big black horse that was hard working and dependable. Fox was a smaller, frisky bay and always ready to do the unexpected He looked more like a racehorse than one that pulled a plow. But we had to use what we had and match them as best we could.

Dad assigned me to plow one section of the 260-acre field while he worked in another section. My plow dug deep into the soil making furrows and ridges. Above the plowshares sat a container holding seed. In the bottom of this container was a disk with holes that rotated allowing seed to drop down at intervals through a flexible metal tube planting the seed in the furrow

By the time the sun had climbed high in the cloudless sky, I was bored and sleepy. That is until the plow went through a snake's nest. The light brown sand racer took off as fast as it could up and down across the ridges and into the furrows. At that moment I remembered bull snakes got in hen's nests and swallowed eggs robbing us of the delicacy for breakfast. When Dad caught a snake, he'd grab it by the tail, whirl it around his head, like popping a whip, and snap it's head off. I pulled back on the reins and the horses stopped. At that instant, I jumped off the plow and began chasing the snake thinking it to be harmless.

When I reached the snake, I grabbed its hard, pointed tail hoping to snap off its head as I'd seen Dad do with bull snakes. But this sand racer was smarter than I anticipated. He jerked his tail from my right hand, turned the tables on me and began chasing me. I ran as fast as my legs could carry me over the ridges into the furrows and mounted the seat on the plow before my intended victim could catch me. We parted company forevermore.

When the sun was directly overhead, I saw Dad heading toward the house while sitting on the seat of the plow pulled by Lake and Fox. That was my signal to lift the plowshares out of the ground with the lever and follow him. We met at the water tank by the windmill. The horses drank their fill and we unhitched them from the plows and headed for the house where Etta and Jessie had lunch waiting.

Mother with her bulging tummy was helped to the table. As tired as he was, Dad had to tease her about getting fat and losing the girlish figure she had when he married her so many years ago. She only smiled faintly. Before we ate, Dad used the same words in prayer he always used. (His words were beautiful, and I've often wished I could remember them.)

After we ate, Dad went into the front room, lay on the floor, crooked his large right arm under his head and took a short nap. I lay beside him attempting to imitate him. After the nap, we returned to the field.

During the boring time of plowing, my mind was forever dreaming up some foolhardy contraptions to make farming a bit easier. While I was peppered with hot sunbeams in the spring afternoon, my mind was busy manufacturing a mighty iron horse. It had to have knees and a body like a real horse. The iron horse had to be hollow so a man could sit inside manipulating chains to activate the legs into a forward motion pulling a plow. When I told a member of the family about some of my ideas, it spread to other members and they'd laugh until I'd run from them to hide.

In the spring of 1931 the rain showers came, the seeds sprouted, the plants in the field grew and before long corn and other grain plants were as tall as I was. It looked like we were bound to have a bumper crop - the best ever. Men from the State Agriculture Department came out to inspect our fields and congratulated Dad on his farming ability. Dad was grinning all the time anticipating money from the crop so he could provide better for his family.

But the harsh realities of the valley, the pocket of perpetual poverty, had not gone away. For it didn't rain another drop the rest of the summer. The plants ceased to grow. Instead of the beautiful green, the leaves and stalks turned a dreadful, deadly brown. The ears of corn and the heads of grain never matured. Nothing was left but dry stalks and withered leaves in the field where our hopes lay. After all our hard work, our dreams of better times ahead were dashed. Our hearts sank to new lows.

But there was no giving up. Something had to be done. We still had our cows for milk and their calves, the horses were capable of work, the grass in the pastures, though brown, was there for the livestock. The hogs were still growing. The dead stalks that contained nourishment were still standing in the dry field.

The hardship that faced him brought out one of the many talents Dad possessed. He rummaged around until he found old boards and a long two by four. From these scraps he proceeded to build a sled. On the right hand side of his invention he made a slanting edge. The next step was to find an old hand saw, sharpen the back side of the saw with a file and nail the sharpened saw to the slanting edge of the sled. Dad then fashioned a contraption on the front of the sled so one horse could pull it down the rows of dead standing stalks in the field.

Nobody had ever seen such a farm tool before or since. It was time to see if this invention would do the job intended.

On a frosty autumn morning Dad and I went down to the lot and harnessed old George, the white ghost on the farm, and hitched him to the sled. My Father said to me, "Son I want you to ride this old nag as he pulls this sled up and the rows of fodder. I'm gonna to sit crosslegged, Indian style, on this contraption and as the slanting edge cuts down the dead stalks, I'll gather them in with my arms.

Dad helped me on the old gray horse, and he walked beside him as he pulled the sled to the end of the first row where we stopped. Dad deposited his bulky body on the sled, crossed his legs and shouted, "Giddy-up." The great experiment had begun to see if we could salvage a crop to feed our livestock during the long winter months.

With me astride him, George walked slowly, the blade on the sled cut the dry standing stalks and Dad gathered in the fodder with his agile hands and mighty arms. The fodder was left beside the rows. Later we would come back with a team and wagon and use a pitchfork, fill the wagon with fodder and stack it near the stock pens. The unique contraption proved a useful tool for the situation.

I can't remember how it happened, but about this time a large dog with short fur, black as coal came to live with us. I claimed him as my own which was all right with the rest of the family. We named him Towser. Why? I don't recall for the word was outside our limited vocabulary. Towser became my constant companion. I will not forget him as long as I live. He followed me to the field and chased ground squirrels, rabbits, and swarms of birds that fed on earthworms that were exposed when soil was turned over by the plow.

When I went to school, Towser was close behind and stayed beside the door as if volunteering to guard the entire student body. At recess he followed close to my heels. When I made excursions into the escarpment to explore the mysteries it held, Towesr was by my side. He saves me from of many a rattlesnake by causing them to hiss and rattle before they could strike. Sometime when a snake was threatening, Towser took the snake in his mouth and shook the varmint vigorously until it died. Once he was bitten and the poison caused his head to swell almost twice its normal size. While Towser lay whining and moaning from pain, members of the family took turns tending to his needs, petting and talking to him. Within a week, my constant companion was up regaining his strength.

When we fed the chickens by tossing grain on the ground, they gathered from every direction with the mother hens clucking, calling their babies to the feast. Towser stood guard for the hawks saw the gathering of the chickens as an opportunity for a good meal for themselves. I've seen my dog jump six feet off the ground trying to nab a hawk in his mouth when it dove down to grab a chicken. He never caught a hawk, but he never quit trying.

After we finished harvesting the remnants of the decimated crop, we could feel the cool crisp air of the autumn mornings. The sky and all things of the earth were gearing up for the freezing blizzards anticipated during the coming winter. Animals put on heavier coats of fur. Ducks and other fowls were flying south. I loved to watch the v-shaped formation slicing through the sky as they flapped their wings following the leader. Large numbers of snakes crawled and wiggled their way to a common hole to hibernate together form the cold. Houseflies and all other insects were thinning out. Ground squirrels and other earth dwelling animals were digging holes to protect themselves and their half-grown offspring.

One early morning when I ran to the back pasture to retrieve the cows for milking, I came upon a mother badger and her growing brood scampering around an old unused well dug with pick and shovel by pioneer's decades before. So no man or animal would fall into it, someone had filled the well with huge rocks. Wind had blown dirt over the rocks filling the well almost to the level of the surrounding earth. I stood at a distance watching as the mother soiled her beautiful gray and white coat while digging through the dirt among the rocks preparing a home for her family. Her off spring milled around learning from their mother. While observing this activity, I had to hold Towser for he was etching to attack the wild animals that were his ancestral enemy.

But I had work to do. Soon Towser and I left the family of badgers to their homemaking. We had to find the cows and drive them home. We drove the cattle at a slow, drudgery pace not wanting the wrath of Dad. However, if an animal didn't want to go home to be milked and strayed from the small herd, Towser would block her path and bring her back into the small group. On this beautiful morning surrounded in a sea of cool air, I welcomed the leisurely pace of the cows while watching the sun rise over the eastern rim of the caprock.

When the cows, my dog and I got to the lot where milking took place, Dad was ready to give orders for the day as he made preparation to butcher a hog for our winter meat supply. There were three hogs in the pen, two gilts and a boar. Dad wanted to keep the gilts for breeding purposes, giving us a future supply of pork. Then there was my pig that I received after the plowing I did for Charley White nearly a year before. I'd grown close to this little guy by feeding him, rubbing behind his ears and scratching his belly while he lay in the shade. I always smiled as he expressed his pleasure by low sounding grunts.

Sometime ago, when he was still a pig, Dad castrated him. He had now grown into a 250-pound barrow. At that time, I feared that some day he would be meat on our table. When Dad separated my pet from the others, I knew full well what was coming next. I ran and hid because I didn't want to see my barrow shot between the eyes with a .22.

Dad carried the black wash pot down the hill, placing it near the water tank, not far from the hog pen. He filled the pot with water, and built a fire under it. While the water heated, he proceeded to fashion a tripod from cedar poles that extended about seven feet in the air. At the top of the tripod, he secured a pulley with a strong rope through it. He then cut from a cedar pole, an eighteen-inch piece, about three inches in diameter and sharpened each end with an ax.

Now everything was ready for the slaughter. Dad had to work fast. Knowing what happened when I heard the sound from the .22, I began to cry. My pet had been shot. Dad called for me to help. With tears in my eyes, I came running. With hands clutching each of the hind feet, he dragged the barrow to the tripod and slit the flesh between the tendon and bone just above the hoofs of the barrow's back feet. Quickly he placed the sharp ends of the cedar into the slits, tied the rope around the cedar pole and hoisted the 250-pound barrow to the top of the tripod. It hung in that position with head down.

Blood had to be drained from the body as soon as possible. Dad reached for the conveniently placed sharp knife, with an eight-inch blade, and cut deep into the throat. Blood that gushed out was soaked up by the surrounding soil. After the blood was sufficiently drained from the body, Dad released the pulley and the dead hog fell onto a board beneath that was placed there for the purpose. While still sniffling from witnessing the slaughter of my pet, Dad ordered me to take a bucket, fill it with boiling water from the pot and pour it on the carcass. The hot water softened the coarse hair on the skin of the dead animal. Then Dad worked vigorously to scrap off all the hair from the body while I continued to pour on hot water as tears moistened my freckled cheeks.

Our work was less than half complete. Dad got down on his knees, on the blood-soaked ground, to begin the job of cutting up the hog into various pieces while the carcass laid on the board The sun was shining down on the proceedings. He ordered me, "Empty that tub and drag it over here." As I obeyed, another order came "Run up to the house and bring the china bowl." (Nothing we had was china, but I knew what he meant.)

First he cut off the head of the dead animal; then he extracted the brains and put them in the bowl. These would later be fried for members of the family who dared eat them. He threw the head into the tub. Meat from the head along with the skin would be run though a sausage grinder, and combined with other stuff to make hogshead cheese that was put in a crock container to set for a number of days before eating

With the long knife, sharpened occasionally on a sand stone, the feet of the hog were cut off, scrubbed clean and thrown into the same tub to make pickled feet With the evil-looking knife, Dad started at the throat cutting across the chest down between the hind legs. With his strong arms and hands he pulled the two sides of the animal apart breaking ribs and exposing its insides. He then extracted the lungs, we called lights. The liver and kidneys came out next and he threw all into the tub.

When the tub was full, I received another command to pull up another tub. Dad worked feverishly as he took out the guts and handed the slimy things to me giving the command to throw them in the hog pen for the remaining hogs to eat. Skillfully he cut off the lower part of the legs at the joint and threw the pieces in the second tub. All the time hordes of flies came from the lots to swarm, landing on Dad and the bloody meat to get their portion.

The knife was sharpened again, and while the odor lingered, Dad removed the shoulders, the hams and cut the back into manageable pieces until there was nothing left except the pieces. Dad was in a hurry to get the meat into the smokehouse before the flies laid eggs on the meat. As he took a handle on the side of a tub, he told me to grab the other handle. The tub was heavy and as we raced toward the smokehouse, I stumbled. Dad understood and encouraged me to get up and go at it again. We went back and got the second tub, but I didn't do any better.

In the smokehouse the excess fat was cut from each piece. Some of the fat would be made into soap with the homemade liquid lye, and other portions would be used as shortening and salve for cuts and other wounds.

After every piece was washed and made as clean as possible, Dad took salt and rubbed into each piece hoping this method would preserve the meat and keep the flies from laying their eggs. For these eggs would produce maggots that would contaminate the meet making it unfit for our consumption.

After the cows were milked late that afternoon, the horses fed and watered and the hogs slopped, we were tired to the bone. We ate supper and Dad went down on the living room floor, put his right arm under his head and took a nap. I laid down beside him hoping to rest, but the twins, Ray and Raymond were still feeling frisky. They wouldn't allow me to take a nap, so they pestered me until we got to wrestling interfering with Dad's nap. He finally said, "If you boys want to wrestle, you can go outside."

Now the twins had turned seven and I would soon be ten. We went out in the yard and they both began to take me on. Heretofore, I handled them with ease by taking one hand, putting one down and with the other hand laying the other on top of the first. But I hadn't realized how much they had grown and their strength. In the yard they tackled me and held me to the ground This time it wasn't the twins hollering "calf rope," - it was I.

While Dad slept, Jessie kept looking at the middle finger on his right hand. It had been cut off at the first knuckle. All his offspring had wondered about it, and up until now he had never explained how it happened. When he awoke and all of us were gathered in the light of the coal oil lamp, Jessie, whom we supposed to be his pet of the litter and could get away with just about anything, asked, "Daddy, what happened to the short finger on you right hand. You've never told us about it."

In the dim light, Dad looked a little embarrassed, but finally said, "Oh, well. It's no secret. It's just some fool thing I did when I was growing up in Arkansas."

We were all ears and eager to learn the mystery of the missing finger. All said in unison, "Tell us about it!"

"Well, as I said. It ain't no secret. So I'll tell you." We all leaned forward as we scooted closer to him. "I guess I was about nine or ten years old, and my brother Ed was a little older. We were chopping wood for the stove one frosty morning. That would have been back in about 1890.

"It was Ed's turn to chop so he had the ax. But I was tryin' to tell him what to do - how to chop a certain piece of wood. Now Ed was a cut-up and liked to do crazy things. So he asked me where to cut the wood. I pointed to a spot on the limb he was cuttin' and said, 'Right there.' And he said, 'that ain't good 'nuff.' If you want me to cut this stick, you gotta tell me the exact spot.'

So I stooped way over and put my finger on the wood where I wanted him to cut. When I did, Ed came down with the ax and cut the tip of my finger off."

Jessie got up, went to Dad, hugged him and patted his massive shoulders. She said, "That must have hurt awful bad." Did you cry?" Yeah, I guess I did." "Did uncle Ed get a whippin'?" "Don't remember, but I guess so."

"Is that the end of the story?" "Not really." "Tell us the rest!" "Well I remember my Dad took a chew of tobacco from his mouth, put it on my finger, wrapped it with a rag and told me to go chop some more wood. Remember when Gene ripped the flesh from his finger on the barbed wire when we lived on the Gibbs place." We all nodded 'yes.' "Well, I did for Gene what I learn't from my Dad."

"Now let me tell you somethin' else," Dad said. "When you kids do some crazy thang and I want to take off my belt and give you a good whippin'. I look at my short finger and remember I was a kid once myself. And I did some pretty crazy thangs. It helps me control my temper. That keeps you kids from havin' a red bottom so much of the time." We all laughed as Mother sat in her cane bottom chair with a weak smile on her face for she had heard the story before.

Jessie asked, "Daddy, what did you do with the part of the finger Uncle Ed cut off?"

"The same thing you kids did when you thought that pig was dead and it ran off across the field after it hit the ground." Dad explained. "We put the finger in a metal snuffbox, and Ed preached its funeral. Then we buried it." Dad hesitated for a while and continued, "But it didn't get up and run off - like your pig did." We all laughed.

When hog killing time was past in the fall of the year and the crops were almost laid by, it couldn't be long till spooks appeared and tricks were played on neighbors at Halloween.

Churchell walked down through the breaks from the plains where he had been working in the wheat harvest. After we greeted him, he noticed Mother's pregnancy and began to tease her about eating too many watermelon seed. Dad noticed she was embarrassed, and told his oldest son to stop.

To change the subject, he pulled from his pocket a fist full of bills. He told us it was the money he'd earned during the fall and summer harvest. The value of the bills was small by today's standard. Nevertheless, I'd never seen so much money in all my life. My eyes bugged out in awe.

My big brother talked about shocking the wheat after it had been cut and tied into bundles by a row binder. The shocks all over the wheat fields looked something like a small wigwam some plains Indians made for homes. After the wheat in the shocks dried for a few days in the desert sun, my brother's crew drove a team hitched to a wagon. Using a pitchfork, they rammed the tines into each bundle and pitch it into the wagon. This was repeated until the wagon was full. Then the load was hauled to the threshing machine that usually stood near the middle of the field. Here the grains of wheat were separated from the stalk and the husk. The grain was hauled to the barn and kept in a granary until it was time to transport it to an elevator where it was sold.

The husks and the stalks with their brown leaves were left in the fields and raked up forming haystacks. In winter the cows and horses could eat from these stacks that often were higher than the animals themselves. Churchell said that sometimes the farm animals ate huge holes in the stacks that were big enough to shelter them during the blizzards in winter. As big brother held my undivided attention, I was amazed at the difference wheat farming on the plains was from our row crop farming in the valley. By this time the stock market had crashed, and our nation was well into the Great Depression. My big brother was bragging because he was able to make one dollar and fifty cents a day working in the blazing sun from daylight until dark. Such was *The Pre-Atomic Age.*

Etta had returned home after picking cotton on the high plains of West Texas. She had made enough money to buy that new $2.98 dress she wanted, and she had a little extra. I can't remember how it came about, but somebody invited her to a dance near San Jon where we attended school for one year. After Jessie fixed Etta's hair, she put on her new dress and powdered her face She looked pretty as a picture when she stepped into her date's 1930 model car. They were off to her first dance. Dad didn't think much of the idea of her going to a dance with someone he hardly knew. She was seventeen and head strong, made her own money, and didn't care much what Dad thought.

When Etta returned home, she painted such a beautiful word-picture of the evening, I still remember it vividly. A large dance floor had been built in the open air a short distance from the few streetlights in town. Candles furnished glimmering light for the dance. The silvery moon was shining bright down on the merry-makers. Cowboys picked guitars and sawed on fiddles as the girls, trained in high school choirs, sang of lonesome cowboys herding cattle and little doggies out on the prairie in rainstorms or winter blizzards. Some songs were of depressed sweethearts sitting in a prison cell far from the girls they loved wishing, hoping, praying for the day they'd be free. The girls wearing new dresses in the romantic setting danced with boys sporting ten-gallon hats, fancy shirts, blue jeans and boots with sharp toes.

Enamored by the music of the era, the moonlight and the sway of the couples on the dance floor, the crowd kept crying for more. They enjoyed themselves till the wee hours of the morning.

When Etta's date brought her home as the faint light in the eastern sky brought the dawning of a new day, Dad was waiting for her. As she entered the door, Dad began to bawl her out good and proper as he did me when I forced the cow to run while holding her tail. He was so upset, he could hardly contain himself. Etta paid him little mind, and went to bed dreaming of a night she would never forget.

Halloween was approaching and Churchell was busy trying to figure out what mischievous thing he could do that would aggravate one of our neighbors. Turning over outhouses was old hat. He had done that many times before, and he wanted to try another trick.

It wasn't until the late afternoon on October 31st when he saw Herbert Gibbs riding his saddle horse toward the setting sun as he usually did when his chores were done. When my twenty-year-old brother saw our neighbor, the lone cowboy, riding his horse at a slow pace, with his head and shoulders bent slightly over the saddle horn, he cried out, "I got it. I know what I'm going to do this Halloween night."

Mother asked, partly in anger as she sat in her favorite chair holding her protruding stomach, "What are you going to do, young man? I hope you're not going to do something that will hurt somebody."

"Now Mom, you know I wouldn't hurt anybody," he said.

Mother had reason to ask the question, for Churchell had come home sometimes with face bruised and black eyes. She wasn't as much concerned about her son's safety as she was the other person's for she was persuaded with his intelligence, strength and agility, he could take care of himself.

When the sun was cut in half setting on the western horizon painting the edges of dark clouds crimson and gold, big brother grabbed my right arm forcing me into the front yard. It wasn't my favorite thing to go anywhere with him, for I wasn't fond of his company. So I jerked loose from his hold on me and raced toward the back of the house. He caught me, and I struggled not wanting to go. He grabbed my right ear twisting, pulling it and demanded, "You're going with me to play a trick on Gibbs whether you want to or not!" Dad was still at work in the field and Mother had no control over her oldest child. Struggling behind him, he must have dragged me by my ear halfway to the Gibbs' house - a considerable distant from ours.

When we got to our neighbor's house, all was silent in the twilight except the lowing of the cows, the grunting of the hogs and the wings of chickens flapping to get upon a roost.

Churchell whispered, "We've gotta hurry up and get this job done before dark." He helped me get on the roof of the porch, and then climbed up behind me carrying gunnysacks with him. He stuffed the sack into the chimney, knowing when Mr. Gibbs built a fire in his fireplace the next morning smoke would fill his house.

My big brother crawled off the roof, opened the unlocked door and proceeded to dismantle Herbert Gibbs' bed. With this accomplished, he handed the bed, piece by piece, up to me. When the complete bed was on the roof, Churchell crawled up on the roof and began to reassemble the bed hoping to leave it there as we escaped back home. This was my brother's imaginative idea of having fun while pulling off an unusual Halloween trick

Well, it didn't work as he wished. While he concentrated on putting the bed back together on the roof, Mr. Gibbs returned home. When we finally looked down, our neighbor was sitting astride his horse in the yard looking up at us.

Now what? Should we apologize, jump off the roof and run. What was Mr. Gibbs going to do? Would he draw his gun, he carried to kill rattlesnakes, and shoot both of us? It was unlikely that he would challenge Churdhell in a fistfight, for he knew my brother's reputation as a brawler. To take neighbors to court was unheard of in our valley.

For a moment, without moving a muscle, we gazed down on the man on horseback, and he looked up at us. Neither party spoke a word. Just gazed at each other in silence. I was transfixed, wondering what would happen next.

Finally, Churchell, knowing he was completely in the wrong and subject to any action Mr. Gibbs wished to pursue, meekly crawled down leaving the bed on the roof. I followed close behind. Neither person spoke a word. As brother looked back at the rider as we walked away gingerly. But when we got around the corner of the house, we struck out in a dead run like scared rabbits.

SEVERE DUST STORMS

Little did we realize what lay ahead for our valley and the Great Plains of these United States of America. In this broad expanse of farmland, the drought of the previous summer continued. Early in the morning we saw the first blue northern of 1932 coming toward us. The air was charged with electricity. I could tell Dad was feeling something strange as he scanned the sky and paced back and forth across the yard.

As I observed him, he said, "Son, that shore don't look good at all. I don't know what it is, but I think something bad is about to happen. I can't figure out why that cloud is so dark. I never saw anything like that before." Seeing Dad nervous, made me nervous.

He looked at the windmill, and said, "See the windmill. It's twisting in the wind. Facin' one direction then another. That means the wind is also twistin', changin' direction as if it can't make up its mind which way to blow. And it's gettin' stronger. Son, you'd better run down there and shut the windmill off."

I took off running barefoot across the stony ground as chickens flapped their wings to get out of my way. Coming to the windmill, I reach up for the iron pipe lever to pull it down. My arm strength allowed me to bring the pipe only halfway in a parallel position. So I laid my stomach across the lever and the weight of my body forced it down until I could put it in a wire loop to hold it. The large rotating fan of the windmill was drawn close to the tail, that kept the fan facing a twisting wind, and it stopped turning.

When the cold front hit, it brought icy winds and a fair amount of fine sand that got in our nostrils. For the first time, we experienced a gritty sensation in our mouths. This was only a harbinger of things to come.

It wasn't long after this that Mother began to have contractions telling her that her tenth child would soon make his solo entrance into the world. One of the neighbors who served as a midwife, was called to our home, water was heated and plenty towels, made from flour sacks, were made ready for the birth.

Ray, Raymond, Jay and I were hustled off to stay with a neighbor family. Etta was close by to make sure warm water and towels were available. The midwife stayed by Mother's bedside, and Dad tried to comfort her by holding her hand and talking to her.

Much of the ordeal was over for Mother when she delivered a healthy baby boy kicking and squalling. What little hair he had was blond and his skin was fair. Mack and Katy named their new son Charles Quentin Charles for Mother's father, Charles Miller. I don't know where the Quentin came from. The tenth and last child born into our family was a lovable, cuddly little guy that all his older brothers and sisters wanted to hold. Charles was spoiled early in life and he loved the attention.

Mother did not do so well. She was sick and weak for a long time, and a large, deep sore developed on her left breast that swelled much larger than its normal size. It was extremely sensitive. The slightest touch of a garment proved to be painful. Sometime she sat in her favorite chair with the breast uncovered except for her hand held slightly above it. Home remedies, such as hog lard and tallow, and other concoctions were used to cure the sore. Eventually it went away.

About the same time I was plagued with a series of boils that appeared on the back of my neck. They, too, were painful particularly when I turned my head. Dad said it was because

I had bad blood. So I was given sulfur mixed with molasses to build up my blood. The same home remedies, used on Mother, were rubbed on the boils. This procedure continued until the boils came to head. Then Dad squeezed the boils between his fingers and out came the corruption that had built up.

But this was wintertime and between a group of beautiful, warm, sunny days came the black northerly fronts bringing cold winds with more and more fine sand. We had no name for the storms at the time, but as they grew progressively worse they came to be known as Sand Storms. The entire Great Plains became known as the Dust Bowl.

The cold north winds occasionally brought a few inches of snow. Even in the freezing weather the chores had to be done. My job was to grab a bucket early in the morning and late in the afternoon and head for the lot to milk the cows. Since we had no barn, my work was done outside where the winter winds howled. Sometimes after the storm had passed leaving the snow, I could hear the whistle of the train seven miles to the north and see the smoke rising from its stack as it traveled westward parallel to Highway 66.

There was a slight rise in the earth between our house and the farm where the Massey family lived. This rise hid their place from ours on ordinary days. But when the snow covered the ground and the atmospheric conditions were right, I could see their house. Knowing nothing of the science that explained this phenomenon, I simply pronounced it as "funny" that such occurred. This phenomenon and many others in nature intrigued me.

When my work was completed, I carried the bucket filled with milk to the house leaving it with the girls to strain the milk and put it away. Without a word, I would rush to the stove to thaw my hands that were aching and stiff from the cold. By this time, the stove was red-hot from the fire within. It felt so good to back up close to it and warm my shivering body.

Jessie was home from school in Wheatland, and she brought with her the book *Uncle Tom's Cabin* by Harriet Beecher Stowe she had checked out from the school library. After the chores were all done, on several of those cold winter nights, all the family left at home gathered around the large table where we ate to listen as Jessie read from the book.

At thirteen, with her dark pigtails dangling around her shoulders, in the light of the coal oil lamp, Jessie's reading held the undivided attention of the entire family. Dad was completely engrossed by the story. He was now 50 years old, and the top of his head was bald. But a patch of gray hair curled up around his head just above his ears. I watched him as he leaned his bulky frame toward Jessie as she read. Dad had both elbows on the table holding his chin in his hands. The roll of white hair around his head reminded me of a halo.

From my recollection, none of us children had ever seen a person of color, yet when Jessie read of the trials, suffering and human dignity of Uncle Tom, and the death of Little Eva, we all cried. As I bring to life the scene around that table, I can see Dad raise one of his massive, powerful hands and wipe away a tear that rolled down his cheek. Mother, with hair rolled into a bun on the back of her head, listened intently. The reading, the listening, the emotion went on night after night until Jessie finished reading the book. Except for the Bible and a Hymnal, that was the only book our family, as a group, ever listened to.

I had grown to be about the same size as Jessie. We became very good friends exchanging secrets, playing jacks on the large flat rock that served as a step-up into the kitchen door, pitching horseshoes and often working together. She liked to tease me about the freckles all over my face. Dad had told me several times how he got rid of the freckles that covered his face when a boy. He said if you will go out on the first day of May, wash your face in the dew, and with your hands still wet rub the portion of your body you want the freckles transferred to, they will leave your face and go to the placed rubbed. To prove his point, Dad would bare his shoulder and say, "See, after I washed my face with dew and rubbed my shoulder all my freckles went to my shoulder." Brown spots did actually cover his shoulder.

I was very skeptical of his story, believing he was pulling my leg with some old wives' tale. So when the first of May rolled around there was a slight trace of dew on the grass in low places around the farm. I didn't want Dad to believe I fell for his tall tale. So in early morning on the first of May, I slipped from the house, found a patch of dew and washed my face and rubbed my shoulder. After waiting several days, I looked in a glass. The freckles were still on my face and my shoulder was clear.

I watched the chickens scratch in the cow lots searching for food. They seemed especially fond of rummaging in manure piles dropped by the cows. The fowls ate the grain what no human would dare eat, but come Sunday dinner that same chicken, fried to crispy brown, tasted so good. Knowing the grain from the manure pile made the chicken grow meat we called thighs, breasts and pulley bones, I was curious about what caused the detestable to turn into something so delicious.

On a late spring morning with the bright sunlight flooding our valley, some of us stood in the doorway watching a mother skunk sniffing her way among the weeds and grasses. As she searched for breakfast, five of her babies strolled behind in a single, straight row. This family, each with fur black as coal and a white streak from head to tail, presented a challenge to me. I knew of the awful stinking spray an adult skunk could spray on an unwanted intruder, but I'd been told that the younger ones had no such protection.

Thinking I could steal one of her babies for a pet, I ran from the door where we were standing, crouched low to the ground attempting to sneak up behind, grab the trailing baby without the mother seeing me. Well, my strategy did not work! The mother skunk, like any good mother, was watching over her brood to protect them from all harm. As I approached, ready to snatch the last baby in line and run with it, Mrs. Skunk let go, in my direction, the powerful spray the Creator gave her. She sprayed me with the terrible liquid from under her tail. Her children were safe from my kidnapping attempt, but I was stunned by the terrible odor and the fumes caused me to cough and my eyes burned.

I ran hastily back to our house, but my family would not let me come in for the stinking odor lingered, and they didn't want me to contaminate the whole house - perhaps for days. A pair of old pants was thrown to me, and I was told to go behind the smokehouse and change. While I was changing, Dad spotted me and wanted to know what happened. When I told him, he laughed aloud for a long time. Finally he said, "Son, the only thing you can do is to get a shovel, dig a hole and bury your clothes for you cannot wash that odor out. When you get through with that job, you'd better go down to the horse tank and wash yourself off before coming to the house."

Coyotes were an enemy to every farmer and rancher in these parts. These thieves would catch chickens and small calves and eat them. As a result the family income was diminished and meat for the table was made scarce. To cut down on the number of these animals, several of our neighbors kept pot hounds. At night, during a slack season, the owners would put these black and brown dogs on a leash and set out in the darkness of night to find coyotes, badgers or skunks they considered to be predators that destroyed our 'bread and butter.' These dogs had very sensitive smellers. When they discovered the scent left by the wild animals on their trail, the hunter turned the dogs loose. The dogs began running down the path. With the noses close to the ground and with every leap the hounds would give out a very distinctive howl. Their howl set the pot hound apart from every other hunting dog. Some hunters swore up and down they could tell, just by the sound of the howl; when the dog was getting closer to the wild animal or when the dog had chased the varmint up a tree or in a hole or when the scent was lost.

Sometime I was allowed to tag alone on these hunts.

During busy times, the dogs were turned loose to hunt by themselves. When they found a coyote scented trail, they started the howling that could be heard for miles on early, clear mornings. But the wild critters were smarter than the dogs. The coyotes would run in pairs in a large circle around the entire neighborhood. The howling could be heard in all directions as they made the circle repeatedly. The sneaky coyotes wore out the dogs by their relay running. One coyote would run with the dogs in close pursuit until it got tired. Then it would leave the trail and hide in the brush. At that point, the first coyote would leave the circular trail and his partner, would begin running the marathon in the same path Since the scent of the two wild critters was near the same, the dogs thought they were chasing the same animal. This continued until the dogs were exhausted. They gave up, going back to their home with tongues hanging out and breathing hard.

In the fall, when harvest was near and the grain in the fields was ready to gather, great flocks of blackbirds came to feast on the crops. It seemed they came to steal our crop we'd worked so hard for. It was them against our family. We were bigger, but their number could easily defeat us in the fight if some definite action was not taken. It was their survival or ours. So, when their craws were full and puffed out in front, our enemies liked to sit on the barbed wire fence while their gizzards work in the digestive process.

It was then Ray and Raymond, Dad or I would slip quietly behind the birds, generally all faced in the same direction, grab the wire, pull it taunt, let it go before the birds could fly. This unexpected action caught our enemy off guard before they could take off. By this method, we killed many blackbirds.

If this sounds inhumane, remember they were destroying our cash crop and the feed we hoped would keep our livestock alive. The horses, cows, hogs and chicken were needed for our existence. We had to fight, often in unconventional ways, to make a living.

In the summer of 1932, when the crop in our 260-acre field was about knee high, an influx of grasshoppers attacked every green thing that was edible. They started at the end of the rows gorging themselves until every leaf and most of the stalks were devoured for about one hundred steps into the field. This made a large portion of the crop incapable of producing. Had we not fought this enemy, the entire field may have been destroyed. This also was our livelihood, absolutely necessary for our existence.

There were some pesticides on the market, but they cost money that we did not have. If we had the money to buy pesticides, we had no way of spreading it in the field. Dad thought he had to do something, even if it were useless. His method of fighting this enemy, the army of grasshoppers, was to give each member of the family some kind of large cloth. All of us marched, with rag in hand, to the farthest point in the field to which the enemy had eaten. There we began waving rags hoping to drive our adversaries from the field, across the fence into the pastureland where they would do less damage. This method of warfare was only successful to a very small degree. Our field was larger and such maneuvers could not possibly do much good. Beside that, we could not stay on the battle lines indefinitely. As soon as we left, the grasshoppers were back in the field eating away driven by their insatiable appetites.

In the fall of that year, Churchell, who was a hard worker, returned home to help harvest the remnant of the crop that was left. We prepared the wagon, making it ready to receive the heads of maize (not corn) filled with reddish grain. The wagon was fitted with sideboards. The sideboard on the left side of the wagon was about three feet higher than the one on the right side. This expedited the gathering of the crop, for we didn't have to be so careful when we cut off the heads of maize and throw them into the wagon as it was pulled down the row by a pair of horses. We had no knives to cut the heads off the stalks that were about as high as my head. Again, Dad showed his ingenuity by taking a chisel and hammering out knives, with curved cutting edges, from an old handsaw. He fashioned wooden handles for the knives that fit snugly in our hands.

Everything was ready to go to the field. I took the row nearest the wagon and my big brother took the next row from the wagon. We began cutting heads of maize off and throwing them against the highest sideboard on the opposite side of the wagon letting them fall into the bed. Churchell could work faster than I, so to help me keep up, he'd reach over into my row and cut off the heads and throw them into the wagon. We kept at this monotonous work day after day until the field was harvested. This assured a small income for the family to buy necessities we could not raise on the farm such as sugar, white flour, salt and vinegar.

Our front yard was as bare of plants as the asphalt on the surface of the narrow Highway 66. We dug a hole in the yard and enriched it with manure. A single castor bean was planted in the hole. Members of the family took turns nurturing the seed by watering it and keeping animals away. We watched it grow from a small plant to one with beautiful, green leaves. It grew to be about my height, and the chickens scratched for earthworms in its shade.

We needed to build a chicken house so the skunks, badgers and coyotes could not sneak upon them at night and make a midnight snack of them. For a foundation, we took the wagon to the breaks and filled it with rocks of every size. When we got the rocks home, they had to be hewn to fit together. Dad proved his skill as a rock mason by using a hammer molding each stone into just the right shape and size. A wall about three feet high was built on the foundation. This wall needed to be about four feet higher before the roof went on.

We decided to finish building the walls with adobe bricks. So we went beyond the windmill where the grass was thick, dug a wide hole leaving the loose dirt in the hole and poured ample water into the hole making mud that contained the grass and roots. While us boys did this, Dad was busy making wood frames the proper size to mold the adobe bricks to fit the stones in the lower part of the chicken house. When the mud was poured into the frames with the grass and roots to hold the adobe bricks together, they were left in the hot sunshine to dry for a few days. Dried to sufficient hardness, we finished building the walls and then put a tin roof on the chicken house. Next came a fence surrounding the structure to keep out the varmints that might want to make our egg-layers into a good meal.

At first, when darkness was approaching, we had to bribe the chickens into their new home by sprinkling grain in a narrow path in front of them. They followed the path clucking and pecking one another as they swallowed the grain. Without knowing it, they were in the house, and we shut them up. Before many nights passed, the chickens would make a beeline for their house without being coaxed. Apparently they came to realize it was better and more secure to spend the night in their new home rather than sleeping, taking their chances, under the yucca, mesquite and beargrass plants.

Even with this protection, some wild critter wanting an evening meal would dig under the fence. Sometimes, in the middle of the night, we would hear the chickens flapping their wings, scrambling in all directions, making awful sounding noises. They were scared for their lives. We knew some predator was in the henhouse seeking to devour our precious flock that produced eggs for us to eat and sell. Some member of the family would rush through the darkness, in his night cloths, toward the chicken house calling Towser as they ran. Our faithful dog would either kill the intruder or chase it away. The chickens would settle down, and we could go back to sleep.

When I had time off from work or school, I'd usually head for the hills in the escarpment with Towser, my constant companion. He chased rabbits, prairie dogs and ground squirrels, not that he wanted a meal, but for the sheer joy of running. He would return from the chase with his tongue hanging from his open mouth and panting hard. I sometimes thought I could see a smile on his face because he was happy to be out in the wild. While Towser sniffed bushes and investigated burrows of animals to chase, I checked the steel traps we set to catch badgers, coyotes and other beasts. This may seem cruel to many, but for us, in those Depression days, it was another source of money with which we could put food on the table and buy a few clothes. When an animal was caught, it had to be skinned, all the fat scrapped off the inside of the pelt and stretched on a board to dry. It was worth fifty cents to a dollar on the market, if we could sell it at all.

Also, I'd take a look at the quail traps to check if any birds were inside. A quail trap was a plain box, but some were fancy, about 18 inches by two feet and about a foot high. To set the trap, we'd lift one end up about eight inches and put a trigger inside with grain on the end of the trigger. After this was accomplished, we hoped that a mother quail would come inside the box and call her brood to share the grain with her. When the chicks gathered around the mother, they'd began pecking at the grain. It was then the trigger would activate allowing the box to fall around the entire family of quail. This operation did not always work, but occasionally it would. When it did, we'd kill the quail, take them home, dress them and have fried quail for supper. If this sounds cruel to you, remember this was the Great Depression and good wholesome meals, for us in the *pocket of perpetual poverty,* were few and far between.

On one occasion, when I was exploring the mysteries of the hills with my companion, we were tired from running over the ridges and down into the canyons. I sat on a huge rock to rest and my faithful dog sat beside me on the ground with his tongue hanging out and breathing rapidly. I had found a large drop of dried resin still attached to a pine tree, and had been chewing it as gum. I spit it out and chose a smooth white stone about the size of a marble and put it my mouth to quench my thirst. While we were resting, I noticed a king snake had crawled up into a nearby bush. I kept an eye on the creature as it worked its lips in various distortions. As I watched, the snake began to wiggle out of the old skin that had covered its body. I kept looking at this strange action until all the old skin was left in the bush, and the snake, with its beautiful, shining new skin, crawled on the ground out of sight.

I returned home and told my family what I'd witnessed. None, not even Dad, believed me. I told what I'd seen at school, but none, not even Mrs. White, believed me. All had seen dried snakeskin lying around on the pasturelands and on farms, but none had ever seen a snake crawl out of its skin making my true story hard to believe.

In my earliest days as a youth, I enjoyed observing the distinct characteristics of people and animals. Animals like humans have different personalities within each species. Two swine may look exactly alike physically, but their keepers can easily tell them apart by their personalities. One will be lazy and the other may be active. Each will have different habits in eating while associating with other hogs. Someone, who has studied the subject more than I, will have to explain why this is true. When we were youngsters, Jessie and I noticed a hen that was large in front and associated her with a buxom woman that visited us. This lady we associated with a squirrel for when she ate food, she'd take small bites, chew fast barely separating the upper teeth from the lower.

A cowboy can tell one White Face cow from another a quarter mile away by the way she acts. Some bulls are belligerent, and others a more gentle. We noticed our milk cows had different characteristics that distinguished them from stall mates.

Probably the most noticeable of all was the characteristics of our four horses. Though they were easily distinguishable by color and size, they were just as different in their personalities. Lake was a big brownish-black horse, strong, laid back and dependable. Fox was smaller, red in color, fiery in character and as stubborn as any mule that ever pulled a plow. Occasionally Fox would absolutely refuse to move. We could coax him by putting food just out of his reach, but he refused to move forward a few steps to eat. We could whip him with a leather strap, but it did no good. One day during one of his stubborn spells refusing to move, Dad became exasperated with the horse for he needed him to work. Fox just stood in his tracks like a statue. Finally Dad said, "I'll make him move." So he got some kindling wood, put it under Fox's belly and set the wood on fire. It wasn't long before the horse jumped and was ready to work.

Our black horse, Mose, was slow moving and would do whatever he was asked at his own pace. The white ghost, we called George, liked to play around with other horses and sometime he'd bite the cows on the neck making them run so he could chase them.

The roof on our house was covered with corrugated metal that was silver in color. On a hot autumn day when the sand cranes were flying south for the winter, one must have gotten lost from the others. This lone crane probably thought our roof was a pool of water. For it landed on the hot tin roof. Instead of flying off immediately, the confused fowl stood there on one foot, at the end of a very long leg, until it got so hot he could take it no longer. At that point, the crane would put the other foot down and draw the first up into the feathers that covered his body. I watched him for quite a while as he continued this little, slow dance. Without even giving a honk, he flew away in search of his mates.

I felt the pain of the creature trying to cool one foot while standing on the other. For on bare feet I had crossed a patch of sand heated by the summer sun almost to the boiling point. It was a painful experience. I'd dance from one foot to the other until I reached soil that was a little cooler.

THE HARD, SIMPLE LIFE

Mother's health had improved. She was smiling and laughing more and her limited sense of humor returned. Yet, when we saw her alone, it was evident from the look on her face, she was wondering if her large brood could be fed, clothed and schooled. Once again, she controlled the reins in her household with her gentle manner.

When spring rolled around, she made sure each of her children, who still lived at home, took a round of Black Draught Tea. Each of us hated the very thought of drinking the absolutely terrible tasting medicine. Perhaps four-year-old Jay hated it more than all the rest. I can see him now dancing up and down on the splintery floor, waving his arms and crying loud at the very thought of swallowing the nasty tasting brew. Mother said it would clean our insides out for the year. So she insisted. It must have worked for I don't remember any of us children getting sick from stomach trouble. In addition, the medicine caused us to run, and I do mean run, to the outhouse frequently. If it were occupied, there were plenty of mesquite bushes we could hide behind to do our business.

However each of us did suffer through childhood diseases. When one got chicken pox, measles or mumps it ran its course by infecting all of us in turn. Mother's experience through the years taught her that each of these diseases lasted a few days. About the only thing a mother could do in those days was to keep the diseased child quiet as possible. I remember when I had chicken pox. I was 'imprisoned' in the bedroom, where all of us children slept. Heavy quilts were put over the windows making the room dark as night in mid-day. Mother thought darkness would keep the light from damaging my eyes while recovering.

Women had raised the hemline on their dresses from ankle length to just below the knee. Mother thought this was a shame. With egg-money. she bought material and made herself a new dress on her Singer sewing machine. The dress was ankle length. She wore it the next time she went to Broadview where she was known by many of the farm-wives who came to the small town to do their Saturday shopping. These ladies, who were more modern than Mother, began to ask, "What in the world has happened to Katy? That old fashioned dress looks very odd for these modern times." Mother got wind of the remarks, so when she got home, she cut the bottom of the dress off to just below the knees.

In those depression days our Mother saved her pennies, nickels and dimes until she accumulated a dollar She thought it was time she did something for herself instead of giving everything to members of the family. The next time she went to town, she spent the whole dollar to buy a purse for herself and herself alone. Having no money to carry in the purse did not keep her from feeling a little taller with an extra spring in her step. I can see her now, as Dad drove the team and wagon homeward, sitting in the spring seat with her husband wearing her flowery hat over her long black hair made into a bun. One-year-old Charles Quentin sat between them. As the wagon bumped up and down on the long, narrow road, Mother held her purse firmly in her lap, enjoying the sunshine, breathing deeply of the clean air and watching the cattle graze in the pastures and wheat fields. She was feeling good and enjoying life. Occasionally Dad glanced at her. Seeing her joy made him smile.

Her younger sons were in the back of the wagon scuffling, laughing and teasing one another. Ray and Raymond read a road sign that warned, "Tractors with lugs keep off the road." They teased me saying, "You're a big lug, so you shouldn't be on the road."

After we got home, Dad and the rest of us teased Mother for weeks because she bought a purse but didn't have any money to carry in it. She took it all with good humor.

President Hoover had been voted out of office, and President Roosevelt had begun to govern the nation from the Oval Office. Politics and the new President were the talk everywhere people gathered in our valley. The stock market, which I knew nothing about, had already crashed and prices for cattle and other farm produce had diminished to the point it hardly paid to put in a crop and gather it. But we kept trying, working spring, summer and fall hoping we could make a few dollars to buy absolute necessities. Most people put their hope in Roosevelt as our savior from the Depression and hoped even that he would do something about the sand storms that were growing more intense with each devastating wind that engulfed us.

The new president wasn't in office long before he instituted many changes. History tells us of the Bank Holiday in addition to the program of giving commodities to families in need. Dad, a proud and fiercely independent man, was forced by circumstances of the period to sign up for the cans of food wrapped in white paper with bold letters telling what they contained. I followed Dad's pride and independence and came to hate the very word commodities for it told our friends and neighbors that we couldn't make it on our own. Hating the word didn't diminish my like for the meat and vegetables in the cans when my stomach was growling for more nourishing food because I was hungry. Though I no longer hate the word, even to this day when I see "commodities" in the newspaper, thoughts conjure in my mind of those days when my family could not make it on our own.

Work as hard as we did in those dark days of the Great Depression, it was impossible to make ends meet on our half section of rented land. Our crops could not produce because the blowing sand either cut the plants to pieces or covered them up. The grass in the pastures was covered by the blowing sand. Some of our cattle died from mud in the stomach after attempting to nibble the grass covered by the fine sand. Young watermelon and cantaloupe vines could not produce because they were blown out of the ground or covered up.

Earnest Leach, the youngest son of Mary Leach who owned the farm we worked, told me in recent years the taxes on the place was $1.75 a year. But the share for Mrs. Leach from the crop one year was not enough to pay the tax. She had to reach down into her own purse for the money.

Our government led by President Roosevelt began paying farmers and ranchers $12.50 a head for men to come out, round up chosen livestock and shoot them. I remember watching cows shot between the eyes and falling dead as I sat astride the bare back of old Mose. Dad wanted to butcher the beef for our own table, but that wasn't allowed. The carcasses remained where they lay and rotted. Maggots were allowed to consume the remains.

But our lot was better than some poor souls. An old man, who had been walking for days, came to our door. He was scary looking with bushy hair and a white beard reaching down to his belly button. He told us he was hungry and needed a meal to get him on down the road a little way. He was welcomed to come in to share what we had. Mother put a ham hock in one of her metal cooking vessels with plenty of water. It was put on the cook stove fired by cow chips and mesquite wood. After it had boiled for a few minutes, she ladled it out into bowls for the family and our visitor.

The old gentleman, who reminded us of Moses of the Old Testament, entertained us through the meal with strange, exciting and funny stories. In all his trials, he had not lost his sense of humor. He told us a story of the American Indians that

I've never forgotten. (True or not, I can't say.) He made the story exciting and funny. According to him the Indians ate their dogs when they had too many or when the dogs were too old to work. As he talked, he took the ladle Mother used. He dipped it to the bottom of the vessel that contained the pork stew, and said, "Dig deep, pup in the bottom." He meant the dog meat (supposedly eaten by Indians), which was the better part of the watery stew, had sunk to the bottom and he was digging for it.

After the meal, our visitor expressed his profound gratitude, and we thanked him for the entertainment that helped us forget our own plight for a short period of time. When he left, we watched him as he walked down the lane making his way over mounds of drifted sand. We knew sooner or later he'd find another family with whom he could share a meal and entertain with stories accumulated from his wanderings.

Even to this very day, when the children and grandchildren of Mack and Katy (They have been gone for more than forty years) meet to share a meal, and the table is set, someone invariable will say, "It's ready, so 'Dig deep, pup in the bottom.'"

Sometime a lone cowboy came by riding his horse with everything he owned in this world tied in a bundle to his saddle. We'd shared what we had and he'd ride off into the unknown.

These difficult times were not so much concern to me because all the families in our *pocket of perpetual poverty* were in the same shape. Perhaps the Tuckers had more. Except for what our schoolteacher told us, and what I read in schoolbooks, the world was no bigger than things I could see from horizon to horizon. When there was no telephone, newspaper, television or books, knowledge of the world beyond was very limited. I had a faint recollection of Arkansas with the tall trees and running brooks, but it was hard to translate that to our valley. The arroyos would swell up to overflowing with rushing water after a cloud burst, but they were dry again within an hour. Dwarf pine and cedar trees inhabited the beaks in the escarpment, but they did not compare to the majestic trees in the forests of Arkansas.

Though our primitive lifestyle was of little concern to me, it must have been a devastating concern and worry to Dad and Mother. The great weight of raising children in such conditions surely weighed heavily on their hearts. With all his abilities, talents, intelligence, mental and physical strengths, Dad seemed to be a loser in everything he tried. The times and circumstances in which he lived just were not for him. He must have thought of his predicament many times. If he did, he never mentioned it that I remember.

I was free from all my parents' worries and concerns. Work, school, family and a few friends in the valley and on the plains were all my life. That's all I knew. I took advantage, when time permitted, to run wild and free with my dog, Towser, across the prairie and over the hills chasing rabbits and dodging the strike of rattlesnakes. Sometimes on hot summer afternoons we'd come upon an earthen tank that held water for the cattle. With no soul in sight, in the thinly populated valley, I'd take off all my clothes, and Towser and I would cool off, with the cattle, in the tank with mud on the bottom squeezing up between my toes.

Early one night, when the sky was clear as ever it was, with the heavens filled with stars and the moon absent, lights began to flash along the horizon from east to west as far as we could see. With no communications with the outside world, Mother, not knowing why these bright lights like huge fans swept across the sky, had additional worry on her mind. As she paced the kitchen floor calling all her family to her side, she announced with fright in her voice, "I just don't know what's happening. This might be the end of the world." Dad tried to calm her down by saying, "I don't think it's the end of the world. I don't know what it is, but it's probably something the government has done."

After watching the flashing lights for more than an hour with no catastrophe occurring, Mother calmed down and we all went to bed. Later we learned it really was the government's doing. Beacon light had been planted from coast to coast to guide airplane pilots across the nation at night.

Mr. Johnson lived a couple of miles west of us past the schoolhouse over a bridge that crossed an arroyo. He was a single cowboy who lived in a small white house beside the lane on a mid-sized ranch. He took a liking to Jessie and gave her a swatch of multicolored wallpaper. It wasn't much of a present and worthless to many people. But Jessie treasured it very highly. It motivated her imagination to new heights never before reached. Sitting in our three-room house with its bare walls, she leafed through the swatch thinking how beautiful our house could look with walls covered in wallpaper. This simple deed by Mr. Johnson planted a seed in Jessie's heart, and later, after she married Raymond Vanderslice, a building contractor, she became one of the most sought after home decorators in Oklahoma City.

Charley White was our most frequent visitor. He usually came after the late afternoon chores were complete. Having received a dose of mustard gas during the first war with Germany, he stuttered as he told stories of his experience in World War I. These stories were sprinkled with curse words that our family didn't use at home. I don't remember how it came about, but one day Mr. White and I rode horses along the base of the escarpment southeast of our house. As we rode alone, he said, "Son, I want to show you something that few people know about." He led riding his horse, and I followed on mine. The horses went up a steep incline into the breaks hitting their hoofs against the many rocks that lay in the trail. When we came out of the warm sunshine that early morning into the shadow of the eight-hundred-foot mountain to the east, Mr. White drew his horse up to a complete stop. When I got even with him, I pulled on the reins, and my horse came to halt beside his.

"Dismount," he said, "I want to show you something that you'll remember the rest of your life." After we got off the horses and tied their reins to a small tree, I followed him up the rocky path as we dodged the thorny branches of mesquite bushes. Finally we came to a few dwarf cedar trees with some small pine trees scattered about. He held his broad brimmed hat on his head with his left hand to keep it from being knocked off by the low hanging branches. I had no such problem, for I didn't wear a hat. We worked our way through the trees and bushes until we came to a cave in the side of a hill. As he said, "Follow me," Mr. White got on his knees and began to crawl into the cave. I was close behind.

It was about as dark inside as the early morning dawn. We could still see three mounds of dirt: Two long ones and one very short. Mr. White began telling me the story an elder of the valley told him when he was about my age. I listened carefully and patiently as he revealed the mystery of the three mounds with his stuttering voice. He told me the three mounds were three graves that contained the remains of a husband and wife and their little child. This young family was killed by the Indians when the white man first came to our valley not long after the American Civil War. In his slow, stuttering manner he told me of the hardship the early pioneers experienced. Many of the settlers who came into the San Jon valley after the Civil War were associated on one side or the other in the civil conflict. Some were for the North. Others who came to our valley were Pro-Confederate guerrillas under "Bloody Bill" Anderson or Quantrill's Raiders in the Missouri and the Eastern Kansas conflict. The families wanted to start over settling in an area where they were not known. But some of them brought their tempers with short fusses with them.

Gunfights among neighbors happened. In addition to gunfights among themselves, the settlers had to fight the Indians.

Among the settlers was the notorious Black Jack Ketchen who was the last of the great train robbers. He was killed in Quay County, near Tucumcari, in 1901.

Once or twice a year Mother would invite some of the neighbor ladies in for a quilting party. She'd have Dad drop a quilting frame down from the ceiling of the living room until it was about three-and-one-half feet off the floor. She washed flour sack, with the faded lettering still visible, and sewed them together. Then they were stretched on the frame from foot to head and from side to side. When the ladies came in, they all had to catch up on the latest news and gossip in the valley. (This was the time for men and children to find something else to do.)

On top of the stretched flour sacks that were stitched together, they would put a layer of cotton to increase the weight of the finished product. If they didn't have cotton, they substituted a worn out quilt or something else. Each lady brought a bundle of scraps to sew together for the quilt top. The scraps were usually parts of men's breeches that did not wear out such as the upper part of the leg and the part below the knee. The seats and the knees of the pants were always beyond use in the quilt - too many holes.

It might take several days to make one bed covering. It all depended on how much talking was done. But some parts of winter were slack times for all of us. It was a good time for the women to make quilts for all the families.

This slack time was a good time for Dad and me to repair harnesses, the wagon and the fence around the place. We didn't have the money to buy axle grease for the wagons and plows. So we put green hog rinds around the axles and slipped the wheels over that. This procedure had to be repeated often for the rinds did not last very long.

It was during quilting time that Etta and Jessie cleaned the house and did the churning in a tall crock. When it was ready, they'd put the butter in a wooden molder making cakes about three-and-a-half inches by two-and-a-half by four inches.

The girls ironed the clothe with real irons. The irons were put on the heated stove, the wooden handles removed so they wouldn't burn. When the irons were hot enough, the handles were reattached by a metal mechanism. To test for the right temperature, one of the girls would put some spit on the tip of a finger then quickly and barely touch the smooth side of the hot iron. If the spit sizzled, it was ready to iron the clothes.

When we caught up with work, Dad would take a nap, Jessie and I would play jacks on the kitchen table and Etta would join the ladies making quilts. If it were warm enough, Ray and Raymond would be out side chasing around. Five-year-old Jay would be trying to keep up with his older brothers. Charles Quentin would be crying for somebody to give him attention.

Charles Quentin's blue eyes, curly blond hair and cute smile made him the darling of everybody that saw him. It must have been uncle Lee, who lived on the plains, who bought his two-year-old nephew a sailor suit with a cap to march. In this outfit he was "cute as a bug in a rug." Everybody wanted to hold him. He sensed that he was the center of attention, and became spoiled. Charles Quentin was the last of the children and our parents were getting older and they tired after raising so many children. Even from the beginning of his life, Dad and Mother did not given him the discipline they gave the rest of us.

In the long winter months there was school, but on weekends there was little to do and with few visitors. We got fidgety and lonely. Sometimes one of the children would say in jest, "I wish someone would die so we'd have some place to go." Mother would quickly say, "You know you don't mean that. You ought to be ashamed of yourself for thinking such a thing."

The child would reply, "No, Mom, I don't mean it, but it does get lonesome around here."

On sunny days, some of us would sit on the big rock that served as a step-up into the kitchen door and watch the road that came down from the caprock. If a car or wagon started down, we could see the dust long before we saw the vehicle. When the vehicle came to the valley floor it traveled down a lane about a mile east of our house. Most of the people that traveled this lane would keep going north. Once in a great while friends from the plains came to see us. If they did, they turned west on the lane that passed our house. We always greeted them with great joy.

One Saturday, Mother's brother, Uncle Jim Miller and his family came from their farm on the plains to see us and to show off their new model A. He had several children. Among them was Chloe who was about my age. When she and I got together, we always "hit it off," for we liked one another's company.

Dad called the day a holiday and the old people sat around and caught up on the latest news and gossip. The children played jacks, pitched horseshoes or pitched washers by pitching them into holes from a distance. Each entered the contests with much vigor. We showed our visitors the new calf born recently or the new litter of piglets.

Dad had caught a large yellow cat in one of our traps. This was a big cat with a long tail. It was different from any animal we had caught before, and Dad doubted if we could sell the hide. Now the seat of one of our cane bottom chairs was worn out and became useless until it was repaired. So Dad, with his wild sense of humor, skinned the cat, and after the hide cured, he put it in the seat of the chair with its long tail falling behind the chair.

When any young lady came to visit us, Dad would always offer the chair to her getting a big laugh when she turned around to see the long tail hanging down behind her. So before our guest left, Dad invited Chloe to sit in the chair. She was pleased with the attention Dad gave her until she turned around and saw the tail. She was embarrassed and her face turned a cherry red.

Both families got a jolly laugh at Chloe's expense.

Before Uncle Jim's family left in the middle of the afternoon, I felt sorry for myself wondering if I was loved and appreciated. Maybe I was also feeling that I was not getting the attention I deserved. I kept feeding my ego with selfpity until I slipped away form our family and the guests and hid in a clump of beargrass (Spanish Spear) lying down curled up on my side completely out of sight. Still I could see and hear all activities going on.

While Uncle Jim's family was loading into their car to go home, and my family was hugging them good-bye and telling them how glad we all were that they came, Mother looked around and failed to find me. She asked, "Where is Leslie? Does anyone know where Leslie is?

(She always called me Leslie and everybody else called me Gene.) I could hear them talking and saying none had seen me in some time. I kept quite as a "church mouse."

The group kept calling my name. The longer they called the louder they got. They looked in the chicken house, the outhouse and the smokehouse and the lots where the livestock were kept down by the windmill. They even looked in the house and under the beds. All the time I was quiet making sure they loved and appreciated me.

I heard Dad said, "We've gotta find that boy!"

And Mother was about to cry, saying, "I don't know where that boy could be. It's not like him to wonder off without telling us."

Dad said, "I'll get on a horse and go out in the pasture and the field. Maybe he wondered off out there." And he ask, "Jim, will you take your car and go up and down the road to see if you can find the boy?" Uncle Jim cranked his Ford and started to leave. That's when I came from my hiding place making my appearance.

Everybody rushed to me, hugging me and expressing delight that I was safe. "What happened? Where have you been?" And many other questions gushed from my loved ones. Dad was so glad to see me that he put those powerful arms around me, and said, "Son, I'm glad you're safe." He was so joyful that he forgot to scold me for the dirty trick I'd played on my family, uncle and cousins.

All doubts of love and appreciation for me were erased from that time on.

After spending the next day in the late spring in the sweltering heat of the schoolhouse under the tutelage of Mrs. White, I said good-bye to my classmates, tied a cord around my books, threw them over my shoulder and started walking the quarter-of-a-mile home. Ray and Raymond had grown up wrestling with me and with one another and playing pranks on me and other members of the family. I wanted to go straight home without their playfulness, but they kept pestering, insisting that I join in their games. They hit me on the shoulder and ran wanting me to chase them. When I refused, they put handfuls of sand in the empty galvanized bucket in which I had carried water in the morning for the teacher and students. The twins were full of life and glad to be out of school. Since I would not participate with them, they threw rocks at ground squirrels as they scampered to their burrows, and they tried to hit birds on the fly.

It was Friday and Mother smelt the sweat, mixed with dirt, that had accumulated on our bodies the past weak. Over our protest, she demanded that we take baths. While the twins fetched water from the tank down by the windmill, I got the wash tub that hung on a nail driven into the outside wall of our house and took it to the back bedroom. The boys poured the water into the tub until it was about two thirds full. With the homemade lye soap, each of us took a bath in the same water. After the three of us had bathed, the twins took the handles of the tub filled with dirty water, carried it out to the barbed wire fence and poured the water out.

Dad came in from the field with his face and clothes covered with dust raised from the horses' hoofs and the plow as it was pulled row on row across the field. The sweat from his body smelled strong. Mother detected the odor the moment he stepped through the door. "Mack," she said, "you've got to take a bath before we eat supper." I retrieved the tub taking it into the bedroom while the twins filled it with water. Dad took a bath as Mother insisted.

With the afternoon chores done, we all sat down at the supper table and Dad said his usual prayer of thanksgiving. I always thought his prayer contained such beautiful phrases. I never learned why he didn't teach his children to say the blessing. We were well into eating supper when Dad said, "I'm going into Bard tomorrow to get some corn ground to make mesh for the hogs and bread for our table. I was wondering if Gene and the twins would like to go with me?" A chorus went up from the three of us and with exuberance, we said, "Yes, Sir!"

Dad said, with a big smile on his large face, "I often wonder if you boys will ever amount to a hill of beans. You always want to go so you can get out of work here at home. Okay, we'll get up early in the morning, and after we do the chores, we'll hitch the horses to the wagon and go to watch Henry Ford's new Model-As parade down Highway 66. And while we're at Bard, we just might get a little work done."

The next morning the twins and I were up early. We gulped down breakfast and rushed to do the chores, harness the horses for our all day trip there and back. Ray and Raymond each grabbed a bucket and rushed to feed the hogs and milk the cows. As they milked, the cows swished their tails, laden with cockleburs, from side to side to keep the pesky flies from tormenting their bodies. Sometime these tails, would slap the boys in the face. It was then the boys would use words, learned from adults, that Mother did not approve.

While the boys milked the cows, I was busy harnessing the horses. First the bridle went on, then the collar that fitted snugly around the neck and fitted nicely on the shoulders. After that, I put on the harness with a long linked chain on each side of each horse to be fastened to the two single trees on the wagon. After the harnesses were secured on each horse, I led them to the wagon. The horses knew work was about to begin, so I had a little trouble guiding Fox on one side of the long tongue of the wagon and Lake on the other side. Lake was always the dependable horse, but we never knew what Fox would do. He pranced around for a while but soon settled down. I clipped the harness on each horse to the three-foot pole at the end of the wagon tongue. Following that, I hitched each horse to a singletree. Each sngletree was attached to the dubletree that was fastened to the wagon at the rear of each horse.

The horses and wagon were coupled together and ready to go. I drove them up to the house where Dad was leisurely sipping a cup of coffee. I shouted, "Hey, Dad, everything's ready to go." He hollered back, "It's a little early. Come in and rest your weary bones awhile." Knowing that if Fox started jumping around or trying to go forward, Lake would stand still, I left the wagon and team to go into the house to finish breakfast. The twins came in with their buckets of milk and Mother took over from there.

After we struggled to put gunnysacks filled with shelled corn into the wagon, we took off on the slow journey to Bard with its general store, United States Post Office and grinding mill On the first leg of our journey, we traveled east down the lane hemmed in on either side by a barbed wire fence. In less than a mile we came to Charley White's place and turned north on to another dusty lane. While Dad sat in the spirngseat driving the team, the twins were scuffling about, and I was counting fence posts and noting the farmhouses and the number of cows feeding on the grass in the pastures.

Mr. Aston's ranch was on the left and his cattle grazed peacefully as we passed. I noted the many structures on the ranch the Tuckers managed. It was on the right side of the road. As we traveled, we came to the lone windmill and water tank in the middle of nowhere. By this time, the sun had made its journey upward to a forty-five degree angle in the eastern sky. Cows with their baby calves had their fill of grazing, and had come to drink and chew their cuds while lying down this cool spring morning. The calves frolicked about. The cows took leisure naps. This reminded me of young people running and playing while the older people sat around and talked or took a nap.

We left the windmill and the cattle gathered around it, and proceeded to cross over a cattleguard and climb a long hill. I watched the muscles in the horses' thighs bulge under the strained to pull the wagon up the slop. On top of the hill, to our right, was a wash that led about one hundred feet down to a flat plain where the Chatman ranch was located. A little further down the dusty road, I looked to the right and saw the tombstones and the iron fence that encircled the graves of the family that was killed about thirty years before. As the wagon bumped along down the dusty road, I wondered about death and what happens afterwards.

As he drove the horses, Dad kept watching the thunderheads in the west. He talked about their rapid buildup and the boiling action within them.

An hour later we came to the dry arroyo we had to cross. Just a hoop and a holler beyond the arroyo ran the T & M railroad that we had to go over before reaching the Bard general store and Post Office. It was owned and operated by Mr. Heckendorne.

These buildings sat beside US Highway 66. The mill, where we took the corn to be ground, was nearby.

Before we pulled up to the millhouse, we saw a thin gray curtain of rain coming down from the distant thunderheads. Dad's experience told him the rain was over San Jon about five miles to the west and approaching Bard at a rapid pace. The curtain of rain became more dense and a darker blue the nearer it came to us. When the mighty thunderheads got over the mill and the general store, it seemed that some giant hand took a huge knife and ripped the bottom of the clouds open. They dumped millions of tons of water on the tiny community. The clouds moved east after flooding the landscape with oodles of water filling the small creeks that led into the arroyo we had passed through a short while before.

Within a half an hour the dry arroyo became a raging river one hundred yards wide sweeping along everything in its path. Dad, Mr. Heckendorne, several other men and us boys stood on the elevated bed of the railroad and watched the angry stream rushing to an unknown destination as it carried bushes, cattle and railroad ties tumbling past us. We all marveled what such a sudden change could come about in the desert land.

A soaking wet cowboy came riding his horse down the same road we had traveled earlier in the day. He stopped at the edge of the rolling waters. Threatening to ride his mount across the raging stream, the men on our side kept yelling to him, "Don't try it. You may be drowned if you do."

But the young cowboy, strong in body and heart, proud of his accomplishments, thinking he could beat any odds, forced his mount into the turbulent stream as he sat in the saddle straight and arrogantly. The horse did a good job swimming until he got about twenty five yards from our side of the stream. There the pony was about to put his feet on the ground and walk the rest of the way through the raging water. But there was deep trough in the arroyo where the water ran extremely swift. Here the rider was separated his horse and began to fight for his life. We witnessed his broad brimmed hat float down on the muddy, turbulent water. With his clothes soaking wet, it was difficult for the cowboy to swim. He went under the water as he was carried by the tremendous force of the flood.

I watched Dad with the versatile farmers, ranchers and storekeeper form a human chain by clasping hands. The leader led the chain out into the mighty stream and after much difficulty clasp the hand of the young cowboy and the men pulled him ashore. Wet, tired and scared the rider lay on the ground breathing hard. Finally he said, "Thanks fellows for saving my life. I don't think I could have made it without your help," His horse and saddle were swept downstream and with much effort the pony reached land.

The mill owner ground our corn, and Dad gave him one-fourth of it for his labor. But the rolling waters had not receded much when the darkness closed over our valley.

Fearful of starting home while receding waters still rolled in the arroyo, Dad decided that we should stay in Bard for the night. We had no telephone or other means to communicate with Mother. She was left to wonder and worry until we got home about noon the next day. But such was our life on the farm in the valley - *the pocket of perpetual poverty.*

DAD PUT ME IN CHARGE

"Stop it," Dad ordered as he brought the heavy scissors down on my head. "You're squirming around like a worm in hot ashes."
"Ouch," I retorted, "That hurt."

"Be still, so I can finishing cutting you hair. If you're goin' to be my preacher son, you got to look nice."

"I don't want to be no preacher. They holler and scream to much."

I soon forgot, and turned my head to see the activities of my younger brothers who were waiting for their turn. After the second whack on the head, I sat still.

The ritual occurred ever few weeks when Dad had time to cut all his sons' hair.

This was early spring and the nights were still cold on the high plains of Eastern New Mexico. I had gotten up early that morning to build a fire in the barrel stove that set in the living room. I can still remember getting out of a warm bed and putting my feet on the cold, splintery floor. My body shivered as I tore the pages from a Montgomery Ward catalog, crumpled them up and put them in the stove. Sticks of kindling were stacked on top of the paper followed by larger sticks of wood. When that was done, I lit the paper with a match. As the paper burned, it set the kindling on fire and in turn the flame spread to the larger sticks. After this chore was complete, I ran and jumped back in bed with the twins until the whole house was warm.

Since I'd gone barefoot most of the time for the past several years, the soles of my feet were as tough and thick as rawhide. Their bottoms' were like soles of shoes. Despite the condition of my feet, shivers ran through my body when I stepped on the cold floor.

Jessie turned 14 last December. Her interests were changing. We no longer wrestled as we use to. I often saw her sitting silently looking off into space. I wondered what was happening to her. I still remembered when she made her dolls by taking a piece of cloth, rolling it up at both ends until the ends met. Then she'd tie a string a ways down from the top to make a head for the doll. She'd take a piece of charcoal and paint eyes and mouth for a face. She would take the doll in her arms and rock it back and forth. But she didn't do that any more. She didn't like to run and play outside as we did. She was different. I didn't understand.

I guess I was changing. I had turned 11, last November. I didn't like to make my cars as I did before. That's when I'd find an empty spool Mother had discarded. Put a rubber band through the hole in the spool. And twist the band with sticks until it was tight, I then put it down and watch it travel across the floor.

Jessie and I learned from youngsters on the plains that clear water had an invisible skim on the surface. We spent our time carefully dropping a needle parallel to the surface of the water and watching it float We would take a piece of string, tie the ends together and with our fingers make crows feet.

These things didn't seem to be as much fun as they once were. Jessie seemed to like to daydream. I guess she was thinking about her future and getting married as our older sister, Annabelle, had done.

I wanted to be with Dad more of the time, ask him questions and hoping to be as smart as he was. More and more I liked to leave the house with my dog, Towser, and watch him chase rabbits, ground squirrels and prairie dogs. He seemed to get such a delight with the chase. When Towser got tired, I'd lay on my back, with him beside me, and watch the clouds change into different shapes while my imagination saw animals, castles and angles in the sky.

Perhaps watching my big black dog and the changing formation of the clouds caused me to observe more closely the domestic and wild animals in their daily activities. After watching Dad dig up seed that had been planted in furrows in the field to inspect them, I began to study more carefully seedlings sprout and grow. I wondered how one seed planted in the ground could produce hundreds of other seed. How could they produce feed for humans and livestock. I wondered about the hills, canyons and valleys in the escarpment. How did all these marvelous things do what they did?

When I was recovering from a childhood disease, I stood in our yard looking across the level field and saw the children playing in the schoolyard less than a quarter-of-a-mile away. I felt alone in the world as if I were transplanted in some distant place, and the children were far, far away and I was gazing down on them in their play.

I wondered why vultures circled high over dying animals, and why after their bodies swelled up, burst and begin to decay the birds would swoop down and eat the decaying flesh until they were full. If other animals ate the maggot-covered meat they'd die. Who taught badger and coyote mothers to love and care for their babies? I had many questions, but few answers.

In was the time of year for the dust storms to reach their peak; ready to do the most damage to farm and pasture lands Since we had no communications with the outside world, it was impossible to tell what kind of weather was coming down from the north until we saw it with our own eyes. But there were a few signs in the heavens Dad had learned from long experience, or he had learned from older heads. Sometimes these signs foretold future weather conditions accurately and sometimes they failed.

Nevertheless, Dad pointed out these signs to us boys, and warned us of the possibilities of bad weather ahead. When he saw a sundog (parhelions), "a bright circular spot on a solar halo," he would warn us boys "that we just might be in for a bad spell of weather. So get prepared for it." Cirro-stratus clouds high above the earth were "characterized by a composition of ice crystals appearing as whitish and usually somewhat fibrous veil, often covering the whole sky so thin as to be hardly discernible." To Dad these clouds were also harbingers of bad weather to come. However, if cirrus clouds, called mare's tail, appeared, that was indication of fair weather on the horizon.

Dad warned Ray and Raymond and me, all who worked in the field and had a tendency to wander and explore beyond the borders of our own place, to keep an eye out for sand storms that came down from the north with increasing regularity. He told us, "If you are in the field, or wherever you are, if you see a sand storm coming, hightail it to the house. Those dark devils that stretch from horizon to horizon can travel faster than we can run." We took Dad seriously. When we saw that dark brown curtain reaching five miles into the heavens barreling down, we struck out for home in a dead run. We learned to fear the turbulent winds twisting and churning great globs of sandy clouds inside like an evil witch's dark brew boiling inside a giant cauldron. We'd drop everything and run for the relative safety of our home.

If we got caught in a sandstorm it was very easy to get lost even in familiar territory. Anyone could get disorientated for the winds blew so hard a person could not see an extended hand held in front of his face. Nor could he stand up straight. It was much like trying to find one's way in a freezing snowstorm with gale force winds roaring across the landscape. In a blinding sandstorm you may step into a hole, wonder into a barbed wire fence, or fall into a cactus or a lump of beargrass (Spanish Spear) before you ever saw them.

A sandstorm could last for many hours. If a person got caught out in one of these storms without the protection of a house, he may walk in circles until he got hurt. Some have been known to suffer through the night and found, in a daze, the next day by family and friends.

The high winds in the storms broke tumbleweeds from the mooring of roots causing these monster-looking things to bounce across the fields and prairies until they lodged against the fences, barns and houses. Topsoil was picked up from the plowed fields and scattered over the pasturelands and caught by the tumbleweeds where they stopped. When the topsoil in the fields was blown away, nothing was left but a hard crusty base with little or no nutrients for a crop to feed on. Sand covered the fences making it possible to walk over them as if they were little hills strung around fields and along the country lanes. Hopes were dashed for raising a crop for a growing family to sustain life. Again, Dad had failed, by circumstances beyond his control, in efforts to provide a comfortable existence for his own. I never learned how he felt, for he never complained. He showed courage, strength and faith by his actions. Something had to be done.

When a sandstorm of such magnitude hit, Mother would wet rags and put them over the faces of Jay and Charles Quentin for they were in danger of breathing dust into their tender lungs and contracting 'dust pneumonia.' This disease was caused by the accumulation of dust in the lungs making it difficult to breath. If it were not checked, a child could not breath and would eventually die. The rest of us had to get our own wet rags and put over our faces.

By this time, Churchell had left home settling in Ponca City, Oklahoma where some of Mother's relatives had moved. This left me, a twelve-year-old, to help Dad run the farm.

There happened to be two major projects beginning in east-central New Mexico at the time. Administration buildings, dormitories and academic buildings were being built in Portales. These were the beginnings of Eastern New Mexico University. This project was about 75 miles south of our place.

In addition, the PWA was building a dam about 70 miles northwest of us on the Canadian River. This was called the Conchas Dam Project. Besides giving men work, this project would supply water for farmers to irrigate crops and furnish recreation to draw vacationers and fishermen to the area.

Substantial rumors was making the rounds that men were leaving their families at home, traveling to the Conchas Dam Project, camping there just hoping to get a job to send money back home for their loved ones to live on. In many cases, even entire families were in such dire circumstances for money to buy food, they left everything behind to camp out at the site praying for work to make enough to keep body and soul together until things got better.

The men who got work were willing to work hard, ten and twelve-hour-days, through winter when water they were trying to corral was freezing, and in the hot, sweltering, dusty days of summer. They knew if they slacked, men who arrived daily from Kansas, Colorado, Oklahoma and New Mexico were eager to step up and take their place at the workstation. There was no complaining from the man with a job, for he was so glad to have work to provide for his family. When families came, they lived, ate and slept in wagons, tents or in open space contending with the wind, the dust, the cold, the heat and the pesky flies. Such citizens, and their sons and daughters, from across America were later labeled *"The Greatest Generation."*

Since he could not make a living for the family on the farm with all the topsoil blown away and stacked against fences, barns and homes, leaving only a hard baked pan in the field minus nutrients, Dad decided to go to the Conchas Project in search of work.

Before Dad could make the long arduous trip in a wagon, he first had to set everything in order on the farm. He kept busy for several days bringing things up to his satisfaction. He put me in charge of the wind-swept farm and told Ray and Raymond, who were nine, to help me.

On the morning he was to leave for the Project, Dad harnessed Fox and Lake and hitched them to the wagon. Then he put the frezno, we called a slip, into the wagon. He wished to use this implement to move dirt that was surely needed to build a dam. Perhaps he'd get a little more money by using his own earth moving equipment. The last to go into the wagon was sleeping supplies and food for the journey. His food consisted of dried apples and dried meat that had been cured on the tin roof that covered our house.

This was a sad day for us. After everything was ready for him to begin the 70-mile journey for work he hoped to get, Dad came to the house to wish all good-bye. Tears were flowing freely as he hugged each of us and gave Mother a kiss. He told her, "I don't know how long I'll be gone. Perhaps it'll be six weeks, two months or even longer. It all depends on what happens, if I get a job and how long it lasts." With his arms wrapped around Mother, who had stayed by his side through all his failures and bore him four daughters and six sons, Dad said, "Katy, you know how hard it for me to leave you and these five young boys. I'd rather somebody would beat me with a bullwhip. I just don't know what else to do. I've got to do something. It won't be long before Jessie will be home for good from Wheatland School. And Etta will come home from her job. Both of them will be here to help out." With his big rough hand, Dad wiped tears from his heavy jowls as they rolled down.

Mother, still in his tender grasp, replied, "I know, Mack. Something's got to be done. We just can't go on like this. While you're gone, me and the boys will keep things going as best we can. I'll think about you every day you're gone."

As we all wept, Dad hugged each of us in turn.

After the good-byes, Dad reluctantly, with a heavy heart, crawled up into the springseat of the wagon and started on his long journey that would take several days. As he drove the wagon down the lane filled with banks of sand, we all watched him, waving until he disappeared from sight Silently we walked slowly back into the house feeling all alone in an uncertain world filled with one catastrophe after another. The valley seemed to have no mercy on us or our neighbors.

The one consolation I held was that if Dad got a job, he would make a good hand. He had proven his durability to me and all who knew him through difficult times and hard work Holding on to this thought, despite the tough assignment he had given me, helped me endure.

The cows were losing weight and giving less and less milk because they lacked feed and much of the grass was covered with sand. Blowflies constantly swarmed around the cattle, tormenting them leaving eggs on their backs. The eggs produced larvae that bore through the skin making large welts and sapping energy from the cows.

The two remaining horses, Mose and George, got thinner and thinner until their backbones looked like two-by-fours covered with hairy hide. Their energy level dropped considerably. There were no weeds to feed the hogs, and stored grain was getting scarce. The swine were losing weight. Calves produced by the cows were scrawny, and some of them died.

There was no reason to plow and plant the fields for the topsoil had blown away. While the days and weeks passed slowly, Mother worried more and more not knowing what would become of us. Occasionally a letter came from Dad with money in it. He was always healthy, doing fine and working every day until he was dead tired at night. He wondered what was going on at the farm. Mother would write him, unloading her great concerns on him. She knew Dad's work was dangerous, and constantly worried about what would happen to her and six children remaining at home if something happened to him But she seemed to have confidence in me, Ray and Raymond to do the best we could under the circumstances for Dad had trained us well.

These were serious times for me also for I felt the weight of responsibility on my youthful shoulders. In the late afternoon when I went to get the cows from the back pasture for milking, I no longer grabbed a tail, striking the cow with a stick making her run with me behind gliding through the air with long strides. I was subdued and sober. I keenly felt the burden Dad had placed on me. I felt that I had to be a man in a boy's body with a child's thinking ability.

The playful boy that ran wild and free with my dog, Towser, across the fields and prairie, and through the hills and canyons in the escarpment, was no more. Instead of playing games and wrestling with the twins, I had to turn my attention to keeping the livestock from dying, tending to baby calves and new piglets. For these were what we relied on to exist. My joyful, carefree mind turned serious and contemplative. Because of the circumstances, I had to grow up in a hurry. There was no other way if I wished to carry the responsibility Dad gave me. It was my complete intention not to disappoint him. I had observed his work ethic, his dedication to family by working hard when times were lean. I knew it was impossible for me to fill his shoes or walk in his steps, but I felt it my duty to try.

When I thought of Dad's dedication, how hard he was working, long hours each day spent on a dangerous job, I was more determined than ever to work hard on the farm that was growing less and less productive with each passing day.

Ray and Raymond, who were about three years younger than I, had to do much of the work around the place. But they were not as serious as I, nor did they feel the responsibility. They were more interested in playing and goofing off. Often when I'd tell them to work at some chore that needed to be done, they'd talk back by saying, "We don't have to do that. You're not our boss." I'd remind them of the instructions Dad gave before he left. Even then they sometimes refused to help out. It was then that I would go tell Mother, and when she told them they honored her enough to obey.

The grain and fodder produced from past crops to feed the farm animals was getting low with no prospect of producing more. The sand storms stole all the topsoil. Depletion of these feeds was growing more severe with the passing of time. I consulted with Mother about the situation. She didn't know what to do, but suggested I go talk to Charley White about the sorrowful state that had developed.

I was worried as I walked over the mounds of sand piled in the lane that led to Mr. White's house. His wife came to the door when I knocked. I told her I wanted to talk to Mr. White. "He's in the blacksmith shop behind the house," she said. I walked around their small adobe house to the shop he had built in the clay bank of an arroyo. Mr. White received me with neighborly cordiality, if not equality.

I told him of the problem that I could not solve. He began by stuttering and swearing at the "lowdown luck" we all were having. "Son," he said, "you know, and I don't have to tell you, that I'm having the same problem, and so is every other family in this valley. But I'll tell you what I'm doing."

"What are you doing, Mr. White?" I asked.

Still stuttering and swearing, Mr. White answered. "I've had to cut back on how much I feed my animals. If you ration the amount you let them eat, your feed will last longer. This way you just might be able to keep your stock alive until these dust storms stop, and we can get back into the fields to raise more feed."

Charley White looked at me, as he shook his head, he said, "Boy, you're a mighty little feller to have such a big worry on your mind."

I thanked Mr. White and left.

On my way home I got to thinking that the Government was killing cattle and hogs of farmers and ranchers who had more stock than they could feed. But our herd was so small that we needed all of them for our living if we could just keep them alive. I wondered if I could go to the neighbors who had some of their animals killed by those government men, and borrow some feed for our stock. On second thought, I didn't have the courage to ask knowing the possibility that we could not pay them back. I had enough of Dad's character that I refused to beg. Therefore, we'd just make out the best we could. I said to myself, "I hope we can last until Dad gets back home."

The twins and I gave the livestock smaller portions of feed though the cows bawled for more and the hogs kept grunting for more grain. The horses, Mose and George, nudged us with their noses begging for more fodder and corn. They were going hungry. But, so were we, for the cows gave less milk and what milk they gave was not so rich making less butter. The meat Dad butchered last fall was about to run out so we rationed it. The ground corn for making cornbread was running low.

The dust storms were growing in intensity as they rolled across the valley and the plains with regularity. When they hit, we all huddled in the house with wet rags held over our faces until they passed. The storms could last for several hours With their passing, they took with them more and more of the farm we rented and left us with less and less hope for future crops.

Baby Charles Quentin lost the spark in his eyes and had become lethargic. He coughed more as the days passed. From the theories passing around in our valley, the baby boy had dust pneumonia.

The cows and horses coughed up mud balls after eating the blades of grass in the pasture that were barely sticking up above the sand blown in during those frightening 'black blizzards.'

After four months, just as we got out of bed, we saw Dad coming home in the wagon. Mother began to cry and her sons were shouting for joy. We boys ran down the road to meet him. When we got to the wagon, we climbed into the slow moving vehicle chattering away to Dad telling him how glad we were to see him. But Dad was dog tired, and so were the horses for they had traveled all night. When Dad got to the house, he took Mother in his big arms and held her for a long time even if he had not shaved or bathed in several days.

After breakfast, when all had settled down, Dad showed us a stack of cash that must have amounted to more than a hundred dollars. Mother smiled and then began to cry again this time for joy knowing that many of her worries would be diminished and Dad was home for a while at last.

Ray, Raymond and I filled the washtub with water for Dad to take a bath. After he shaved, he fell into bed and slept the rest of the day. After he awoke, he looked like the strong, vigorous man we knew all our lives. Supper was over and Dad gathered us all around the long dining table to tell us of his plans for our future. He knew Etta was eager to go back to work making her own way for she would soon be eighteen. It was uncertain whether Jessie would go back to school in Wheatland.

It was autumn and there no crop to gather for the dust storms took care of that. The garden down by the windmill produced good crops of vegetables, watermelons and cantaloupes because it was protected by the fence from the fierce winds and blowing sand. When ripe, the melons and cantaloupes would be stacked in the smokehouse and eaten when needed. Etta, Jessie and Mother would can the vegetables for the coming winter. On Dad's trip, he learned wild cherries grew on the banks along the Canadian River near Logan about ten miles north of Bard.

It was Dad's hope, the next time we went to Bard for groceries and to get corn and wheat ground for bread, we'd take a few days more to go there and pick berries for canning.

Money Dad earned during the four months he worked on Conchas Dam would tide us over for a while. With it he planned to buy grain and fodder for the livestock when our supply ran out. Part of the money would go to Mr. Heckendorn to decrease the debt we owed him for groceries bought on credit. We would still have money left over to buy needed supplies and clothes for the coming school year. (During the Great Depression a few dollars went a long way).

Dad was on the Punkin' Center School board for several years. Two years before he told the family we were in danger of losing our school if the attendance went any lower. So he looked at five-year-old Jay Bertie and said, "Young man you're goin' to school this fall. You're goin' keep our school open." With this announcement, Jay's big brown eyes sparkled and a broad smile lit up his round face. Mrs. White was retiring.

The experiences, the worry and the apprehension while Dad was gone had a life-changing effect on me. Since I had a taste of responsibility of running the farm life in those Depression years seemed much more complicated.

Having to face the stark realties of making a living for a family and worrying if we could possibly come out of these circumstances alive, I grew up in a hurry. I became much more serious-minded. Wrestling with the twins, and playing jacks with Jessie were activities of the past. I didn't laugh as often. Nor did I like to play jokes on others. My sense of humor was tattered.

The world was changing before my eyes. One or two families had already left the valley. I was sure Dad was contemplating the same thing.

Before, working in the field and going to school was a part of life for that was all I knew. Now I was still a boy thinking

151

and worrying about adult problems. It didn't take a very smart boy to see what the dust storms had done to the farm knowing it was all we had. I felt the pains in my stomach when it craved food that was rationed. I often saw Mother cry because she didn't know what was going to happen to her children.

The black demon dust clouds kept coming carried on winds traveling fifty, sixty and seventy miles an hour with thousands of tons of soil and sand twisting, churning forming dark curtains reaching high into the air These dreaded storms that inundated us came with regularity. (It is doubtful that anyone who has only read about them, and not lived through these storms, can understand the devastation they left on farms, ranches, human health and soul.) The best, the strongest people were affected in a very negative manner. For those of us who experienced this period, it was a time of trial and bitter discipline. Some people cursed God for the devastation and gave up, while others refused to abandon life's trials and tribulation and forged ahead These brave souls, believed, trusted that there was purpose behind it all. The purpose was that we were being prepared and made tough for some greater event that lay ahead

Adolf Hitler was appointed Chancellor of Nazi Germany, January 30, 1933.

HARD TIMES AND GOOD TIMES

The world kept on turning, and we kept on yearning, working, striving for better times to come. But better times were in the far distant future. We wondered if diligence, patience and prayer would ever pay off. There was absolutely no way for us to give up. Hope, dim as it appeared at times, was always present in our hearts.

The yucca plants, we called beargrass, were as thick as fleas on a mangy dog. They grew all around our place and spread throughout the valley. These plants named Spanish Spears were beautiful in late spring and early summer. It was this time of the year when stems grew from the middle of the plant four to six feet high and produced beautiful white blossoms. The prairie was awash with these flowers and bees were busy gathering their nectar.

Before the beautiful blossoms died in the fall of the year, they produced hulls containing seed. Ugly brown hulls on dead stems were left. All this grew from a bulb in the ground. These numberless bulbs, about double the size of a man's fist, scattered over the countryside, gave Dad an idea.

Early on the cool fall morning after he came back from work on Conchas Dam, Dad left the house carrying a grubbing hoe on his shoulder. I was trailing close behind in faded overalls and bear foot. "Son," Dad said to me, "I've figured out how we can have a limitless supply of feed for our cattle without paying for it."

This puzzled me, so I asked, "How?"

Dad answered, "You and me have a lot of work to do. We're goin' to grub up this beargrass, stack them in a big pile and burn off the spears. The hot bulbs will remain in the ashes. While the bulbs are still warm, we'll rake them out of the ashes, find an old stump, lay them on it and cut them up with a hatchet for the cows to eat."

"How do you know the cows will eat them?" I asked.

"Oh, they'll eat them all right. And I'll bet they gain weight."

Dad and I worked all day digging up beargrass bulbs while fighting the sand collected around the plants. Without gloves, blisters sprang up in the palms of our hands as we swung the grubbing hoe with its long handle. The tops of our hands were bleeding by being pricked with the sharp ends of the green spears that grew thick and long about eighteen inches from the bulbs. After several days, we stacked the beargrass into a pile about as high as the smokehouse. We left the stack alone until morning, went in and ate a supper of pinto beans, corn bread and milk prepared by Etta and Jessie.

After a refreshing night's rest and a breakfast of redeye gravy and toasted wheat bread, Dad and I rammed a needle in the blisters in our palms to drain the pus and water that had collected in them overnight. Now we were ready to finish our job with the pile of beargrass that was stacked far from any buildings.

We dug dead grass from the sand dunes, stuffed the grass near the bottom of the stack and set it on fire. Before long the entire stack of beargrass was ablaze. I watched the flickering flames for more than an hour as they devoured the stems on the bulbs. I watched, as the fire chased the chill from my shivering body.

By mid-morning the flames had done their work, and nothing was left but hot bulbs in a bed of ashes. The next job was to separate the bulbs from the ashes. After raking the bulbs into a pile about as high as my head, Dad brought a cedar stump previously hauled down from the hills, with a hatchet and told me to cut the bulbs into quarters when they were cool enough.

It wasn't long before I sat down beside the stump with hatchet in hand beginning to chop the bulbs in quarters and throw them out onto the ground. A sweet aroma wafted through the air. The hungry cows and their calves smelled the food and came running to its source. They gobbled the quarters faster than I could chop them. With a constant diet of bulbs the cows did gain weight, as Dad predicted, and their milk was richer and more plentiful. So this procedure continued through the winter when the weather permitted.

Jessie had turned fourteen before Christmas. She had been going to the much bigger school at Wheatland. The girls there had visited Clovis learning of the latest hairstyles. My sister thought she was too old for braided pigtails hanging down her back. Dad always frowned on the idea of cutting them off when she asked him. But there came a day when Dad and Mother were visiting friends on the plains. Jessie saw it as the opportunity she had longed for. She got the heavy scissors and whacked off her pigtails just above the shoulders. Then she got the pasty, jelly-like goo the ladies used in the thirties and made a curl that stuck to her forehead.

When she finished, I couldn't make it look like the sister I'd wrestled and played jacks with. She looked more sophisticated. I guess I felt like I had lost the little sister I had grown to love since we grew up together. I couldn't keep from crying. It was almost as if my sister had left and another had taken her place.

When our parents came home, Dad looked at Jessie's change. He must have felt as I did. He knew his youngest daughter was growing up, and it was hard for him to accept. With sadness showing on his face, he took one look at her and turned leaving the house to be alone. Mother was surprised and said to Jessie, "You ought to be ashamed." Jessie took it all in stride, for she expected a more dramatic confrontation.

Not long after this, the Leach family, who owned the place we rented, came down from the plains to visit and perhaps find out how things were going on the farm. Their sons Kenneth, Wallace and Earnest were with them. We left our parents who were discussing the government's handling of the Depression and the sandstorms. Then we huddled in a secluded spot where the Leach boys became very excited while telling us of the radio reports they heard about Bonnie Parker and Clyde Barrow who were shot by G-men in northern Louisiana. This outlaw couple, still in their twenties, had robbed banks and killed at least twelve people. But the G-men stopped them cold when they shot them full of holes on a lonely road. This was heady stuff to us boys, and the more we were told the more enamored and excited we got.

"But that's not all," Kenneth, the oldest of the visiting boys said, "People are taking the car Bonnie and Clyde was killed in around the country showing it off They plan to show it in Clovis pretty soon."

"Is your Dad goin' to take you to see it?" I asked.

"I hope so," Kenneth answered, "if he can get away from the farm."

I spoke up again, "How much will it cost to see the car?"

"The radio said they'll charge a dime."

My excitement was growing to a fever pitch. I was thinking to myself that I'd sure like to see the car all riddled with bullets with the blood of Bonnie and Clyde still on the unwashed vehicle. But I knew, even if I got to go, I couldn't see the car for I didn't have a dime. I could imagine what it must have looked like. Just thinking about the car, owned by outlaws and chased by G-men, filled me with awe. It was exciting.

All the time, so many other things were happening. School, in our one room building was functioning. To keep the doors open, Jay Bertie enrolled. I was not going regularly for work was my first priority. As a result, my grades were barely passing. I was promoted to the next grade each year by the skin of my teeth. As I recall, that wasn't much of a concern to me. I was learning much from Dad who was my hero and his formal education stopped at the fourth grade. So I didn't worry about it. But Mother and Dad did worry about it, for they both wanted me to advance in school as far as I could They knew circumstances prevented me from making good grades.

With Mrs. White at the helm, school was running smoothly, and the children were doing as well as possible. Though my attendance was sporadic, and my grades were below average, I do believe she laid the academic foundation for all I have learned since.

Mrs. White was a pioneer, who came to the rough and rugged west with her young family when the New Mexico Territory politicians were killing their opponents for advantage Indians still roamed the land, and outlaws from Missouri and Texas came to the Territory to escape punishment back home. Justice was still determined, in large part, by the man or party that could draw guns the fastest and shoot the straightest. If a drifter or a man with a bad reputation was killed by a neighbor, that had "proved his worth," lawmen figured the dead man got what he deserved, and that was the end of the matter.

The Punkin Center schoolteacher taught us more than what was found in textbooks. She made sure her students understood the problems, sorrows and excitement of helping build a new community in the San Jon Valley. She and her husband, J. T. White, rented an emigrant railroad car around the turn of the twentieth century and put their furniture, farm equipment, hogs, cows and chickens in the car. The train took them only as far as Hereford, Texas. In this small Panhandle town, they bought a freight wagon to haul their belongings across the plains into the valley where they settled.

The wagon was heavily loaded with the cows tied to the back following behind. On their way, they were caught in one of those downpours of rain. After the cloudburst, they attempted to cross an arroyo. But the water had soaked the mud in the bottom of the creek. The wagon wheels became buried in the mud. The team could not pull the wagon out. Mrs. White and her small children were stuck there for several days while her husband went for help.

Arriving in the area that became San Jon, the White family acquired a home adjoining the present town site just south of the railroad right of way. The train would furnish transportation to haul their produce to market.

In the early days the closest post office to San Jon was in the community of Rivuelto about eight miles west as the crow flies. There was only one barbed wire fence with a gate that had to be opened when traveling between the two places. In order for the folks in San Jon to get mail, somebody had to ride horseback to retrieve letters and packages. One cold winter day the lot fell on Mrs. J. T. White to fetch the mail.

The snow was peppering down and Mrs. White saddled her pony named Pet. She put an oversized blanket under the saddle so it could be turned back over her legs and feet to keep her warm. Leaving her infant child with her sister, she began her journey through the snowstorm as high winds piled snowdrifts up to the mare's belly. The lady was determined to make the trip, regardless of the sacrifice, to bring the mail back to friends and neighbors for she knew they were anxious to receive correspondence from loved ones back home.

Without incident, she reached Rivuelto within a couple hours. She, her horse and blanket were all covered with snow, and her face was red from the cold. She jumped off Pet, tied her to a hitching post and ran into the Post Office to get warm while the postmaster tied the tops of three second-class mailbags and one first-class bag. But there was a problem: How could they get four large bags of mail on the pony so they would stay while going through the windy snowstorm. The debate continued until it was suggested they tie the tops of the mailbags together and swing two bags on one side of the horse and two bags on the other side. By putting the bags behind the saddle, they reasoned, the balance should make it comfortable for horse and rider.

With this task complete, Mrs. White mounted her pony and started no her way back home while the wind kept swirling the snow. Giving a gentle tap in the sides of Pet with her spurs, the pony, knowing they were headed home, jumped to start the journey. When she jumped, the bags not securely fastened, turned into the ponies flank and Pet began to buck and pitch. The bags and Mrs. White hit the ground. The crowd that had gathered at the general store, where the Post Office was located, began to laugh and holler slapping their western hats against their legs. The men cried out, "Ride 'em, cowgirl!"

While the men were still laughing, our future teacher brushed herself off and replied with a smile, "That's all right, boys, just you watch me. I'll get this mail home in good time in spite of a spooked pony, the wind and the snow."

With this said, Mrs. Smith proceeded to re-arrange the mail bags - two in front of the saddle and two behind - tying them more securely. She took off through the snowstorm determined to succeed on her own "pony express." She had noticed that Pet was nervous as they traveled. When they came to the only fence, she got off the horse to open the gate and led Pet through. Something frightened the pony. She jerked the reins from the rider's hands and started running and pitching across the prairie toward home about five miles away.

Mrs. White began immediately to wonder what her husband and sister would think if the horse came home without her. They would be worried and frightened for her safety and probably send out a search party pronto. Because of the pony's twisting and bucking, the saddle turned to a position under Pet's belly. Not knowing what to do, the pony braced her front legs and stopped. The rider could barely see her mount through the blowing snow. Mrs. White ran, caught the horse, re-arranged the mail and saddle and rode eastward through the blinding storm to deliver the mail.

This is the character of the lady who taught us in the one-room schoolhouse. But Mrs. White, in her younger days, taught the generation that preceded ours. Though her family lived on a ranch close to San Jon, she drove her ancient car fourteen miles over rough, rutted roads through untamed ranchlands to Punkin Center to teach students long before I was born.

The San Jon Sentinel and Quay County Times of New Mexico recorded the following:

Friday, February 18, 1921: "The Fairview schoolhouse burned Saturday night about ten o'clock, together with the entire contents. E. W. Whinery, who lives a short distance from the building, and J. O. Smith saw the fire and hurried to the place but it was ready to fall in when they arrived. They were unable to save any of the books or furniture. Mrs. White, the teacher, got as far as Grandpa Barnett's on her way to school Monday morning not knowing the building had burned...... the fire was thought to be of incendiary origin."

In 1933 Mrs. White was close to retirement. Even in her last year she kept attempting to pound knowledge into the heads of her backward, 'punkin headed' students. There is no doubt that she succeeded to a large degree. For most of her charges were better prepared for adult life than our parents or even our teacher thought we would.

I was able to go to school more often for it was impossible to do much in the field after the topsoil was all blown away. For this reason the sand storms may have been a good thing. For the foundation Mrs. White laid in my academic learning became more firm and lasting. I spent hours analyzing sentences by drawing diagrams on the blackboard and on paper. At first this exercise made absolute no sense to me. Nouns, pronouns, verbs, adverbs, adjectives, conjunctions and all the rest were not important. What difference did ain't, aren't, and weren't make as long as I could make myself understood. I was a farm boy and all this high-falutin' city grammar and language was foreign to me, and I didn't think I'd ever need it for most of my friends talked about the same way I did.

"Later on down the road of your life, you will need it," Mrs. White kept telling me. She kept pushing and pushing hoping I and the other students would understand the truth of her statement. It was difficult for her to get through to us the necessity of what she was teaching. Because we respected her and wanted to please, we kept trying. With much persistence on her part, her adolescent students finally began to understand. A little light in our darkened minds began to shine dimly. As school days passed, and with her encouragement, the light brightened.

Our teacher drilled us on spelling by making us write words on paper until our fingers cramped. We had many spelling bees. As I recollect, I never won a single contest. We were forced to perform in little plays. After we practiced until each word was pronounced correctly and our timing was what Mrs. White expected of students our age, parents were invited to watch the play.

With very limited resources, she wanted to expose each of us to various fields of endeavor. Science was touched on in school. To demonstrate osmosis, she had each of us bring a boiled egg to school Each student peeled his egg and from the ink well on our desks, we were instructed to put a drop of ink on the peeled egg. The egg quickly became permeated with the blue liquid. "Now," we were told, "this process s called osmosis." (I've never forgotten that word or the process.)

Our dear teacher wanted us to know something about astronomy. When one of her students asked how the moon hung way up in the sky without falling down, she talked about gravitational pull of the many objects in the universe. Then she suggested a simple experiment we could do. "When you get home," she explained, "take a bucket, fill it with water and whirl it around hour head. If you do this fast enough you will notice the water does not spill out when it is upside down."

When we arrived at school later, some of us were excited about the experiment and desired to talk about it. Mrs. White informed us that when we whirled the bucket of water over our heads, we created centrifugal force that held the water in the bucket. None of her students became a scientist, but she did whet our interests and imagination to ponder and continue a life-long desire to learn more about the natural phenomena all around us.

It must have been Mrs. White that gave me the only book I ever owned as a boy. (The book is still one of my prized possessions.) It pictures city boys, girls, bears and other animals, all in color, with notations, roller-skating, and playing hopscotch etc. But what makes the book decidedly different is that each page is sectionalized into four equal parts. This makes it possible to put the head of a child on a skating bear. There were as many funny combinations to be formed as a boy my age could want. I spent many hours with this little book using my imagination wondering what life must be like for boys and girls that lived in the city.

Our teacher spent her young adult days on the last frontier of America - Southeast New Mexico, the last place in the Lower Forty-Eight European people settled. Because of this experience and knowing the Great Depression was still with us, she knew her students would have a hard row to hoe in their adult life. I'm persuaded she was preparing us for our tough times ahead. She knew the only way we could be prepared was to stuff all the knowledge in our heads she could and to toughen us up to face future difficulties with courage and self-confidence.

But it wasn't all hard work. Mrs. White made sure there was fun and excitement in school. It has already been pointed out that recess was fun for us. She took us on long hikes pointing out different plants and animals telling of their habits and how they made their way in the wilds. She allowed us boys to run to the arroyo behind the schoolhouse and jump off the twelve-foot bank into the sandy bottom.

Perhaps the most exciting experience of all and the most frightening, was when her son Clark came to Punkin Center to demonstrate his hobby. Clark was attending Arizona State University but still lived with his parents when he was on leave from school. In the basement of their home he kept a variety of rattlesnakes. These, the most feared varmints in the wild in our valley, were his pets. At the University Clark dressed up like an ancient wild man and put on a show featuring his pets for the students and faculty. In the early 1930s his was one of the most popular shows on campus.

Mrs. White persuaded her son to bring his show to our country school. Dressed in his ancient garb, Clark carried several rattlesnakes in a cage into our schoolroom. Before the thirteen students, ranging from the first to the ninth grade, Clark took his station in front of the excited students body that squirmed uneasily in their seats. Very gently he took the defanged snakes from their cage and wrapped them around his neck. Then he began to dance a jig before the wide-eyed students who with screwed-up expressions of fear on their faces, reared back into their sets ready to run at the moment they thought one of those slimy creatures got loose.

All went well for Clark White was one of the few men, if not the only one, who had perfect rapport with rattlesnakes. He handled them as most of us could handle a gentle kitten. He could detect their change of temperament. He knew when a snake was gentle and responsive, and he could tell when his pets were angry and ready to strike. He handled them in different manners depending on their mood. They were his pets, and he treated them kindly and with respect.

Mrs. White was pleased with her son's performance, and the students clapped and screamed as Clark put his pets back into their cage.

Side note: Clark bought a home of his own in anticipation of marriage. He transferred the rattlesnakes into his own basement When his new wife learned that she would be living in a home with rattlesnakes crawling around in the basement, she put her foot down and announced with much certainty. "I will not live in a house with those varmints." Clark made other arrangements for his pets, and the couple lived together until death in their old age.

While Clark was at our school, his mother persuaded him to put on another show for us during recess. He never did anything unless he could do it better than others. In this he was a perfectionist. He never carried a gun for a slingshot and a pocket full of round stones served him well. On the grassless schoolyard he demonstrated his skill and quickness with the slingshot.

Clark pointed out a fence post about 25 feet from where we all stood. All the boys were standing around him, looking up at and admiring our new hero. He said to me, "See that corner fence post." I nodded. He said, "You begin counting when I say 'go,' and we'll see if I can hit that post with a rock before you can count to 10.

"Ready?" he asked me. "Yes, sir," I said "Then go," he said.

I began to count, "One." His hands began to fly so fast we could scarcely see the motion. The showman jerked the slingshot from its place, inserted a stone in the pocket, pulled it back and the stone flew through the air straight as an arrow and hit the post dead-center before I could say 10.

The only thing his spectators could say was, "Whew, that was fast!" When he got on his horse and rode away, all the students yelled and waved good-bye to the man who had

164

entertained us more lavishly that we had ever been entertained before.

Our teacher was pleased with her son's performance, but she was even more delighted that her charges received a taste of the world beyond the narrow confines of our daily routine.

Not long after Clark's visit to our school, Mrs. White retired.

With the dust storms intensifying and farms and ranches producing less, families began anticipating moving from the valley. Parents and students in our thinly populated area wondered whom, if anybody, would come to our desolate region to teach in our Fairview school best know as Punkin Center.

NINETEEN-YEAR-OLD TEACHER

In the summer of 1934 we knew that Mrs. White was not coming back as our school-teacher. So Dad, who was on the school board with two other men, worked feverishly trying to locate a teacher for our rural school. Teacher's pay in those days was often nothing more than a promissory note stating that if the county or state ever received enough tax money the teacher would get paid their very small salary. It was never a guarantee the pay would be forthcoming.

With all the farmers and ranchers in our valley 'flat out broke,' they could not pay taxes and were constantly threatened with foreclosure. The school board decided the best bet they had of securing a teacher for the year was to find a young single person who still lived with parents. Mr. Heckendorne, who owned the store and was postmaster in Bard where most of the board members traded, had a son, named Melvin whom they had seen grow up. Melvin had finished high school and had one year of college under his belt and wanted to be a teacher. He was probably the only prospect they could find to keep the Punkin Center school doors open for the coming year.

This nineteen-year-old young man met the state's requirements for teaching in a school such as ours. He was single, lived at home and had few if any expenses. The three members of the board zeroed in on the Bard store to persuade Mr. Heckendorne to allow his son to drop out of college to teach in our school. When approached, the storekeeper and postmaster said with much doubt in his voice, "I don't know about that. My boy wants to teach, but he wants to finish college first while he's still young with few responsibilities."

One of the board members said, "Now you know Mr. Heckendorne, we've been friends a long time, and we've traded with you all these years."

The storekeeper laughed half in jest and half in doubt, "Yeah, I know you've been trading with me all these years, but most of it has been on credit and I'm not sure you all will ever be able to pay me back."

One of the board members wishing to change the subject replied, "You know experience is a valuable thing when you go looking for a job. Now if Melvin had some experience teaching, when he goes looking for work in a larger school, he'll have a leg up on other teachers that have no experience."

The postmaster gave his rebuttal, "But my boy has made good friends with the boys in college. In fact some of them are here right now to be with him here at home. They ride horses almost every day over these prairies. They take their .22s and go rabbit huntin' and have a great big time together. I'd sure hate for him to lose contact with them. They seem to be a good bunch of boys. They have a good influence on Melvin."

The discussion went on for a couple of weeks. Finally Mr. Heckendorne gave the board members permission to talk to Melvin. After presenting the same logic to the college student, Melvin decided to take the job. He reasoned, "My college friends can come any weekend they want, and we can still do the same things together." Perhaps the argument that struck nearer home than any other was the experience factor. For he knew it was going to be difficult to find a school to teach in that paid a sure salary during the Depression. Experience would be an edge on others seeking employment.

The Fairview School, better known far and wide as Punkin Center, had a teacher when school opened in the fall of 1934. Parents and children in the neighborhood rejoiced at the news.

For most families, being assured of a schoolteacher was about the only reason we had to rejoice.

The first day of school the young male educator rode his big sorrel horse the seven miles from his home in Bard to the little white schoolhouse. As he approached the building, he surveyed the location with a keen eye. Much of the paint on the building had curled up from the extreme heat in summer and the blustery winds in winter. The playground was bare of any vegetation and hard as any packed soil could be. The sand storms had left drifts in many places.

Both outhouses were leaning to one side in need of repair.

The shed in the back, where wood was kept for burning in the potbellied stove, was about to fall down. Young Mr. Melvin Heckendorne, our new schoolmaster, must have felt depressed after getting an eyeful of the place where he'd promised to teach at least for one year.

Melvin slowly dismounted, pulled off his big Stetson and hung it on the saddle horn while he tied the bridle reins to the barbed wire fence. After going to the university where buildings were made of brick and kept in top condition, this must have been a big letdown. He retrieved his hat and put is gingerly on his head covering a thick crop of black hair.

He spotted me coming down the lane carrying two galvanized buckets full of water. Not having seen Mr. Heckendorne since he was in high school, and then only a few times, he appeared like a giant to my twelve-year-old eyes. He had a slight swagger as he approached me with my burden. "What have you got there?" he asked.

"Water," I replied as politely as I could.

"What for?"

"It's for us to drink while we are in school."

"You mean there's no water well here at school?"

"No Sir," I said, "I've been totin' water for about four years when I come."

With a look of bewilderment on his face, our new teacher took the buckets from my hands and carried them the rest of the way. Inside, he placed the buckets of water on the shelf attached to a wall. He took the dipper that hung over the shelf, and asked, "Does everybody drink from this same dipper?"

"Everybody except Billie Sue. Her parents gave her a collapsible cup."

"Haven't you all been warned about spreading disease?"

"I think so. But we've gotta do with what we've got."

I began to get nervous in his presence because I thought I detected a tone of disgust in his voice. If my thoughts were correct, it was a reflection on, our school, my family and me. But when he extended his big hand to shake mine and said, "I'm Melvin Heckendorne, your new teacher," my nervousness left.

"I'm Gene Fooks," I said. "I live in that house you can see through this front door."

Other students began arriving. The girls in home made dresses. Some of the dresses were made of washed-out flour sacks, and the boys wore overalls or coveralls faded and patched. Some of the students had walked as far as three miles. There was one exception. Mrs. Tucker brought her daughter, Billie Sue, to school in their car. I watched as her mother kissed her good-bye. When she stepped from the car, I thought she was the prettiest person I'd ever seen. She wore a tailored blue velvet dress, and she was more sophisticated than any one else in school. When she entered the schoolhouse, she smiled at me and my heart fluttered. Her family, the Tuckers, had moved to our valley from Amarillo, Texas to operate the ranch owned by a relative. The kinsman was a tailor who made the clothes worn by the pretty, young girl.

Mr. Heckendorne looked at his pocket watch, saw it was time to begin the first day of school and rang the hand bell.

All the children scurried to line up outside the front door. My five-year-old brother Jay, the only first grader, was first in line that formed a stair-step formation until the oldest in the highest grade stood at the end of the line. Mr. Heckendorne occupied the doorway. When all the boys and girls had settled down, our new teacher said, "Now you may come in and take your seats."

We marched in quietly and sat at our desks with the slanted tops with a groove in the center for pen and pencil. An inkwell was in the upper right corner of each desktop. The postmaster's son appeared unsure of himself as he took his place in front of the student body. He introduced himself in a mechanical manner by saying, "I'm your new teacher for the coming year. I'm here to keep discipline and help you learn."

It was evident to the older students that he was at a loss to know where or how to begin.

This was so unlike Mrs. White who had perfect control of both herself and the classroom situation Some of the older boys began to snicker and laugh trying desperately not to be heard or seen by the new teacher.

With all eyes on him, Mr. Heckendorne took his seat behind the big white oak desk before his charges. Some of the students had to crane their necks to see around the potbellied stove in the middle of the room. Our teacher was silent and the children were getting restless wanting to be told what to do. Finally Lorene Massy, an eighth grader, was called to Mr. Heckendorne's desk. We knew why she was called, and the laughter and snickers were harder than ever to control.

A few minutes passed and the conference with Lorene was over. Our teacher rose to his feet and announced to the thirteen students present, "All of you will take your books from your desks and study them to acquaint yourselves with their content. You will do this for thirty minutes. After that I will call you to my desk one by one and make assignments. Now if while you are looking over your books, you need help to understand something, you may call one of the older students or me and we will help you."

All of us made it through the first few dreadful weeks of school while Mr. Heckendorne was learning more than any one of his students. Our young teacher was intelligent and soon caught on to the routine of teaching in our small school. Before long he seemed to enjoy riding the seven miles observing the antics of the prairie dogs, the scampering of the coyotes and the hunching of the baby calves at their mother's teats for more milk. These early morning rides in the cool autumn breeze were refreshing and invigorating to him. When the children began to arrive at school, he was there ready to greet each one with a friendly smile asking about families. We began to look on him as a big brother. But he was still only nineteen-years-old and acted the part most of the time. During recess, he played ball and other games with us and taught us the actual rules of each game. Before our new teacher arrived, we made our own rules.

Dad, who never lost his sense of humor, visited school often and learned that Melvin still had not matured completely. He planned to play a practical jokes on or new teacher.

Knowing our teacher got to school before any of the students, early one morning Dad filled a bucket with water and took it to school. He opened slightly the only door to the building, and balanced the bucket of water on top of the door. Then he hid behind a mesquite bush on the edge of the playground.

A short time later Melvin came riding on his big sorrel horse whistling one of the popular tunes of the time. He dismounted, hung his big hat on the saddle horn, tied his horse to a fence post, retrieved his hat and ambled to the schoolhouse. He stepped upon the flat stone that gave him entrance and noticed the door was ajar. The teacher said, "I thought surely I closed the door yesterday afternoon when I left." He hesitated a moment and said, "Well, maybe not," and opened the door. Two gallons of water and a bucket fell on the head and shoulders of the schoolmaster. He was startled. Our teacher was drenched with a downpour. Since he was taller then most men and the bucket didn't have far to fall. He was not hurt. Since Melvin had played plenty of jokes on others, he determined, immediately, to get even with whom ever it was that did this to him.

While Mr. Heckendorne was shaking to remove all the water possible from his clothing, Dad walked up and asked what happened. The teacher said, "Somebody put a bucket of water over the door and when I opened it, the bucket fell on my head. Look, I'll have to wear the wet clothes all day."

Dad doing his best not to laugh, his heavy jowls quivering, said, "Now who would do a thing like that?" By this time, the youngsters began to converge on the school, and it was time for the teacher to get his students settled down But he wouldn't forget the incident.

The little diversion of fun didn't keep Dad from worrying about keeping beans, cornbread and milk on the table for his five growing sons still at home. And there was Mother. Etta had become pretty well self-sufficient. Jessie was home part of the time from the Wheatland School. where she lived with our older sister Annabelle to help with her three children. Churchell had 'flown the coop,' a couple of years before.

Dad still had that nagging concern for his remaining family. Since we gathered no crop last year, grain and fodder for the livestock were getting very low We continued to grub up the beargrass, burn off the spears and cut open the bulbs for the cattle to eat. This did not prove enough to keep them gaining weight and giving the amount of milk our family needed. Our four horses were still losing weight and getting gradually weaker. Supplies of dried pinto beans, corn meal and home canned foods were all diminishing fast. Mr. Heckendorne's store in Bard continued to sell us foodstuff on credit. We were depending more and more on commodities doled out by the government. I disliked more then ever those cans of food with the white labels. I'm sure Dad and Mother did too. With the dust storms getting progressively worse and the fields lying fallow, there was nothing else we could do. Our prospects to keep body and soul together were not bright. Yet there burned within the heart of each of us that flickering light of hope. Would that light soon be extinguished? We did not know.

The five of us boys slept in the bedroom behind the living room. Dad and Mother slept in the far end of the long kitchen/dining room that was separated from our quarters by a thin wall. Since Etta and Jessie no longer slept in the room with us boys, we often roughhoused before going to sleep making a lot of noise until Dad yelled, "You boys better settle down and go to sleep before I come in there with my belt and use it on all of you."

When my younger brothers were asleep and all was quiet, I was still awake worrying about the future for our family. I wasn't the only one with very deep concerns, for when I was lying there in the darkness and all was still as a tomb, I heard Dad whisper to Mother, "I just don't know what we're goin' to do. I think I've worked as hard as any man alive to provide for this family, and look where we are. We have to depend on government handout for food, our livestock are getting poorer everyday and there is simply no way we can raise a crop with this drought and the sand storms. We haven't made enough to pay taxes on this place."

Mother, attempting to console her distraught husband said, "Now Mack, I know you've worked hard all your life. You've been a wonderful husband and father. I don't know why things have turned out as they had. There's nothing we can do about it............"

My parents were still whispering about hard times when I drifted off to sleep.

The physical things around school were as they were when Mrs. White taught, but the atmosphere, attitude and emphases on learning had all changed. Mrs. White ran a tight, orderly ship, now things were loose and almost playful at times. The older students picked up on this and did not take school as seriously as in former times. Mrs. White stressed penmanship, grammar, spelling and sentence structure, while Mr. Heckendorne emphasized arithmetic and recess. Instead of a strict fifteen minutes for recess, sometimes our teacher would be on the grounds playing ball with us and the period would run thirty minutes or more.

One hot, drowsy afternoon shortly after lunch, when the students were struggling to stay awake, one of the older girls hid behind a book with an open mirror on top of her desk. With head down as if she were studying, she was looking into the mirror and applying lipstick. I saw what she was doing and since her desk was close to mine, I passed her a note asking for her lipstick." With a question on her face, she handed it to me.

To draw the attention of the children around me and (perhaps to keep from going to sleep myself) I pretended to apply the red stuff to my own lips without touching them. The students' eyes were focused on me, and that's when Mr. Heckendorne noticed what I was doing.

Our teacher called me to the front of the room. He took the tube from my hand and ordered me to face him while standing still. I obeyed. All eyes in the school were glued on the scene before them. One could feel the apprehension in the room. Mr. Heckendorne, with lipstick in hand, printed "fool" in large letters on my forehead. Everyone burst out laughing as our teacher told me to take my seat.

I felt the two Os he had printed. Since my last name has two Os, I thought I was branded me with my last name. But during the afternoon recess, while we were playing in the yard, the youngsters were all calling me fool. None told me why.

When I got home that afternoon, I saw in the looking glass the word "fool" scrawled across my forehead in huge red letters.

I refused to wash it off hoping to embarrass the teacher the next day.

The following morning I carried the buckets of water to school. After lifting each bucket upon the shelf, I turned to face Mr. Heckendorne. He gasped in surprise when he saw the lettering still above my eyes and said, "I see you are still wearing what I printed."

I replied boldly, "Yes, Sir."

He asked, "Why?"

Stubbornly I said, "Because I want to."

He had grown agitated with me, and ordered me to go home and wash it all off.

As I walked down the lane alone to our house, I wondered what I could do to get even with my teacher. He not only embarrassed me before the student body, but he also did me an injustice, I mistakenly reasoned in my mind. So I decided not to go back to school that day. I realized later my actions did me more harm than they hurt Mr. Heckendorne.

Under Mr. Heckendorne we were drilled on adding, subtraction, dividing and multiplying numbers. We had contests by going to the large blackboard on the wall all students faced while at their desks. Who could add a long list of numbers the fastest. Who could divide 73 into 1,049 the quickest. Who could multiply 49 x 914 faster than all the other students? In these contests, hands, with pieces of chalk, were flying all over the blackboard. The girls were usually the first to get the correct answers.

Everything at school rocked along pretty well until one hot afternoon when one of those terrible dust storms hit. Mr. Heckendorne asked that all windows be closed. Even then the dust that got inside was so bad it caused some of us to cough and spit out mud.

As time passed the air in the building got stuffy with all the children breathing the same dusty air. When the teacher's back was turned Leon, a boy about my age, raised the window by his desk about four inches.

Our teacher noticed the raised window and walked lightly to Leon sitting at his desk and said in a voice sweeter than sorghum molasses, "Leon would you like to do me a favor?"

Leon shook his head to clear it from drowsiness. With exuberance he replied, "Yes, Sir."

"See my horse out there tied to the fence."

"I sure do, Sir. It's a little hazy, but I can barely see him through the foggy dust."

"I wish you would go out there and get one of the reins of the horse's bridle."

Leon jumped to his feet, raced to the door, opened it and slammed it behind him. The students watched him through the windows as he fought the gale-force wind and struggled to run against the swirling gusts. As he took two steps forward and one step backward, leaning into the wind, his tasseled hair stood out straight behind him. Like some drunk, the wind caused him staggered from side to side.

When he finally reached the horse, Leon untied the leather rein from the bridle and raced back to the schoolhouse in a zigzag fashion. He was puffing hard when he came through the doorway. He stopped a moment to get his breath. He then walked up to the nineteen-year-old educator and handed him the rein not yet realizing why it was needed.

The teacher took Leon gently by the arm and led him to his desk. "Now bend over your desk!" Mr. Heckendorne ordered. It was then Leon understood the purpose of the strap. He looked up into the teacher's face with the expression of a whipped dog His pride was wounded, and his self-importance diminished.

As he came down hard with the leather strap on Leon's backside, he said in a tone loud enough for all to hear, "This is for raising the window when I told you not too. You've got to learn to obey your superiors."

Wounded, but refusing to cry, Leon was determined to prove his toughness to his classmates. We all took note and afterwards acted more circumspectly in the presence of Mr. Heckendorne.

At home I worried along with Dad and Mother for I knew things were getting in awful bad shape for us. We never discussed our dire circumstances with one another. I took note that my parents' faces were drawn and their countenance was melancholy most of the time. After Dad talked to other school board members, he hitched the horses to the wagon and was gone for several days. I figured he was planning something that would have a profound affect on the family. Even my dog Towser had lost some of his playful attitude. He must have sensed something was about to happen.

In all of his anxiety, Dad had not lost his desire to have a little fun once in a while. In early morning on April the first, 1935, before we went to school, he came to the lot, where I was alone milking the cows.

Dad waited until I finished milking the last cow and I stood before him holding the bucket half full of milk.

He began, "Son, I suppose you've noticed that I've been up tight the last few weeks. I'd like to be relieved from worrying about our troubles for a while. Thought you and me could play a little April fool joke on your teacher."

"Whatcha driving at, Dad?"

"I figured that I will come to school today during the noon hour while you kids are playing in the yard. I'll tell Melvin that I have important business to talk to him about, and we'll go in the schoolhouse by ourselves. Here's where I need your help. Now while we're inside with the door closed, I want you to tell all the youngsters to leave the school and not come back all day. Tell them they can go home or any where they want, just don't be around when we come outside."

To my young mind, it seemed strange that a school board member and the father of almost half the children in school would want us to skip school. However, I agreed to go along with the April fool trick.

So while Mr. Heckendorne was on the schoolyard playing with us during the noon hour, Dad came walking up and called our teacher to him. After a short whispered conversation, they went inside and closed the door. That was my signal to call all the children together and tell them what Dad had cooked up. It wasn't difficult to sell them on the trick, and we all scattered like a frightened covey of quail.

When the two men could no longer hear the joyful screaming and laughter of children at play, Mr. Heckendorne became alarmed, excused himself. opened the door and saw not a single child. The schoolmaster was worried for he knew the children were his responsibility as long as they were at school. He ran around the house looking everywhere for his charges but none could be found. He rushed back in and reported to his school board member. It was then Dad began to laugh hilariously, and said, "April Fool!"

Melvin's face flushed with anger for a moment. But when he realized no harm was done, he began to laugh along with his boss.

Dad had been making plans for some time to leave the valley. He and Mother had not confided in me. Knowing we couldn't continue as we had for several months, and his absence for days caused me to think something was in the wind.

The harsh realities of the valley – *the pocket of perpetual poverty* - had defeated us as it had defeated the generation before us.

FORCED TO LEAVE THE VALLEY

Since we had not harvested a crop for two years, money was non-existent. The cows were giving less and less milk because grass was covered with sand. Feed supply was very low. The horses were thin as rails, and we had slaughtered most of our hogs to keep meat on the table.

Our family subsisted on what we grew in the garden, government commodities and what we could buy on credit from the Bard store. Many times, we went to bed hungry. Dad still cut his sons' hair and Mother patched our clothes. The black blizzards were still coming with increasing regularity.

Neighbors were in the same condition and worried about what they were going to do. There was strong talk about leaving the valley, and closing the school. But, if they left, where would they go? The bright dreams of the second generation of valley settlers had vanished like the visions of the generation that preceded them in this *pocket of perpetual poverty*.

Because Dad didn't want to over burden Mother and us boys with worry, he worked secretly with men in the valley and on the plains that he had known since he was a young man. The Leach family understood our plight and stood by us all the way. Their help was limited, for they also suffered from the drought and sand storms.

We all knew in the early spring of 1935 the one room school was closing for lack of students. Dad and Mother had decided we were moving. When brothers Ray and Raymond, Jay and I were no longer attending Fairview School, there simply would not be enough students to keep the school open. It was sad to think about, but the over riding thoughts that occupied our minds were getting away from the dreadful storms where we could have a comfortable place to sleep, enough to eat and a good school.

Mother's health was only shaky at best, but Dad was still strong in body. His spirit was just about broken. Love for family and the dire circumstances compelled him to continue the search for an answer to our dilemma. I had turned thirteen the previous November and passed to the seventh grade when school was out. With conditions on the farm as they were, I worked less in the fields and was able to go to school more often making better grades. The twins were now ten and passed to the fourth grade. Jay was probably the smartest of the bunch, even at six, and he was crowding the rest of us. Jessie was home from the plains and had finished the ninth grade.

Our existence was in a flux of turmoil and confusion. After corresponding by letter with Churchell and other relatives in Ponca City, Oklahoma, the decision was made that we were moving there. This city in the north-central part of the state was close to the Arkansas River that was always flowing. The area had escaped the damaging sandstorms that eroded the farms of western Oklahoma, the Texas Panhandle and eastern New Mexico. We had visited relatives there in 1927 when we had to leave Arkansas because of Mother's health. Dad must have taken a liking for the place.

When thousands of families left Oklahoma heading for California, I can only speculate why Dad chose to take us to northern Oklahoma. A contributing factor may have been that E. W. Marlin, a millionaire wildcatter, started the Conoco Oil Company there several years before. The company's headquarters with a large refinery was located in Ponca City. Dad may have had hopes of going to work with Conoco.

After the decision to move was made, I wanted to spend more time with my big, black dog, Towser. I knew he couldn't go with us, and told Towser that we were moving and it was impossible to take him. He seemed to understand and clung more closely to me than ever before. While Dad made arrangements for transportation out of New Mexico, my furry companion and I took long walks climbing over sand dunes that covered the fences. On hot days in late spring, we'd make trips up into the hills and sit in the shade of a scrub pine tree together. I'd stroke his straight back with my left hand while rubbing the lose skin under his chin with my right hand.

I pondered the age of the escarpment. When finding a rock with the shells imbedded in it, I wondered about time. I thought about the ancient sea creatures that roamed the hills eons before I was born. This made the cogs in my head grind away contemplating things I couldn't possibly understand. When I was thirsty, I'd pick up a smooth stone and put it in my mouth to quench the desire for a drink of water.

Towser and I hiked over the hills and the deep depressions between them. We hid in a cave washed out by water that came with sudden cloudbursts. The stream that was formed rushed with great speed down the miniature mountain into a deep gully often causing large stones to tumble and uprooting small trees and bushes. It made a beautiful waterfall as it tumbled down over a cliff into a dry gulch below. On the days we walked and ran over the rugged escarpment, it was dry as the bleached bones of cattle that had died in time past, scattered over our portion of the great Chihuahuan Desert.

While hidden, I imagined my dog and me where the only creatures in all the world, and I was king over the rugged landscape and the flat, dry land that stretched out before us. Towser was my faithful helper and companion. We stood ready to go forth and conquer. However, as the sun began to sink lower and lower in the west, I knew it was time to return home leaving my kingdom of my imagination.

As I walked toward home through the ravines and over the hills with Towser close by my side, I stopped occasionally and turn to drink in memories of past excursions into the hills that I loved, knowing we'd soon be leaving and wondering if I could ever see them again. What would our new home be like? Could I ever adjust to city life and big schools with hundreds of boys and girls? In the Punkin Center School, I knew every one and they looked to me to lead them in play. Would any one in city school follow me or even know that I exist?

When I got home, Mother and Jessie were folding all our worn clothes and placing them carefully in the huge trunk that was a fixture in our family since I could remember. This trunk, three-and-one-feet wide, three-and-one-half-feet deep and five feet long, had a shelf six inches deep that fit snugly inside.

Towser took his position outside the kitchen door, lying down on the ground in the shade, to wait for me the next time I left the house. As I entered Mother called out, "Leslie, where have you been? We could have used you to help around here!"

"Towser and I decided to go up in the hills and hike around," I responded.

One of the few times she ever scolded me, she said, "Well, that's not good enough. You know we're getting ready to move. And you're out there gallivanting around with your dog."

"Sorry, Mother. What can I do?"

"You can get a bucket, and go down to the windmill, and bring back a fresh bucket of water."

"Okay." I grabbed a bucket, exited the house and ran down to the well with Towser romping beside me.

Ray and Raymond were helping Dad who was preparing the horses and cattle down at the corrals for the auction that was scheduled in a few days. Jay was helping around the house. Charles Quentin was wearing his sailor suit and cap crying for something to eat as he pulled at Mother's dress.

It was lunchtime and Dad and the boys were called from the lots to eat. They washed their hands and faces in the pure clear water in the stock tank before coming to the house. While they walked from the tank to the house, their hands and faces dried in the dry desert air. All of us sat down to the long table. Dad led us in a prayer of thanksgiving. Jessie served each of us a bowl of ham hock soup.

After eating, everybody went back to the same job he was doing before the break. Everybody except me. My mind was occupied by reminiscing about the past and contemplating the future. I'd found a long piece of twine used to sew up the open end of a feed sack, and I sat in a cane-bottom chair while twisting the twine around my fingers making a "crow's foot."

Again Mother had to scold me, insisting I help prepare for our move. I disliked the thought of moving. Move we must, and I came to recognize the fact and be reconciled to it - but not with grace.

Reluctantly, I grudgingly walked down to the corrals to see if I could help in the preparation for the sale. In the mood that had captured my being, I wasn't much help. I felt nobody cared about how I felt because the entire family seemed joyful and hopeful that we were leaving. I just couldn't accept that for I wasn't sure I'd ever see this valley again where I had grown from a little boy to one who was beginning to understand life. Memories filled my head and I was sure the umbilical cord that anchored my conscious self to this lonesome valley would never be severed.

The old trunk was filled. Cardboard boxes full of other items sat beside it. The day for the auction had arrived. When the men with their families came to bid on our meager belongings, I became more aware than ever before of the reality of our move. I went to a secret place apart from all the others and cried until Dad began to call me. When I approached him, he saw my eyes were red and my face was stained with tears. Dad showed his love for me by putting a huge hand on my shoulder, and said, "That's all right, son." I think I understand."

The auction wasn't really an auction at all but a very informal affair with men walking about looking at the horses, cows and the farm implements with Dad trying to follow each one.

I stayed on Dad's heels to learn what I could about such things and to be near him, for I knew this was exceptionally difficult for him.

A man from the plains looked at old Mose and said to Dad, "I'll give you $20 for that horse."

Dad replied with a note of pity in his voice, "I thought I'd get maybe $30 or $35 for him.

"Now, Mack, I ain't saying he ain't worth what you expected, but you know I've been hit by these sandstorms just like you."

Dad spoke with disappointment, "That horse has served me well. He's always ready to work at anything you want him to do. I need more than $20 for him."

"I know he's worked for you a long time. I figure he ain't got more than three or four more years left in him. Beside I never saw a horse with so little meat on his bones."

I saw Dad's lips quiver for he was thinking about making the long move and taking care of his family after we got to Oklahoma. Knowing the horse's poor condition and that he didn't have many working years left, Dad stuttered, "Aright, Johnston, give me twenty, and the horse is yours."

Mr. Johnston had put up some of his own livestock for collateral at a Clovis bank for the hundred dollars he carried in his pocket. With the deal made, the man from the plains pulled from his pocket a small roll and gave Dad four five-dollar bills. No papers or receipts were exchanged. A simple trade was made, and that was that, for a man's word was good enough.

Dad stuffed the money in his pocket and sauntered to another man looking at the milk cows. He said to Mr. Polk, "Considering the terrible weather we've had the last few years, the cattle look pretty good," a hitch in his voice caused it to drop, then he continued, "don't they."

Mr. Polk noticed the change in Dad's voice and looked at him with some doubt. "How much milk do each of these four cows give?"

"They give about a half gallon each. We milk 'em morning and night; so that makes a full gallon each day from each of the three cows. At the present, we don't milk that old brindled cow. As you can see, she's due to calf in a few weeks."

"I see. How about these other cows? Are they bred?"

"I think so. Gibbs has a bull and when I think they are ready, I drive them over there and leave them a few days. But, you never know if its goin' to take or not."

"Do you get a calf from each of these cows each year?"

"I can't say every year. But I get two or three calves a year from the bunch."

"Your cows sure look like they'er in poor shape. What do you feed them to keep them alive?"

"The boy here and me grub up the beargrass, burn off the spears and cut up the bulbs that remain and the cows eat them."

"I notice some of your neighbors have started doing the same thing." Mr. Polk held his chin in his right hand for a few seconds and said, "Mack, I'll tell you what I'll do. I'll give you $12.50 for each head. That's what Uncle Sam will give you if he takes them out and shoots them. I remind you $50 will take you a long way down the road toward Oklahoma."

The deal was struck and Dad pocketed the cash. There was more haggling before each sale was made. Every man present put full trust in the description Dad gave them of each animal and each implement. Each bidder knew his character.

When the sale day was over Dad counted his money and the total was a little more than $300 for everything sold. A few things were left when the buyers left our place about sundown. The next morning Towser and I went to the lots to bid the horses and cows goodbye before the new owners came to take them away. My dog was nervous, and tears rolled down my cheeks.

Nobody bought the old wagon that had hauled us around since we had to get rid of our Model T a few years before. The wagon was precious to me for memories of trips made in it filled my mind. I remembered riding in the bed of the wagon, lying on a pallet on my back counting the stars as Dad drove the team up through the escarpment at night to a revival on the plains. I recalled the time Dad loaded the wagon with supplies and left to work on Conchas Dam leaving us for several months without transportation. And the time when Alta Marie was born leaving Mother bedridden for some time. Our little sister died after three days. That's when Dad made a little coffin out of scrap lumber and took her away in the wagon to bury in some unknown grave as I watched until he was out of sight.

Through the years, the wagon's wooden wheels would become dry from the hot desert sun and shrink allowing the iron rims to get loose. Before the rims fell off, we would take the wagon to an earthen water tank driving it in the pond leaving it until the wooden wheels swelled up and the iron tires fit properly.

The godevil was not sold. In a way, I was glad for I had ridden it to plow the field since I was six years old. I knew why it was not sold. Plows came on the market that did a better job. Most farmers bought the latter models. When I saw the plow sitting there alone, I had to approach it, rub my hands over it, sit on the seat and imagine the horses, Mose and George, were pulling the plow down a row in the field as the smell of rich loam entered my nostrils. The hot sun bore down on my head covered only with a mop of nearly white hair of my youth.

I looked to the east, south and west and viewed the "everlasting hills" that formed the ancient escarpment where I had spent so many unforgettable hours with Towser. I desired to drink every memory into the depth of my soul.

During these hectic days, Mother and Jessie packed all of our patched and faded clothes in the bottom of the big trunk. Our Sunday-go-to-meetin' clothes were packed in the shelf on top. So was Mother's big hat she wore on special occasions, keepsakes, especially the rubber ball Dad kept from the days he worked at the bankrupt tire plant in Texaco where I was born.

We were almost ready to begin our journey from the valley eastward down Highway 66 into an unknown life in the future that was waiting for us. Final details had to be worked out with Mr. Kerr our neighbor who lived in the half-dugout with his family. Dad had been talking to him for some time, but they had not worked out the expense agreement. Who was going to pay for what and how much each would pay.

Fred Kerr owned a Model-A truck. He had already agreed to haul us to Oklahoma. Dad didn't want to spend any more of the $300 than necessary. He knew it would be sorely needed for family expenses when we got to Ponca City. Mr. Kerr didn't know how he was going to pay for gasoline that was 12 cents a gallon, repairs on the truck and tires - one or two were bound to blow out on such a long trip.

Dad invited Mr. Kerr over to our place to look at plows, harness, and other farm equipment. Two calves left over after the sale. He was anxious to learn if our long-time neighbor would make the-thousand mile roundtrip for the remainder of farm equipment and livestock we owned. After much haggling Fred Kerr said, "Okay, I think I can use those plows and that old wagon after I do a lot of work on them." He stopped short of sealing the deal. I could tell Dad was getting nervous for his finger- with the tip gone- began to twitch. Finally, Mr. Kerr said, "Mack, it's a deal." They shook hands and the contract was solid and irrevocable as if a dozen lawyers had witnessed it.

We spent a few days bidding goodbye to our neighbors and friends who had experienced the same hardships and disappointments. Most of them were making plans to move out of the valley that upon first inspection promised so much but had produced mostly disappointment and failure for two generations. This valley, the *pocket of perpetual poverty* has won the battle against the invasion by man into the sanctuary of ancient nature where wild coyotes, badgers, prairie dogs, snakes, all kinds of birds and other creatures reign supreme. Today there is not a soul living in the entire township. Almost everything has returned to its natural state as it has been since creation. However, man left his marks upon the land just as the Anasazi Indians left traces of their civilization when they disappeared from the Chaco Canyon in northwestern New Mexico nearly a millennium in the past.

The visible marks we left on the desert landscape are tumbled down houses where children were born and families grew in those dire circumstances and desolate times. We also left barbed wire fences and unpaved roads that are still traveled with care by adventuresome souls who dare.

The day finally came, in that Pre-Atomic Age, for us to load up and begin our long trip into the unknown. I visualized our future as jumping off a very high cliff into a dense fog having no idea where we would land or what the conditions would be when we landed.

Early the morning agreed on, Mr. Kerr backed his truck up to our front door just as the sun was coming over the eastern hills. All of our meager possessions, left after the sale, were securely packed in boxes, bags and the big trunk ready to be loaded. Mother was most anxious to leave hoping to escape the poverty that had captured us. She also wanted to see her sisters and brothers who were already living in and around Ponca City.

The entire farm, especially the lot where the animals were fed, looked more abandoned that I'd ever seen. The men who bought our livestock and farm equipment had already hauled them all away. The two calves that now belonged to Mr. Kerr were bawling to be fed. We had nothing to give them. I looked toward the schoolhouse that could be seen easily from our yard. I viewed it with a nostalgic feeling. It was in that old schoolhouse where Mrs. White taught me to read, write, add, subtract, divide and multiply. There I said the one line in the school play. There I learned to diagram sentences on the blackboard. My mind was filled with memories of playing in the yard, and Mrs. White's kindness and thoroughness in teaching. I thought of the fun we had and the discipline while Mr. Heckendorne taught us. I wanted to cry knowing I may never experience such again.

After a short conversation as to how to proceed, Dad and Mr. Kerr began the task of loading the truck Mother insisted they put the cook stove in the bed of the truck first next to the cab to minimize damage. Next, under Mother's direction, the men got behind the big trunk and scooted it across the floor through the door. The lady of the house wanted the family treasure placed beside the stove. After much heaving, staining and struggle, the heavy trunk was placed in the truck beside the stove. Mother was pleased.

Next, we broke down the beds and put the coil springs in the floor of the truck bed, and on top of the springs, we placed the mattresses. We carried the boxes and bags out the door and stuffed them in holes and crevices around the stove, trunk and beds. The unsightly, but very practical heating stove made from a fifty-five gallon metal oil drum, was not moved from the middle of the living room where it has sat or stood (take your choice) for years. This piece also had a sentimental value for it had kept us warm in the freezing winters when the howling north winds blew and the snows fell.

The last things to go into the truck were boiled eggs, a big pot of cooked beans, cooked roasting ears of corn from the garden, a pot of prepared beef and another pot of pork ready to eat. We hoped this was enough food to last on our 500-mile trip, for Dad didn't want to dip into the $300 he carried on his person to make sure none was lost.

While all this activity was in progress, Towser followed me around looking sad and forlorn. I'm persuaded he knew we were leaving and by necessity, he had to stay behind.

When all was ready, and it was time to leave the farm, where we had sweated, labored, planted and gathered crop after crop, Dad and Mother got in the front seat with Mr. Kerr. Jessie, Ray, Raymond, Jay, Charles Quentin and I climbed into the back with all the furniture. I watched Towser as he sat on the ground watching, taking it all in. In my adult life as a Christian minister and chaplain for many years in a nursing home, I've seen many sad faces. I've never seen a face that looked as sad and that was more indelibly impressed in my memory then the face of Towser, my dog. As the heavily loaded truck labored on it's way down the dusty lane, I watched Towser, through tearing eyes. He grew smaller and smaller as the distance grew between us. Soon he had vanished, but he will never be forgotten.

LEARNING AND ADJUSTING TO CITY LIFE

Mr. Kerr, our driver, felt the truck pulling toward the center of Highway 66. That followed by the unmistakable sound of a tire gone flat. He steered the vehicle to the right of the road and stopped. "That's the fourth flat tire we've had since leaving home," he announced.

Dad replied, "Well, Fred, there's only one thing to do. We'll just have to fix it."

As the men got out of the truck, Fred Kerr reached for the tire tools and the patching material. Lifting the vehicle up with a jack, Mr. Kerr said, "I wish some company could make better tires than we've got these days. We spend half our time on the road patching tires."

Arriving in Amarillo, we rolled into a service station for gas and to use the restroom. Soon we were on the road again. With us six siblings cooped in the back of the truck with the furniture for such a long time, we got cross and rambunctious with one another. Occasionally, while we traveled down the narrow confines of the highway at forty miles an hour, Dad had to yell through the open window, "If you kids don't settle down back there, I'll have Mr. Kerr stop this truck, and I'll come back there and let you have it!" We knew what he meant. We would settle down for a while. Before long, we'd be aggravating one another again.

When we arrived in Ponca City, everybody was exhausted. After a search, we found a house to rent for $25 for three months. This place on North First Street was on the alley behind a larger house that faced the street. After the furniture was unloaded, I began to scout around. There was a structure beside the house with grapevines growing up the posts of the structure and over its roof. Since it was early summer, tiny green shoots, the beginning of leaves, were popping out all alone the stems of the grapevines. I visualized the cool shade it would make when the sunshine got hot in mid-summer.

But what would I do all day for there was no work to keep me busy. No wide, open spaces nor hills and ravines to run over with old Towser. I anticipated endless boredom.

Mother took to bed most of the time because she was worn out. Sadness and dejection were itched in Dad's face. He had no job so he could provide for his family and knew that jobs were hard to come by in 1935. The $300, carried in his pocket and checked frequently to make sure it was still there, would not last long. He felt lost and forlorn in a world not of his making.

Hope for him was nearly gone. He never gave up knowing it was his responsibility to look after his ailing wife, and he must see his children grow to be adults when they could wrestle with life's problems. Dad had fought through his life, and it seemed he had lost.

Etta and Churchell came to see us. We had no transportation so our kinfolk came by to see us in their cars. From the looks on their faces and their veiled comments, I believed they felt sorry for us. That was the last thing Dad wanted. Though we were down and out, broken in spirit, we still wanted to keep our dignity and face our difficulties without sympathy from others.

From time to time Conoco Refinery announced they planned to hire a few men to work. Dad would go down each time and stand in a line of fifty or sixty men hoping to be hired for one of the few jobs. Ninety percent of the men went home with hopes unrealized. After a while, Dad resorted to standing on a street corner with a group of other men hoping a contractor would come by and hire some of them. When hired, they would be employed for a day or two at fifty cents an hour doing backbreaking work.

We moved several times before I graduated from high school five years later. Each time the younger boys changed elementary schools. Self-conscious and backward, I enrolled in Junior High School always dressed in patched overalls. I felt completely out of place with the one thousand students enrolled there. Some of the boys would taunt and call me bad names. I was persuaded I could defeat any one of them, having built strength from working on a farm. Since Mother had taught me not to fight, I chose to obey her.

Jessie had a sweet, lovable personality and found a job in a home where she lived. All of us older boys were enterprising enough to pick up little jobs that paid a dime or quarter for watering trees or working on lawns. We gave some of the money for family up-keep. On occasion, we spent our money to go to a cowboy picture show. I was thirteen when I saw the first cinema. Apparently, it was shot in Africa. Tigers, lions and other wild beasts jumped toward the audience with their mouths open, teeth showing and their claws stretched out in front of them. It frightened me.

Not long after I'd enrolled in Junior High School, our English teacher told the class we would be giving an oral book report on a certain day. "So, be prepared," she advised. I had no ideas what "oral" meant. I was at a loss as to the meaning of the assignment. After class the boys and girls were all chatting about the assignment. I was ashamed to expose my ignorance by asking what the teacher meant, so I listened to all the chatter, hoping nobody would notice me.

After learning that we had to read a book then give a review of it before the class, gave me a panic attack. Just thinking about getting before all those "rich students who were a thousand times smarter then me" made me extremely nervous. In spite of my feeling, I did not intend to shrink from a responsibility.

I had never read a book in all my life other than schoolbooks. I finally got up nerve to go to a library for the first time ever. There was stack after stack of books. I didn't know there were so many books in the world. Still ashamed to reveal ignorance, I talked to nobody about my problem. I walked between the endless stacks of books having no idea which ones were for adults or junior high students.

Finally, I pulled from a shelf *The House of Seven Gables* by Nathaniel Hawthorne. There was no reason for choosing this particular book. A book was needed for the oral report, and out of the hundreds of books, I picked this one. It would be stealing to take, without permission, the book that belonged to someone. After watching other students check out books, with great apprehension, I stood in a long line. When my turn came, I laid the book down on the counter.

The pretty lady behind the counter asked, "May I see you library card." I was speechless not knowing about such things. "You know, your card, so I can check out your book." Still speechless, I noticed the lady's sweet perfume tantalized my nostrils. For a farm boy who had smelled the odors of the cow lot and the rest of nature, it was the best smelling stuff ever.

In a lovely voice that matched her perfume, she asked, "You don't have a card?" I shook my head. "Than let's step to the end of the counter, and I'll make a card that you can sign. Then you can check out a book any time you wish." For a boy with third grade reading ability, I had not considered that the book's content was a greater challenge than I could possibly meet. After struggling through the first few pages, I gave up. There was no other preparation before the day of the assignment.

The day came to recite before the class, and I wasn't prepared. The names of the boys and girls were called. The girls, in their frilly dresses, walked boldly to the front of the class and gave their report with ease. The boys, acting like jocks, with pressed shirts and creased pants swaggered to the front and spoke with confidence. When my name was called, I was terrified. To meet my responsibility, I pulled myself from the seat. In patched overalls and wrinkled shirt, I walked trembling to the front of the class. Taking an example from the other students, I gave the name of the book and the author. My report was short and certainly not very sweet. I said, "There was a pretty girl sittin' under a tree." Then I froze. Not another word came from my lips. I stood there like a paper statue in the midst of an earthquake. The room full of students began to snicker. The teacher ordered, "All right students no more of that." Turning to me, she said, "You may take your seat." These were welcomed words. I never wanted to go back into that classroom. Something inside keep saying, "You must go back,"

In a science class, we had a test that asked something about the environment. The questions were written on the blackboard, and we were to be quiet while writing down the answers. I was completely dumbfounded as to what that big word "environment" meant. I sat here pondering while the rest of the students finished their papers, handed them in and left the room. My paper was handed in without an answer. That was the only course I ever flunked.

In junior high, the school was required to give an I. Q. test to all students. The test asked us to name the left side of a ship, the right side and the front and the back. I'd never seen, read about or ridden in a boat much less a ship. We were to answer questions about things, that in my previous experience, I had no relationship whatsoever. Nevertheless, I made an above average grade on the test. However, I reasoned: if they had asked us to name the parts of a wagon or a plow, how to harness a horse and hitch it to a plow, I could have answered correctly.

While in high school, my family moved into a second floor of a two-story, unpainted, wooden building that had been used for commercial purposes. The first floor was empty. We gained access to our floor by climbing the stairway attached to an outside wall.

Bill, Iven, Archie and Roy Essary, boys about my age, lived close by. All became my friends. Evelyn, who lived in the neighborhood, and my cousin, Chloe Miller were close friends. Roy and I spent much time together. His family was in about the same financial condition as mine. Even as a high school young man, Roy was very industrious. In the midst of the Great Depression, he always had one, two or three jobs. One time he said to me, "I'll give you all the money I got in my pocket if you can guess the exact amount." I guessed seven dollars and fifty three cents." He took the money from his pocket and counted seven-dollars-and-fifty-one-cents. (That was a lot of cash in those days.)

Roy got up at three o'clock in the morning to go work in a donut shop and deliver the goodies to the cafes around town. In addition to that job, he delivered the Wichita Eagle on his paper route. This out-of-state paper had a limited number of customers scattered all over town. All this was accomplished before he went to school.

He divided the paper route and asked me to take half of it. After talking with the downtown merchant whom Roy worked for, I accepted the route that paid $1.25 a week for morning and evening delivery. I managed to buy a worn-out bicycle for a couple of dollars to carry papers on my route. The sprocket in the center of the back wheel was forever slipping. Often I had to turn the pedals several times before the cogs would catch. I spent most of my Saturday mornings working on the thing.

I peddled each morning and afternoon from the south part of town to the north side on that old bicycle, with the paper bag wrapped around the handlebars, throwing papers from the street on to customers' yards or porches.

Jessie was married by this time, and her husband Raymond Vandeslice loaned me $5 for a down payment on a brand new bicycle. I promised to pay $1.25 a week to the Western Auto Store. If I wanted money for my own use, I had to sell extra papers at five cents each or get another job.

Roy nor I could take part in extra activities after school hours because of our schedules. Since he was a grade ahead of me, I usually followed his lead for I considered him a good guy. Neither Roy's family or mine had a radio, and television was only a flickering image in some inverter's eye. This left our evenings free after the papers were delivered. While carrying on our several jobs and going to school, we enrolled in boxing classes dreaming of a championship. After we were sufficiently trained, the manager of the gym paid us each $3 per fight when boys from other towns came to climb into the ring with us.

Roy usually won his bouts for he entered the ring with the same eagerness and determination he worked at other jobs. I didn't do so well against other boxers for I couldn't develop the "killer" instinct. This meant Roy got more fights and more money than I did. In 1938 we went to the State Golden Gloves in Enid. Roy was state champion for his weight, and I came in second in my class.

Our city newspaper ran a story about Roy and me winning a prize in the Golden Gloves. That was the first time I ever saw my name in print, and it pleased me.

Girls were not forgotten by either of us. The big difference was that Roy got all the dates and I got none. When he could manage time from work, Roy could always find a girl that would go out with him. One time we were in a cafe where a blond about our age was waiting tables. She was giving all her spare time to my companion and ignoring me. I attempted to learn his secret with the female species and wanted her to give me some attention. I blurted some remark that must have offended her. She dropped everything in her hands and walloped me on the face with an open hand. My face turned redder than the red in the Stars and Stripes. It was another lesson learned while living in a society I knew little about. From then on, I chose my words more carefully, and the tone of my voice was more kind.

Roy had a girl in Tonkawa, a college town about 12 miles to the west of us, and he had a hankering to see her. After delivering our paper routes one afternoon, he persuaded me to ride our bicycles over there to visit the young lady. Being the third party, I stayed in the shadows while he visited his girlfriend. (I think she was the lady he married.) We got home about two the next morning and he had to be at work in the donut shop at three.

I did have one extra activity in school. During the noon hour, I served as the projectionist for the movies showed in the dark auditorium. All the students who wished could come in to watch old movies of Fanny Brice, Charles Chaplin and sometimes a Tom Mix cowboy episode.

Our class graduated in May 1940. When our yearbook called, *The Cat Tale,* was published, all the seniors pictures were in it. Some students had three, four or even five lines beneath the picture to tell all the activities they pursued in school. Mine had only two words: "Movie Club." The editors may have been more correct than I was willing to admit for I had secret ambitions to be a part of the Hollywood movie industry. I even helped form a writer's club.

I accepted the fact that I couldn't buy a copy. The day the yearbook was handed out to the students, all of them were excited, thumbing through their copy laughing and talking about it. That is, all but me. I went silently about my business. A pretty classmate, whom I had admired from afar for three years, came to me and whispered, "Didn't you buy a yearbook?"

I was shocked when such pretty girl spoke to me. My answer was, "No." This lovely girl, whose name was Eleanor Johnson, knew something about our family finances or lack thereof. She was one of a group who brought a Christmas basket of food to our home. The young lady took $1.50 from her purse and gave it to me saying. "Please, go buy one of the extra yearbooks. You'll treasure it all your life." She was right. I have looked at it often and treasure it.

World War II started September 3, 1939 when Germany invaded Poland. Pictures of this awful conflict were shown everywhere in magazines, newspapers and newsreels at the movies. I shuttered with great anxiety seeing men slaughter men in war. "How could men do such things to other men?" Dog fights between fighter planes were shown. Men parachuted out of their destroyed planes and the enemy in other planes shot the defenseless men as they floated earthward. This was absolutely beyond my comprehension. I followed the War closely as it proceeded when England got into the fight. I wondered why anyone would want to bomb innocent women and children in London as the Germans did.

The summer after finishing the eleventh grade, I got a job on a farm owned and operated by a young couple whose name I can't remember - and I don't want to remember. I stayed in their home. The man worked all day in the field harvesting his crops and gallivanted somewhere away from home most of every night. I'm persuaded he wanted me to stay in his home to look after his wife and babies in addition to working in the field all day with him.

The man promised to pay me $15 at the end of each week. At the end of the week, I'd ask for the money owed me. He would give excuses delaying week after week while occasionally paying me a few dollars. Most of the jobs for high school people were already taken, and it would be almost impossible for me to find another one. I needed the work to buy school supplies and clothes for my senior year. I didn't know how to handle the situation.

I worked through the summer getting dribbles of pay for my hard work. I rode the binder that cut the long rows of maize and tied the stalks into bundles. When the cutting was finished,

I gathered the bundles and stacked them in pyramid shocks so they could dry properly. When time had lapsed, we gathered the bundles in a wagon and hauled them to a stationary threshing machine where the grain was separated from the stalks and fodder. The grain was collected in a truck bed and hauled to town for sale. The stalks and fodder were gathered into large stacks for the cattle to feed on during the winter months. All this was done while the boiling sun was coming down and the humidity must have been 80%. By mid-morning our clothes were saturated with sweat.

At the end of the summer, I asked for all the money I'd earned. My employer was free with his vulgar words and cursed frequently. He gave me $15 as he called me names seldom heard before, saying that was all I was worth and besides I got my room and board. As a boy 17 years old, I was at a complete loss, not knowing what to do. I hitchhiked to town with the $15 secured in my pocket, wondering what was to become of the wife and babies who had to live with a man so cruel.

Facing my last year in high school, I went to the library and checked out a book written by Dick Carlson entitled *How To Develop Your Personal Power.* Before I went home, I went by a Five and Ten Cent store and bought a small pad to take notes as I studied the book. By the time I finished, the notebook was filled and I had written in it my resolution for the last year in school. The resolution read: "I resolve for the year of 1940 to develop my personal powers more fully."

I had guarded the $15 religiously. On the last page of the notebook, I posted my budget for the following year. This is my budget verbatim:

	$15.00
Socks & underwear:	$0.75
Hair oil	.10
Shoestrings & Polish	.15
Halfsoles	.10

Pants	4.00
Shirt	.70

Clarence	<u>2.00</u>	(I owed Clarence Larson.
	(Total)	$7.50

School and graduation:

Picture	$0.25
Annual	1.50
Gown	1.50

Typing and writing paper <u>.40</u>

<u>Total $3.65</u>

That left me $3.85, plus my paper route and what ever I could make at odd jobs, for expenses for the year.

Jay and I had been attending church with Mother and Dad at a shotgun type building on Fifth Street for some time. The twins, Ray and Raymond, went occasionally. One hot summer afternoon just before graduation, I was walking alone with a load of books. A car pulled up to the curb and the driver called me. Our minister, Brother Crumbly, told me to get in the car and he would drive me home. After a few pleasantries and a short talk about the hot weather, he said, "Leslie, you seem to be a bright young man with potential."

I responded, "Thank you, Sir. I hope you're right, Sir."

"Don't you think it's about time you were baptized?"

I had always felt and believed that there was the divine Power who created all that we could see and much that we could not see with our physical eyes. I had been taught from preaching and lessons taught by John Hardin in Sunday School that God loves us sinners so much he sent his Son Jesus Christ to earth to live among us. That he died and shed his blood for us, paying the price for the sins we have committed, that we may become the children of God by the new birth. Heaven knew I'd committed sins and had no way in the world to get rid of them by myself. So I said to Brother Crumbly, "I've been thinking about it."

The minister explained a few things I didn't quiet understand and encouraged me to take the step.

Dad, when asked, took the janitorial job at the church for $25 a month. Often on Saturdays, I would help him, and I learned all the nooks and crannies in the building. A passagewaay led from the auditorium down into a cubbyhole where supplies for cleaning and lawn care were stored. A smaller door in the cubbyhole opened on to the back lawn.

I'd seen a few others baptized and after the ceremony members of the church came to the new convert hugged, kissed and expressed their great delight over the decision. I was still shy and wanted none of that.

When I came up out of the water, I changed from the wet clothes into the ones I wore to church. All this happened behind the door that led down into the cubbyhole. After the change, I slipped through the smaller door leading to the back lawn, leaving the church members wondering what happened to me.

Walking home alone under a perfectly clear sky, the stars never looked brighter nor did the air I breathed ever feel fresher. I thrilled to be walking alone with the Creator. That night I have never forgotten.

On the night of graduation, I was the first and only member of my family ever go through such an exercise. All the graduates were told to be at the high school early. We gathered in a room and donned our caps and gowns as the parents filled into the auditorium where I had shown the movies. Having no transportation, Mother could not walk the three miles up the hill to the school. Dad, with all his weight, managed to walk the trail I had walked the last three years.

The nearly 300 graduates sat crowded in chairs on the huge stage behind the desks where Superintendent Howell and

Principle Anderson sat at a table with a few board members. We had a good view of the parents and siblings. The mothers were dressed in their most expensive dresses and hats, and most had corsages. The men wore fresh cleaned suits, ties and white shirts. Dad, dear Dad, did wear a white shirt with open collar. He looked out of place as a fly floating a bowl of gourmet soup. He proved it didn't bother him by the prideful smile that decorated his face. That smile warmed my heart and gave me confidence.

As we walked home together in the darkness that night, Dad kept telling me how proud he was that one of his children had graduated from high school. My refrain was, "Dad it's not such a big deal. You saw all those other students graduate."

He retorted, "It is a big deal. You are my son. I expect you to have it a lot easier life than I've had it."

At home, the room was lighted by a dim electric bulb on the end of a cord hanging from the ceiling. While I explained to Mother the activities of the evening, Dad went into another room and brought back something wrapped in white paper. He handed the package to me and told me to open it. I found a pair of socks that cost fifteen cents. It was the only graduation present received, but it was enough, for I knew it came from his heart.

Etta's husband, Clarence Larson, had taken me several times back to the farm where I had work the summer before. I wanted to collect the money that I had earned as the man promised. My former employer was always gone before, when we went to see him. Shortly after receiving my diploma, we made our last trip of about ten miles in Clarence's old black van. This time we found the man some distance from his house. He and his pickup stood close by a barrel of gasoline. When we drove up, he was attempting to siphon gas from the barrel into the tank of his truck. He was using a metal pipe crook for just such a purpose.

When I got out of the van and told him what I wanted, the terrible man began cursing and calling me every dastardly name that could possible come from his filthy mouth. When I insisted he give the money owed me, he turned into a wild man and threw the crooked pipe in my direction. Well, that was enough. The money wasn't worth risking my life further. I got back into the van and Clarence drove away shaking his head at such a demonstration. That was the last time I ever saw the evil man.

AN ADVENTURE ON A VERY LOW BUDGET

My older brother was sought by police. It was he, who forced me to get out on the hood of the old Model T, when I was six years old, as he drove from the plains on the rough, dusty road, onto the valley floor 800 feet below. Churchell's name was in the local news much of the time while I was in high school. Because our last name is so unique, I felt certain my fellow students associated me with my brother. I was ashamed of his bootlegging activities.

The closest I ever came to a run in with the law was one evening a group of us boys on bicycles were weaving in and out among the traffic on Main Street. Cars were honking and drivers shouting at us. Looking back on the incident it was very dangerous, but we were having fun. When we heard the police sirens, bicycle riders scattered in all directions. I was on the old bicycle with cogs slipping. Yet, I managed to escape in the darkness. My transportation and I lay in a bar ditch until the sirens stopped.

Every time I was out among people, I consciously wondered if citizens thought I was like my big brother. Therefore, I was anxious to leave town to a place where his activities were unknown. Since my sister Jessie and her husband, Raymond Vanderslice, had moved to Oklahoma City, I believed that was the place for me to go.

Soon as things could be arranged, I put my meager belongings in a small cardboard box, bid my family good-bye in early morning and walked to US Highway 77 to hitchhike to Oklahoma City. The only help I asked of anybody was a free ride to my destination. With $3.55 in my pocket, I struck out on an adventure without the supervision of my parents. What lay ahead was a mystery, and I delighted in the prospects.

Before I had traveled the 100 miles to the City by "thumbing it," on the rough highway with its many twists and turns, a half-day had passed. I was not a complete stranger to metropolitan area that was at least ten times larger than my hometown. I had spent at least one summer living with Jessie and Raymond while delivering The Daily Oklahoman newspaper on a designated route while it's regular carrier was on summer vacation.

When I arrived in the big town, the rest of the day was spent looking for a place to live within my very limited means. No prospect for a job was in sight. Being a high school graduate, I felt that l should be completely on my own and not live with my sister's family.

After looking all afternoon for a place to live, near sundown, I struggled up to a private home with rooms to rent posted. A strange looking woman answered the door when I knocked. Her husband, with a protruding stomach, stood behind her. "Yes. What do you want?" the lady asked in a soft voice with a foreign sound. "I saw your sign *room for rent,"* I answered in my best high school manner.

The Depression still had its grip on our nation and shysters of all kinds were roaming the streets and approaching private homes seeking anyway to get by. So the man of the house asked cautiously, in a tone that concerned me, "Who are you, and where did you come from?"

Meekly I replied, "I'm Leslie Eugene Fooks. I just graduated from High School in Ponca City last May."

"You got any references?"

With great uncertainty, I said, "No, Sir."

She pulled her husband back from the open door while they talked in whispers. When their conference was over, the man stepped forward and said, "You look like a decent young man. So come on in and we'll show you the room."

They led me up a squeaky wooden staircase to the second floor. When the door was opened to a small room, I saw a bed and a mirror hanging on a wall. "This is it," the man said. "It'll cost you three dollars a week."

"Where is the bathroom?"

They showed me the bathroom that I would share with a single young man and a mother with her six year old son. The three small apartments were on the same floor.

"Give us three dollars right now," the man crudely ordered.

I pulled the money from my pocket and gave it to the man. That left me with fifty-five cents to live on until I got a job, and I had no idea where one would come from.

After putting the cardboard box with my possessions on the bed, I went to a nearby grocery store and shelled out ten cents for a can of pork and beans and another ten cents for a loaf of bread. Of course, I had to pay state tax that was two mills the equivalent to 1/5 of a penny. After these purchases, I had 34 cents and eight mills to last until I got a pay check with no prospects for a job in sight.

I was very tired when I went to bed and slept well through the night. When I paid the rent, I was told I would be sharing kitchen privileges on the screened-in back porch with the other renters. There was a stove, cooking utensils, plates and silverware that we could use only if we washed each item after using.

Next morning, with the loaf of bread and the can of pork and beans in hand, I walked down the noisy stairs, through a large living room containing ancient but beautiful furniture, and on to the enclosed back porch. Knowing I had to ration my food supply, I wished to make two pieces of toast and warm up a very small bowl of pork and beans to last me through the day.

The other renters were already eating breakfast when I arrived on the porch. After introducing myself, the lady told me her name was Caddo Webb. She worked while her young son, Kermit, went to first grade in a nearby school. Before she moved to the city, she had live in the small town of Choctaw about twelve miles to the east.

I cannot remember the young man's name who rented the room next to mine. I do remember he was about my age. He came from Colorado, was aspiring to be an artist. Eating our meals together, we all became friends. Caddo and I belong to the same church so we had much in common and visited when time permitted. The young artist had different interests than mine. We visited, and he showed me his artwork. We never became close friends.

The six-year-old son, named Kermit, was a bright little fellow who liked to have fun. I teased him, calling him a Guatemalan. He thought that was a dirty word and ran to tell his mother. She explained to him that Guatemalan was a citizen of a country in Central America. He was satisfied and began calling me the same as best his youthful tongue could pronounce the name of the country.

I had to find a job. Any job that I could latch on to would be sufficient. My room was on 24th Street and the many stores and movie theaters on 23rd Street received a call from me asking for a job. Near the end of the day, some kind soul said that I might be able to land a job with Mr. Lincoln. This businessman owned a huge dry cleaning shop with pick-up stations scattered over much of the City. People who needed suits or dresses cleaned would drop them off at the stations. One of Mr. Lincoln's truck drivers would pick up the items, haul them to the shop for cleaning and deliver them back to the station where the customers could pick up their cleaning.

The Depression was still oppressive, and jobs were almost as scarce as gold paved streets. I was smart enough to know the guy that tried the hardest usually got the job. The next morning, bright and early, I appeared at Mr. Lincoln's office that was located in the corner of the large shop where men were already pressing suits, dresses, et al.

I knocked on the office door and a deep voice said, "Come in." The voice frightened me. When I opened the door, I saw a large man sitting in a leather-upholstered chair behind an expensive desk. His costly suit looked like a million dollars, and his diamond ring flashed under the ceiling lights. He was the king of his business empire, and I sensed it.

"Come in," sounded more like an order, than an invitation. Knowing I had to have a job, I stepped into his office with trepidation.

Mr. Lincoln was filling out forms, but looked up to ask, "What can I do for you?"

"Sir," I stammered, "I'm looking for a job."

"What experience do you have?"

"Sir, I just graduated from high school." I hastened to add, "I was raised on a farm, and I know how to work."

Mr. Lincoln mellowed and a smile came on his face. "So, you're a farm boy and know how to work. Farm work is much different than working here."

"I know, Sir, but I can learn."

After much more give and take, Mr. Lincoln said, "All right, young man, if that's what you want, you can go to work here. I'll give you a dollar a day, and you'll work six days a week."

I calculated rapidly in my head: Three dollars for rent and three dollars for food. I could get by on that. "Okay, Sir, I'll go to work when you wish."

As he pulled from his desk drawer and handed me a paper to fill out, he said, "Come to work in the morning at seven." He then lowered his head and began work at his desk.

I walked home happy and proud as a peacock that had laid her first egg.

Before seven the next morning, I reported to the foreman and chief pressman who worked a steamy press. His name does not come to mind, but later I learned his salary was $15 a weak to support his family.

My job was to carry the pressed garments from the several presses back to the designated racks so the truck drivers could gather them quickly and deliver them back to the stations. I was busy all day long going back and forth. The people who worked the presses were constantly busy for when the materials left the hoppers where they were cleansed, they were stacked on tables beside each presses. The press people dared not slack up, for they knew jobless people were waiting to take their jobs.

Everywhere I went, I walked, except when Jessie and Raymond took me with them in their old Chevrolet. Sunday morning I walked to the church on Tenth Street. I walked to the grocery store, to work and downtown that was about three miles.

In order to carry out my resolution for 1940 to "develop my personal power more fully," I enrolled in an Arthur Murry Dance class that met in a hotel downtown. This class met one night a week. On another night, I started taking classes in a Business College that also met downtown once a week. The class met for two hours, and the instructors gave students piles of homework. The Business School allowed us to enroll with no money up front with the promise to pay for our education when we graduated and got a job.

On my feet all day at work, and making two six miles round trips a week to the center of Oklahoma City kept me in good physical shape.

Listening to the experiences of Charley White in World War One while we lived on the New Mexico farm during the Dust Bowl days, and our school teacher leading us in singing The Stars Spangled Banner in the one room school house, caused me to have a great love and patriotism for my country.

I began to get restless with my job earning a dollar a day and the other activities I engaged in. I felt like I was on a slow train going nowhere. I saw little or no prospects in sight for advancement. Even if I graduated from the business college, landing a job was a remote possibility for there were experienced, men with families, waiting in line for any available work.

With these thoughts nagging at my inner being, two months after I turned nineteen, I presented myself in the Army recruiting office and swore to uphold the Constitution of the United States of America by signing on the dotted line. That was February 17, 1941. I was no longer a civilian free to do as I pleased within the framework of the law, now I was a new recruit in the Army Air Corps under orders of that command.

Twenty-one-dollars a month, room and board with medical privileges thrown in, sounded like a pretty good deal for a kid making six dollars a week and none of the other assurances. At my age, I didn't need permission from my parents to sign up.

Was it the money and the privileges that caused me to sign up for the duration? Was it patriotism? Was it boredom? Was it the belief in my own heart that America would soon be in the war that started in Europe almost two years before, and I wanted to get in on the ground floor before millions of other men signed up? Honestly, I can't say why I signed up so early. Probably it was a combination of all the above.

It should be remembered, pictures of those "blood thirst Germans, those awful Krauts," committing terrible atrocities were shown in newspapers, magazines and newsreels. Propaganda was preparing us to enter World War II. Many young men were affected by these news stories and the government releases and joined up early. As it turned out, we were the forerunners for the millions of young men and women who followed into the armed services after Japan attacked Pearl Harbor, December 7, 1941.

The day I joined the Army Air Corps in Oklahoma City, Howard Dull joined the same branch of service in Indianapolis, Indiana. The afternoon we signed, we were put on trains in our respective cities. Traveling through the night, our journeys ended in San Antonio, Texas. We were strangers assigned to Kelley Field for recruit training. When I left Oklahoma City in the late afternoon, the grass was winter-brown and the trees were bare of leaves. The next morning, a different world welcomed me. The warm sunshine revealed fields of green grass and glorious palm trees lining the streets. This change surprised me. I delighted in the difference.

In Kelley Field, we were lined up in alphabetical order according to our last names, and told to count off by eights. Howard Dull and I fell in the same bracket of eights, so the sergeant put us in the same tent with six other guys. After six weeks of boot training, Howard and I chose photography as the branch of service we desired.

Another train ride took us to Denver, Colorado. We ended up in Lowery Field where we studied photography for several months. Seeing different parts of the country that I had only read about and meeting men from many parts of the United States was high adventure for me. I learned the speech pattern of men from Brooklyn, the accent of the men from the Deep South, the pride of Texans and the peculiarities of West Coast men. We laughed at one another's mannerisms, and learned to appreciate others who were different. More than photography, we learned what it meant to obey orders.

All of us were happy-go-lucky buck privates doing kp duty, scrubbing the barracks, going to school, taking pictures on the Field and in the Rocky Mountains. All of this amazed me. We goldbricked when we dared. Being paid $21 month, with free room and board and medical care, was just fine with me. I failed to realize, Uncle Sam was training us to do his bidding in a very dangerous world.

Every man wore khaki uniforms that looked just alike, did the same chores, went to the same classes, ate in the same mess hall and ate the same food. Though the sameness was monotonous, I never felt inferior, as in high school, to any of the soldiers. I was more confident and outgoing than at anytime in my life.

Before the War started, soldiers had Saturdays and Sundays off. After scrubbing the barracks and finishing other necessary chores, most of the men went into Denver to shop and to check the town out. While some of the men came back to the Base soon after sunset, others stayed in town to visit the bars and meet the girls that hung around such places.

When they returned to the Field before curfew, some swaggered from too much to drink. The lights were turned off in the barracks. The darkness didn't stop the soldiers from talking and laughing about their activities while in town.

Their talk of having such a good time, and the joy they seemed to feel, excited and intrigued me. Still, on Sunday morning I walked to the church in Aurora while some of the good-timers suffered from hangovers.

I never heard Christians so joyous after attending church. Many Saturdays after work, my barracks buddies kept saying to me, "Why don't you go with us? We're just having fun. It won't hurt for you to go, so get ready and come with us next Saturday night."

One Saturday I decided to go to town with my soldier friends just to see what it was all about - why the boys had so much fun. I had never even sipped a drop of alcohol beverage. I neither drank nor danced with the girls that night. We got back on the Field just under the wire at eleven. Next morning I slept in and failed to attend church services. My conscience bothered me a little.

Before long, I became a regular on the Saturday night good-time circuit drinking and dancing with the pretty girls. What I learned from my parents and in the little shotgun church-house back home was not forgotten, I just shoved these things to the back of my mind. For the time, I chose to "enjoy the pleasures of sin for a season." The church parties and other activities I participated in while in high school seemed like child's play compared with Saturday nights in Denver.

It didn't take a genius to notice that some of the men who engaged in the raunchiest activities, were the first to come to the aid of a fellow soldier in need. While some who seemed so righteous, would question if the man in need were worthy of their help. By the time they solved their question, the need was met.

All this made me wonder about some of the things taught in church while in High School. Right or wrong, I reasoned if the father had a banquet and a dance when the prodigal son returned home, what's wrong with dancing? If Christ turned water into wine, what is wrong with drinking? I must admit I went overboard sometimes, but "do all things in moderation" was dismissed from consideration.

I was learning everything was not quite as distinctively black and white as I understood while growing up. Life is more complicated. My inquisitive mind was asking probing questions about the world beyond the narrow confines of my youth.

On a Saturday afternoon, without orders from the "brass," our barracks was filled with soldiers lolling around, scantily clad and shooting the breeze. Suddenly all was quiet when we heard the announcement: MAIL CALL. Finally, my name was called which was unusual. The following poem, *A Letter of Introduction,* I wrote, years later, describing the occasion and the letter received:

On a Saturday afternoon, Near the Colorado Rockies,
Mail call ended for a Barracks full of rookies.

I made a fool of my self, For I was eager to show
A letter from an Okie girl I didn't even know.

Naked but for shorts, I stood tall on my bunk.
Soldiers gathered 'round; Some of them were drunk.

I ripped the letter open, And silently I read.
A barrage of pillow missiles Assailed my dodging head.

In cadence the privates yelled, In the speech of G. I. Joe,
"What does the letter say, Is what we want to know!"

From the wrinkled envelope, Her picture fell to the floor.
Some guy grabbed the picture; Looked at it and swore.

I laughed heartily, And began to read aloud.
This letter from a girl, Made me very proud.

"Caddo Webb," she wrote, "A mutual friend or ours,
Thought I should write, To relieve your lonely hours."

The boys laughed and teased. My reading came to an end.
I felt I had betrayed, The confidence of a friend.

I ran though the barracks With the letter in my hand;
Hid in a shower stall, from a jolly soldier band.

In secret, I read her letter. She was barely seventeen.
That seemed a little young, For soldier turned nineteen.

Running proud through her veins, Was Choctaw Indian blood.
Blood running my veins, Caused my heart to flood.

She said she was an orphan, Working her way through school.

Her script was letter perfect; I knew she was no fool.

As I continued reading, My interest began to grow.
I was looking eagerly, To my very first furlough.

Before I answered her mail, I thought it best to tarry.
Never did I realize, She was the girl I'd marry.

After several days I answered the letter from Dorothy Hendrix, the girl in Oklahoma. The exchange of letters continued. I was getting more involved in the night life on Saturday nights and enjoying it.

On Sunday afternoons, we would go hiking in the Rocky Mountains or go to the zoo in Denver to see the animals and watch the pretty girls walking around in shorts.

In due, time our photography class graduated. On August 15, 1941 I received my Diploma that read: *United States Army Air Corps Technical School*: Be it known that Private Leslie E. Fooks, 18050076, 354th School Squadron Air Corps has satisfactorily completed the prescribed Photography course of instruction at the Air Crops Technical School. In testimony whereof and by virtue of vested authority, I do confer upon him this Diploma. Signed Early E. W. Dorcer, Colonel, Air Corps

Members in the school were assigned to different Air Fields around the country to work as professional photographers for the Army. Howard Dull and I had the good fortune of being assigned to Luke Field near Phoenix, Arizona. With graduation certificates securely in hand, we boarded a train at Uncle Sam's expense and headed for our new home. Early in September 1941, we reported to the 90th Air Base Group under the command of a First Lieutenant, whom we had never heard of before, by the name of Barry Goldwater.

STATIONED AT LUKE FIELD

Howard Dull and I walked into the office of Lt. Barry Goldwater, saluted him and presented the proper documents. The Lieutenant, whom we regarded as just another officer, received us cordially, looked over our papers and gave us an assignment. We gave him a departing salute and went to our assigned quarters as proud soldiers in the Army Air Corps.

In the barracks, men of all shapes and sizes, and every conceivable disposition were unfolding army cots, making the beds for inspection, and sleeping. Some of these men seemed to be very bright while others seemed to border on the other end of the intellectual spectrum. Some were laughing and others went about their business very sober minded perhaps wondering why they had joined the Army. Some were nervously talking loud with every dialect scattered from across these United States.

Though we were all different and from many parts of this beloved nation, all had experienced the Great Depression, each had sworn to uphold the Constitution of the United States of America and defend our country against all enemies from within and without. To complete the small space that surrounded each cot, every man tided up his footlocker at the end of his bed. To cap off each soldier's area for his own pleasure, each man taped a picture of his girl friend, or some glamorous Hollywood female celebrity inside the lid of his footlocker. Every time we opened the top of the trunk, we could view scantily dressed Jean Harlow, Betty Grable or Carman Miranda. As these women looked back at us, men in their late teens and early twenties dreamed of many things.

It never crossed our minds that in the future we would be called a part of The Greatest Generation.

Because of personalities and ideologies, it is natural that we wished to associate with people who had like interests. For the same reason, we tolerated others, work with them but never become close friends with them. Howard and I had become close friends, and a young man from southern Oklahoma became a member of our small circle. His name was William Nelson, whom I called Nelly. Nelly was a quiet soldier with a winsome smile. His voice identified him as an Okie from the southeastern hills of his home state.

Howard wasn't as active in the nightlife as I was when we went into Phoenix. I had learned to dance pretty well in Oklahoma City when I attended the Arthur Murray Dance Studio. At the USO Canteen, I could do a fairly good job of 'cutting the rug' with the prettiest girls from high school and college who came to entertain the soldiers. We'd do the jitterbug, dance the waltz and the fox trot, hopping and swaying to the recorded music of Harry James and Tommy Dorsey and many other big bands of the time.

Though I never liked the taste of alcohol and my stomach would often reject it, I'd go to the bars, sit around a table and drink with a bunch of uniformed men while we told exotic lies about the women we had danced with and later dated.

Nelly didn't engage in such things for he had his heart set on a pretty lady from the "everlasting hills of Oklahoma." When the lady came to Phoenix, they were married in the Post Chapel accompanied by soldiers, dressed in their best uniforms, as the couple walked hand in hand beneath arched swords to the alter. It was very impressive.

All the time I was thinking of the high school girl in Oklahoma who had written the letter to me, and looking forward to my first furlough that was coming up in October only a few weeks away.

The photographers' duties on Luke Field were to take picture, with a 4 x 5 Speed Graphic camera, of personal on the base, jump in a Jeep and go anywhere an airplane was down and photograph the crash for investigators to study. These pictures were brought to the lab and developed. All were in black and white in those ancient days. After a while crews sort of specialized in certain areas of the work. Since motion picture cameras and still cameras had a tendency to wear out or damaged somehow, Howard Dull was put in charge of the camera repair shop. I didn't like to be confined to an office or shop, so I was given the job of making acquisitions for camera parts, film and other supplies. I passed the test to drive the big GI truck. I drove the truck to the warehouse where all orders were processed, and brought supplies back to the lab. That made it possible for me to get acquainted with more civilians as well as army personal. I learned that my real interest in life was dealing with and learning about people.

Sometime the pilots would take us up in an AT-6, a two-seater trainer plane. Perhaps the most thrilling ride ever was when the seasoned pilot flew up to Grand Canyon and flew down into the gapping ditch We marveled at those colorful, magnificent walls as we flew 150 miles an hour in the propeller driven machine.

In the compound, Lt. Goldwater did the necessary paper work in his office early in the morning. He was restless and desired to get outside among the soldiers, go where planes crashed to take pictures along side the enlisted photographers. Our commander was also, eager to fly the planes. The whole world learned latter that he was interested in both photography and flying. It was not unusual to see our company commander walking across the compound at a brisk pace, his frame straight as a steel rod. Often as he walked, an enlisted man would walk along side him and they would talk as friends. He made a great impact on every soldier and that is the reason we held him is such high esteem.

On at least one occasion, Lt. Goldwater invited the entire company of around 100 men to his estate in the suburbs of Phoenix. He gave us freedom to use his swimming pool, four hole golf course, tennis court and barbecue pit. It was one of those days, one does not soon forget.

I had no car but another man from Oklahoma did, so we planned our furloughs to start the same day. We decided to share expenses and take turns driving. We left Luke Field, anxious to get home. I was especially eager to meet Dorothy, my pen pal for the past several months.

Money was always in short supply so we drove through the night stopping only for gasoline and eating nothing hoping to save money. Just as the dawn began to break, we followed a truck hauling groceries. We were surprised when a wooden box filled with Fig Newtons fell from the truck onto the highway. Tires on the car screeched making black marks on the pavement. We jumped from the car, grabbed the box and ate Fig Newtons all the way to our destination. (I got sick, and have not eaten Fig Newtons since.)

The owner of the car, (I can't recall his name), dropped me off in Nicoma Park, a suburb of Oklahoma City, where my sister Jessie lived with her family. I was delighted to see Jessie, her husband, Raymond, and their young son, Kenneth. I desired to meet Dorothy who lived with her sister, Opal, in the suburb of Choctaw only five miles to the east. I phoned Dorothy to tell her where I was. With her permission, I hoped to come to see her within an hour. The eighteen-year-old high school senior was so nervous she could hardly respond. Finally, she said it would be all right for me to drop by.

After scrubbing the dead skin and sweat from by body in the shower, I tried to relax while eating the prepared evening meal. I was so nervous and excited setting down was next to impossible. Raymond loaned me the family '39 four-door Chevy. Twilight had crept over the communities when I slipped into the driver's seat to drive eastward. The headlights bore a hole through the darkness leading me to the home of the girl I'd been writing to for some time but had never met.

I was dressed in a khaki uniform with tan tie fixed in a four-in-hand knot and stuffed in my shirt. My hair was slicked down heavy with oil. When I knocked, Opal came to the door. Dorothy stood behind peeking over the left shoulder of her older sister. Opal invited me in, shook my hand in greeting and introduced me to Dorothy who extended her trembling hand and said "Hello" in a low, uncertain voice.

Opal was much more forward, a lady who was well adjusted in life, introduced me to her husband Talmage, her twelve-year-old daughter, Jo Francis, and her nine-year-old son, Calvin. Dorothy, who was destined to be valedictorian of her graduating class the next spring, was shy, standing alone and aloof from the rest of us. When I finally ask her to go riding in the car with me, she looked at Opal for permission. When her sister said, "I think that would be nice," my wife to be replied, "I guess it will be all right." By this time, the full moon had crept over the horizon to about 20 degrees giving the whole landscape a mellow glow. We drove in silence until she began to speak for the first time. She wanted to show me her school. I drove by the big red brick schoolhouse. She began to talk about her teachers, fellow students and the courses she was taking in a more relaxed mood, Dorothy ask, "Do you like the songs that are popular now?"

When told I thought they were great, she began to sing, *Three Little fishes, Little Sir Echo, As Time Goes By, Chattanooga Choo Choo* and many others. Dorothy knew every word of each song. I asked her where she learned to sing with such beauty and loveliness. She related, when she lived in the Tipton Orphan's Home, Brother Shotts formed a little trio of singers and she was one of them. The trio traveled over Oklahoma and Texas singing in churches and asking for donations during the Great Depression. This was necessary to keep the Home open for the children.

She told a joke they told on themselves in those days. This is it, "We bathed in Sweetwater and dressed in Plainview." Dorothy wore very thick glasses that detracted from her beauty and charm when she was singing.

After this first date, I spent some time with my parents in Ponca City and visiting Roy Essary.

Back at Luke Field, I continued in the routine until the latter part of November 1941. I had just turned 20 and two soldiers who owned a car invited me, and a twenty-seven year old Airman, to split the expenses traveling to Los Angeles. Each of us got a three-day pass starting Wednesday morning. With no duties on Saturday and Sunday, we had five days off. With 500 miles behind us, we landed in Los Angeles. This was my first visit to California. After securing hotel rooms, the two 24-year-olds took off in their car leaving me alone with the older guy. My roommate's idea of a vacation, was to get a jug of whiskey, lay around in the room until every drop was gone. I was determined that I wasn't going to stay with him. Striking out alone early the next morning, I wanted to visit sites in this city I'd only read about. On the streets of the strangest and largest city I'd ever been in, many questions had to be asked. By the middle of the day, I had found the Hollywood Bowl. There I sat in a seat and imagined a performance on the huge stage.

For a boy from the farm in the *pocket of perpetual poverty* during the Dust Bowl, I was having the adventure of my life and all alone. I can't remember all the sights I visited, but the one experience I shall never forget was seeing the Pacific Ocean for the first time. The sun was shining as bright as it ever had and the water stretched and stretched and stretched out to the west farther than my eyes could see. A gentle breeze was blowing endless rows of white caps that bounced against the sandy beach and disappeared. I stood, completely lost in astonishment, gazing at the miracles wonders of creation that lay before me.

I'd heard about the beautiful Santa Catalina Island and desperately wanted to see it. When I found a port that was taking vacationers there, I carefully counted my money and found I had enough for the fare. All alone, with people everywhere, I boarded the boat with many other passengers, and we began to sail westward. I don't believe I spoke to a single person on the 25-mile journey. I was excited to see the dolphins play around the boat. They dove deep into the salty water and thrust themselves up through the surface of the ocean time after time. They seemed to enjoy putting on a great performance for the spectators.

After we landed in the harbor of the island, I walked up and down the streets of the village looking into the windows of shops wishing to buy a souvenir but money was scarce and didn't dare. I wanted to ride in the glass bottom boats to see the other fish that inhabited the clear ocean waters. I kept reminding myself that I had to keep enough money to pay my share of the room rent and expenses for the return trip to Luke Field.

I hiked up the highest peak on the Island (that cost nothing), sat down on top to rest and spent the time surveying the Island and viewing the ocean with the incoming and outgoing boats.

The journey back to Los Angeles was just as enjoyable with the dolphins still doing their unbelievable tricks. Boarding the bus to take me to our hotel, I rode through the streets of Los Angeles gawking all the way. There I found the older soldier still nursing his bottle of booze. It wasn't long before the other two men came in. Rushing, we loaded the car and headed eastward racing to get back the base on time. The two men who owned the car occupied the front seat talking and laughing about the women they had seen. Being the youngest of the foursome, my place was in the back seat with the smelly drunk who hadn't taken a bath since we left our home Field.

The next morning after our return, I walked into Lt. Goldwater's office. With the customary salute, our company commander gave my orders. It was my turn to pull guard duty, four hours on and four hours off every day for the next month. This was not for punishment, it was the duty of privates. This beat pealing spuds and washing dishes on kp.

When December 6, 1941 rolled around, I was still on guard duty. Instead of standing post at some location on the Field, I'd been "promoted" to guarding prisoners from 4 AM to 8 AM. I had been on duty. When an armed soldier came to relieve me at eight o'clock December 7, I was dead tired. Finding a cot in the office of the guardhouse, I fell into deep sleep. While snoozing, a soldier violently shook me awake shouting in my face, "The Japs have bombed Pearl Harbor!"

Without rising from the cot, I responded, "You're crazy," pulled the GI blanket over my head hoping to return to sleep.

"Honest! No kidding! We've been listening to the radio. And the commentators keep saying President Roosevelt will declare war on Japan soon."

The next day the entire world sat by a radio listening in stunned silence to FDR's *Day of Infamy* speech that plunged the United States of America into the most devastating war of all - World War II.

The top brass in Washington and the Military were greatly concerned about the possibility the Japanese could bring their aircraft carriers close enough to the West Coast to bomb the military bases inland as far as Phoenix. Now, instead of four hours on and four off, we guardsmen were put on duty for an undetermined length of time. On a moonlit night in December, I had stood guard for 22 hours straight. I sang, I danced, I did military maneuvers with my rifle - any thing to stay awake.

We'd been warned that sleeping on guard duty during time of war was a very serious offence and subject to court martial. About midnight, I saw an unbelievable sight. A rainbow in its entire splendor arched across the starlit sky in the mellow softness of the light of the moon. For some reason, this sighting gave hope for me and for our nation.

In early December, America was at war on two fronts - Germany and Japan. Doubts were rampant. Were we spreading ourselves to thin? As unprepared as we were, could we win wars on two sides of the world? Could these kids who grew up in the Great Depression, many of them mal-nourished and deprived, do the job expected of soldiers, airmen, sailors and marines?

Could American young men who delivered newspapers, did small jobs and worked at anything to keep alive challenge and defeat German and Japanese military men who had been in training since they were little boys? We simply didn't know. We bowed our necks, straightened our backs and with complete determination, went forth to meet the enemy fully resolved to do our dead level best. This was true of the civilian population as well as the military. Every aspect of American life joined into a cohesive force, as never before or after, willing to give life and limb, if necessary, to keep our cherished freedoms alive.

Men of every color, nationality and religion crowded into recruit stations across this broad land of ours, to sign up for military duty, for the duration, putting their lives on the line to keep America whole and free. New military bases and new factories to manufacture weapons of war began spring up everywhere from the Atlantic to the Pacific shores. Men and women moved from their homes to factory towns and cities to work for the common purpose, to keep supplies of war rolling off the assembly lines. That's when Dad and Mother moved from Ponca City, Oklahoma to Wichita, Kansas to work in the Boeing Aircraft Plant.

Songwriters like Irving Berlin wrote patriotic songs to spur us forward. These songs were played by orchestras like the Glen Miller Band and danced to by couples in every small town, city and military camp where citizens were stationed. Artists were busy painting pictures that announced our cause loud and clear: We are Americans and we can defeat any enemy who dares to take away our God-given liberties. Business men, women and many celebrities left their offices and studios to go on the stump encouraging citizens to buy war bonds to keep the noble effort moving forward. Youngsters in high school, junior high and elementary schools got in on the act by collecting iron and metal foils for the war effort. Victory gardens sprang up in back yards, vacant lots and farms across this dedicated nation. Everyone put his shoulder to the wheel and pushed with all his might.

Men came into the Army Air Corps in such numbers that soldiers who had enlisted months before were promoted to higher rank hoping to direct the new recruits. Within a few months, I jumped from buck private to staff sergeant. It was a matter of learning on the job. In early 1942, women were welcomed into the army to form the Women's Auxiliary Corps - WACS.

During this time, soldiers continued going to the Canteen dancing with the girls who came there after completing their shift for the war effort. I began dating a Phoenix native. She was a beautiful, young Baptist lady who loved to dance. We were very compatible partners on the dance floor. We had exchanged 8 x 10 portraits. Her picture set beside Dorothy's on my footlocker. The men in the barracks teased me for having pictures of both women displayed. I took their teasing in a good manner, for I felt I was getting up in the world. I thought this is what Clark Gable and Bogart did - having a girl in different towns.

Well, my bubble was soon burst for I made a fool of myself by attempting things that neither lady liked. The Phoenix lady got another boy friend and gave my 8 x 10 portrait to him. This new soldier brought the picture to me, threw in on my bunk and said, "Your girl friend ain't your girl friend no more. She said she never wanted to see you again." A few days later, I received a letter from Dorothy saying she wanted to break off our correspondence. My ego dropped likes an iron ball thrown into a bottomless pit. What was a man with a wounded pride to do? Still wanting to act like the male movie stars on the big screen, to solve my problems I went to a bar in the city, sat on a stool and ordered a bottle of whiskey wishing to drown my troubles. I poured a glass of the brew, played with the glass while I sat on the bar stool thinking all the while. Finally, I said, "This is ridiculous. If I'm not man enough to take what has happened to me and solve my own problems without this stuff, I'm not much of a man."

The bartender came over and asked, "What's the matter. Don't you like your drink?"

I shoved the bottle and the glass toward him and responded, "You can give this damned stuff to some other poor bastard. I don't need it." With that announcement, I walked out of the bar never to return. I showed the independent spirit I'd been taught all my life. The spirit is: If you have a problem, do everything possible to solve it on your own, and ask for help from others only as a last resort. These nice ladies taught me a very valuable lesson: If you want a good woman, respect her and treat her like a lady.

In the spring of '42, the Army started building Walker Air Base south of Roswell, New Mexico to train student bombardiers. It was a foregone conclusion that crashes would occur and pictures needed to be taken. Regulations called for all personal to be photographed. Photographers would be needed to fly with the student bombardiers to take footage of how near their bombs dropped to the shack in the middle of the circle on the ground that was 500 feet in diameter. The practice bombs were shaped like a real bomb. Only these bombs were filled with sand. A small charge was placed in the fin section to detonate when it hit the ground signaling with a puff of smoke where the bomb landed.

Howard Dull and I, alone with others in the photo section, were transferred to Walker. When we arrived, the streets were already laid out, but they were unpaved, dusty passageways. Periodically water trucks traveled the streets sprinkling water over them to keep the dust from irritating the personnel and so the dust could not obscure the sight of automobile drivers. This cut down on our work, for all automobile wrecks also had to be photographed for inspectors to determine the cause of the accidents.

When we arrived at the new air base, barracks were only covered with tarpaper. The only permanent building was the photo lab.

As stated before, every patriotic American strove to do his part to speed victory over our determined enemy. Some citizens who were to old, or needed in the war effort in civilian capacity or disabled were denied the privilege of wearing the uniform for Uncle Sam during the War. Yet most found something they could do to protect the freedom we enjoyed. Such was the Hayes family who lived in a small wood frame house on East Fifth Street across the railroad tracks in Roswell. Wishing to enhance the moral of the recently arrived airmen, forty-two-year-old Mrs. Hayes phoned the new Air Base stating it would be her pleasure to prepare Sunday lunch for four or five airmen. The personnel officer was glad to accommodate her and sent Howard, me and a couple other guys to her home on a Sunday after church. After we passed inspection, we caught a bus to the Hayes home. Mr. and Mrs. Hayes were wonderful hosts, the lunch was delicious and all went well. Their lovely, friendly 19-year-old daughter, Myrtle, caught the eye of each soldier.

It seemed miraculous, and heaven arranged, because the rapport of the Hayes family and the men from the base was instantaneous. We were invited back many times. (We all remained close friends until the death of everyone but me.) It wasn't long before Myrtle and Howard Dull were going together on dates. I may have tried to horn in on their relationship, but I had not forgot Dorothy back in Oklahoma.

On an autumn Sunday, after we ate lunch at the Hayes home, Myrtle suggested we go horseback riding in the country. She persuaded one of her local girl friends to ride with us. On a very beautiful afternoon while riding rented ponies down a country lane, Myrtle's friend saw a mulberry tree loaded with ripe fruit She expressed, with enthusiasm, her taste for wild berries.

The berries were high in the branches and could not be reached by sitting in the saddle. I was in a khaki uniform wishing to impress the new girl. While Howard held the reins of my horse, I stood up in the saddle, plucked the sweet fruit from the high branches and handed the berries to the beautiful young lady. All went well except unknown to me some berries fell, lodging in the seat of my saddle. I took my position in the saddle, and we rode into town. After turning in the horses, someone suggested we go bowling.

Acting the part of a smart aleck, I heard people giggling every time I took the ball to throw it down the alley. Finally, Howard called me over and asked, "Do you know what is on the seat of your pants?"

"No. Why?"

"Maybe you ought to go into the restroom and look."

In the restroom, I discovered why people giggled. A huge blotch of purple stain from the mulberries covered much of the seat of my khaki pants. I did not return to friends who were bowling. Instead I left, caught a bus back to the base never turning my back to any person I happened to encounter on the way home. Many rough edges needed scrapped off my personality and character. I continued to learn the hard way.

After about a year of working in and out of the photo lab in Walker Air Field, I began hankering to fly the airplanes we had been photographing for almost two years. There were so many pilots killed or wounded in the European and Pacific theaters of war, the army relaxed the requirements to become flying cadets. Up until this time two years of college was required before one could be considered for cadet training. I had only a high school diploma. If anybody could pass the required test, he became qualified for consideration for flight training.

I went to the commanding officer and told him my desire. He said, "You must go through the chain of command." While deciding if I really wanted to go through with all the red tape and tests, Dorothy phoned me saying some of her friends were coming to Clovis, New Mexico on business. They knew I was stationed about 100 miles to the south. She wanted to come see me. Her friends didn't have time to come to Roswell, but perhaps I could get a pass and travel to Clovis to be with her. I assured her I could ride a bus on the weekend to visit. We saw each other in Clovis and worked out our differences. Her beautiful voice sang many of the never-to-be-forgotten songs played by Tommy Dorsey, Harry James and Glen Miller.

This orphan girl, who had been kicked around most of her life, began talking about marriage. I wasn't sure I was ready for a lifetime commitment. If such a commitment were to take place, I certainly had to make more money than at present. These thoughts may have been a continuing factor in deciding to try out for flight training.

I went through the procedures all prospective cadets went through. Took the physical and passed. Took the written test and failed. Disappointed but determined. Studied when off duty for a couple of months, took the test a second time and passed.

No longer a member of the enlisted men of the army, I was sent home on furlough to await an opening in the cadet ranks.

After seeing Dorothy in Oklahoma City, I went on to Wichita where my parents had moved and Dad was working for the Boeing Company making B-17 Bombers. Dorothy got a leave of absence from her job as a receptionist for a foot doctor and came to Wichita. We were together for almost a week before we went to a carnival. Years later I wrote the following poem to commemorate the occasion:

We lived in a different world
Back in nineteen-forty three.
Allies were fighting the Axis,
And none of us was free.
Battles raged in the Pacific,
The cities in Europe were dark.
I took my Choctaw Maiden
To a Wichita amusement park.
I was a likely soldier that
Had learned a thing or two.
Proud of my rank and station,
Wearing the Air Corps blue. *
Her dress was plain and simple,
A red ribbon was in her hair.
Her bright green eyes sparkled;
Glowing lights were everywhere.
Charmed by her schoolgirl wit,
I loved to hear her sing.
Before I returned to war,
We thought we'd have a fling.
Carnival barkers were crying
Of strange, exotic shows,
A man we'd never seen before
With pig-like feet and nose.
What caught my lady's eye
Was the great big Ferris wheel.
From the top and going down
She'd get a thrilling feel.
We were holding hands and laughing
As the Ferris wheel went round.
Suddenly the lights went out,
There wasn't a single sound.
We were stranded on the very top,
Transfixed in a rocking seat.

Darkness was all around us,
The whole world at our feet.
The moon was shining bright,
Every star was in its place.
The day was Good Friday,
We were bathed in heaven's grace.
Could ever there be a better time
To ask for a maiden's hand?
Nervous, I took from my pocket
A golden, diamond band.
If you'll take this ring and wear it
Through every joy and strife,
I'll be your faithful husband;
You can be my loving wife.
Surprise filled her eyes.
When she gained composure,
She hugged my neck and kissed me
And held me ever closer.
She gave me her dainty hand.
The ring slipped on her finger.
We heard voices down below,
We had no time to linger.
Our engagement was complete,
On it, we'd placed our seal.
The engineer turned on the lights
And started the Ferris Wheel.

* Blue uniforms were not issued at that time.

SIX MONTHS FROM BASICS FLIGHT TRAINING TO FLYING THE B-17

After our engagement, I was ordered to Kelley Field in San Antonio for officer training and ground school. Recruit camp was tough, but it was nothing compared to cadets. The officers and upper classmen made it absolutely miserable. Every aspect was hurry, hurry, hurry. When we were not in ground school, which was tough enough, we were running here and running there; changing from sweaty fatigues to spick-and-span uniforms for inspection.

In ground school, they warned us, "If you drop a pencil and have to pick it up, you've already lost a semester's work."

With guards standing over us, we policed the area by filling a gallon bucket with gravel, carrying it a certain distance and dumping it in a pile. We repeated this "useless exercise" until a guard yelled at the top of his voice, "FALL IN!"

We marched under the blazing sun in high humidity until our olive drabs were drenched with sweat. The drill instructor called us every uncomplimentary name he'd learned from the DI before him.

When the drillmaster yelled, "FALL OUT!" cadets ran for the barracks as if the demons of hell were chasing them. We had five minutes to shower and dress in clean khakis and white gloves. On other occasions, upper classmen made us stand at attention against a wall until an outline of our bodies was left by perspiration.

While standing at attention, another senior would place a lighted cigarette so close to the nose you could feel the heat.

If you moved an eyeball or flinched a muscle, you were forced to run around the drill field half-a-dozen times. This kind of treatment went on day after day. When the lights went out at ten, every soldier slept soundly until early reveille the next morning.

I hated this regiment for it all seemed like nonsense to me. Finally it dawned on me that the top brass in the army thought all this was necessary for the men to learn to take orders regardless of circumstances or sacrifice to ourselves, particularly in combat situations.

After eight weeks of this training, some of us were sent to a small makeshift airfield on a rancher's land near the small town of Stamford, Texas. All the buildings showed signs of hasty construction, and the runways were of sod scrapped off by a bulldozer.

I was one of most who had never flown an airplane before. Beside all the discipline, ground school and officer training, we were expected to learn to fly the plywood PT-19 and pass all the tests in the air and in ground school within eight weeks.

Since I had been in the Army Air Corps for over two years and had a staff sergeant rating, I had privileges and made more money than most of the cadets. Dorothy learned of these privileges, and that some of the wives followed their husbands. She wanted to get married. After talking it over by phone and letters, she quit her job in Oklahoma City and caught a bus to Stamford.

While she was enroute, all cadets were quarantined to the base for two weeks because of a polio scare. I couldn't meet her, and Dorothy didn't know a soul in Stamford. Being resourceful, she went to church and told the members of her plight. A family, by the name of Luck, invited her to stay with them. It was a relief to me to know she was in safe hands.

The cadets couldn't go to town, and the wives and girl friends couldn't come on the base. The commanding officer did allow us to meet the ladies at a barbed wire fence that surrounded the airfield. Under the boiling Texas sun in mid-summer, we met the girls at the fence. They were on the outside and we were on the inside with the fence between. To keep our ladies from sweltering in the heat, we brought blankets and pillows. We tied the blankets to the barbed wire and the ladies held the other end over their heads for shade. The girls sat on our pillows to protect them from the over abundance of grass burs. Under these conditions, we could hold hand, but no kissing. Little was known about polio in those days, and the army didn't want to be responsible for the ladies or the cadets getting the disease.

At the end of two weeks, the restrictions were lifted, and Air Base personnel were given a six-hour pass from 4 PM to 10 PM. The news of the announcement spread like a forest fire in a high wind. The base and the small town of about 2500 souls were excited. Merchants prepared for the invasion of army cadets that had been confined for too long.

Dorothy had heard of the news and was waiting when I phoned. A whirlwind of activity was put into play for us. My future wife, with Dorothy Luck, the daughter of the people my Dorothy was staying with, rushed to Anson, the county seat, to get the marriage license and wedding rings. She got the local minister to perform the ceremony.

On August 17, 1943 at 6:30 on a beautiful afternoon five of us cadets, all clad in khaki uniforms, marched into the home of Mr. and Mrs. Luck. Dorothy was dressed in a white dress borrowed from her sister, Bonnie. The minister was ready with Bible in hand. Several new friends from the church were present. The minister said the magic words, the knot were tied and Dorothy and I became husband and wife.

The unorthodox situation still called for a wedding shower for Dorothy. She received a few homemade dishtowels: and that was it. After the short wartime reception, Dorothy and I walked two blocks, in the early evening darkness, to the only hotel in the small town where a room had been reserved for us.

After we became better acquainted, I walked Dorothy back to the Luck home, caught a bus and arrived at the barracks a few minutes before lightsout. The cadets were waiting. They were unmerciful while giving me the third degree. There wasn't much sleeping on the army cots that night. Come morning light, we all stood for dawn reveille.

After the wedding, the $10,000 GI life insurance was transferred from Dad and Mom to Dorothy. Many other changes were made. When I was dog tired after a sixteen-hour day, Dorothy would call me almost every night saying she was lonely with nothing to do. She wanted me to come to town and be with her. It seemed not to matter that I had a job of learning to fly, ground school, marching in parades and a dozen other things that had to be done every day.

All this put an extra strain on me. It became harder for me to concentrate on school, officer training and flying. Pressures built up to the point that I was just about to washout of the pilot program. The pilot instructor was thoroughly disgusted with me. After a few more foul-ups, the instructor said as he swore, "I'm sending you up for a final check ride. If you fail the test, you idiot, we're gonna drum you right out of the cadet Corps!"

The test pilot and I climbed into the little single engine plane with no canopy. Over the noisy motor, he screamed through a rubber tube from the back seat, "Take this thing up to ten thousand feet." After making sure, everything was checked safe before take off, I reved the motor and ascended toward the heavens. When we reached the assigned altitude, the officer yelled through the tube again, "Turn this thing on its back. Let's see if you can fly it that way. I flipped the plane over, and began flying upside down, each of us had on a parachute, but there was nothing holding us in the seat of that flying machine but a seat belt. Looking down toward the ground at that altitude was frightening. Fright had to be forgotten. There were more important things to do. We hadn't flown in this position but a short time until the motor died because it was fed by gravity instead of a motor. I flipped the plane right side up and the motor started ginning again.

Again, a message was telegraphed to me from the back seat, "See that landing field down there?"

"Yes! Sir!" I shouted.

"I want you to cut the motor, make the usual pattern and land this plane in front of that hanger. You had better not give it another drop of gas. If you make a mistake you're gone bye, bye. Got it?"

"Yes! Sir!" I screamed loud and clear.

While the officer filled out the tally sheet, I put the PT-19 into a shallow glide. We circled the field, while keeping a sharp eye out for other planes that might be in the area. My concentration was completely focused on every maneuver. I brought the plane down in a zigzag path until we were about 500 feet above the ground. We flew a dogleg pattern, lined up with the dirt runway, landed with only a slight bump and stopped directly in front of the hanger where my flight instructor was waiting for us. The test pilot gave me a good grade and the instructor said, "Good job." This was about the sixth week of learning to pilot an airplane.

One young cadet was killed along with his test pilot when the plane crashed while on a similar flight. Such incidents caused one to ponder.

Occasionally I had a few moments to think about Dad and Mother and my brothers and sisters, wondering where they were and what they were doing. I thought of my youth on the rented farm in New Mexico, the Great Depression and the Dust Bowl. My experiences as a boy taught me self-discipline and to meet with courage all the hardships life dealt. I thought of the free public schools and our nation of free people that gave citizens the opportunity to rise out of poverty and do what they set their hearts to accomplish. These moments were certainly fleeting but they always warmed my heart giving me the determination to succeed.

When we graduated from the Stamford Air Base, our class 44-B was shipped to Majors Army Air Field near Greenville, Texas. The wives and girl friends followed by bus. Dorothy arrived in Greenville about midnight. It was a cold night in late October, and again she didn't know a soul. At the bus station, she got to a pay phone, found a preacher's name in the directory and called him. He got out of bed wondering who was calling at that hour. She spilled out her needs by saying, "Every room in town is filled. I'm following my husband from air base to air base. I wonder if you could help me out."

V. E. Howard, a businessman and a wellknown radio evangelist, considered her request and after a short silence said, "I'll be right down to pick you up."

Early the next morning Dorothy made a deal with the Howards. Mr. and Mrs. Howard owned a jewelry store where they both worked. They had three young children, two boys and a girl. Since baby sitters were hard to find during the war, it was agreed that Dorothy could stay in a room in their home if she agreed to care for their children while they worked. It was a deal.

At Majors Army Air Field, the cadets were introduced to the Basic Training. We were to fly an all-metal B-13 airplane with a canopy, two-way radio and 450 horsepower Pratt and Whitney motor. This was big time stuff for us, and we were eager to get in the pilot's seat. Ground school and officer training continued at an accelerated pace. These were blended in with all the other activities. Since I had been a photographer, I was asked to be on the staff that prepared and edited the book called, *Basic Leg,* depicting personnel and events while at Majors. We could purchase the book at the end of our training there. With all the work on the field, and Dorothy wanting me to be with her as much as possible, I had to decline the offer.

No time was squandered before we were put to work learning, learning, learning new stuff every day until our heads seemed loaded to the brim. Could anything more be poured into our brains? I began to doubt. In addition to all this, we were introduced to night flying which was another ball game. We were warned of vertigo when the lights on the ground can be mistaken for the stars in the heavens. This could be most confusing to the new pilot. The new pilot must learn to rely on the instruments in the airplane. Two student pilots, Aviation Cadet Millen S. Marshalek and Aviation Cadet Walter F. Bigelow, were killed in basic training. The book we received at the end of basic training was dedicated to them.

While flying solo, we had to land on unfamiliar airfields some of which were nothing more than a dirt runway scrapped off in a pasture by a bulldozer. One time I was ordered to land on such a field. I flew for half-an-hour looking for the strip on the prairie. Couldn't find it. I contacted the officer by radio that was stationed on the ground beside the strip telling him I was lost. He gave the direction and heading to find the place. I still could not find it and had to radio him of my inability to locate him. I dreaded to tell him for fear I'd get another eating out when I'd already received more than I wanted. The officer spoke kindly and told me to fly down low enough to read a sign on some railroad station. I buzzed Hillsboro, Texas at an altitude of about 50 feet and radioed the officer my location. He replied giving the number of the highway to fly over, and that he was sitting on the left side of the highway about ten miles out. He was more understanding the most flight officers. Perhaps he remembered the mistakes he made when learning to fly.

Ground school and officer training were getting more complicated and technical. Could I possible learn all they expected? I reasoned, if other men had done it, so could I.

Dorothy wanted me to be with her more for she said she was lonely. Other wives got together while they waited for their husbands to come in to be with them. Dorothy didn't want to do that, so she sat alone waiting for me to have a few hours off. She kept busy taking care of the three Howard children. At night when the parents came home from work, she had little to do.

When the single men on the base had time off, if not in town, they gathered around in the barracks and talk about flying. They got efficient in using their hands for airplanes to demonstrate the maneuvers they practiced while in flight. They were a proud and eager bunch of men wanting to finish cadet training, get their wings and the Lieutenant bars and ship overseas to join the Germans or Japanese in dog fights. I never developed the intense interest in flying they had.

At the end of basic training, the officers talked among themselves to discuss each cadet's aptitudes, grades in various studies and their ability to fly. These officers had to determine whether each cadet was promoted to fighter pilot or bomber pilot training in advanced schooling at the next level The officers decided that I was best fitted for advanced training as a bomber pilot. Several of us were sent to the new Army Air Base near Frederick, Oklahoma where we were scheduled to fly two motor A-13s and A-17s. We called these planes, covered with aluminum, "double breasted cubs." Perhaps your imagination can tell you why.

These planes had more instruments on the panel. We had to learn and use them in flight. They also maneuvered in a different manner than the single engine planes we flew in basic. It was altogether a new learning experience and a new challenge.

I had been with Cadets Victor W Fincannon, Francis X. Fink, William M. Flanagan, Alton S. Emerson, Loyd A. Extrom, Nathan B. Faulkner, Jr., and Robert. J. Fleming four months. When you sleep in the same barracks, study together, work together, fly together for several months and see two more of your class mates get killed in training, you don't forget them easily. You don't want to forget them for they become very close to you. They may have a different religion, philosophy and a life style than you, but still you love them and want to keep their memory alive.

With four months of training behind, some of us began to think we were hot pilots. Sometime two cadets flying side by side in the trainer plane decided to fly south over the Red River into Texas. They would fly past Vernon to Lake Kemp. To some student pilots it was a delight to fly skimming over the water only a few feet and frighten the fishermen. It was sport, according to some student pilots to give the plane full power, quickly pull up the nose making the rear wheel strike the water. Some time the student pilots spotted a farmer peacefully driving his tractor while plowing his field. They'd "dive bomb" the farmer as he jumped under his tractor wondering why those young smart-alecks wanted to scare the living daylights out of a tax payer that was paying their way to learn to fly.

On an occasion, while flying, I spotted a farm and decided to "strafe" it. I flew down about 50 feet above the terrain. When I passed over the chicken pen, those poor critters were so frightened they scrambled in all directions including up. In their flight, they almost got high enough to reach the airplane. One time of that was enough, for I didn't want to be among the dead cadets.

It had been only eight months since we started officers training in San Antonio, and only six months since we began flight training near Stamford. Now we were ready to graduate as officers and fullfledged pilots in the United States Army Air Corps. After much tension and sweat, we were privileged to wear the officers uniform, the coveted silver wings and the shiny gold bars of a second lieutenant. All the cadets looked forward eagerly to the day of graduation.

All but two of our number managed to graduate from advanced training. The bodies of the deceased cadets, who didn't make it, were sent home for proper burial. Wives of the living were looking forward to pinning wings on the brand new officer uniforms of their husbands and gold bars on their shoulders. All but Dorothy. A few days before the final ceremony, Dorothy decided she had to go back to Oklahoma City to visit her sisters. She was absent for the grand occasion, and a fellow officer pinned the hard-earned wings and bars on my uniform.

On the day of the big ceremony and before we left for our respective homes, another "shave tail" and I thought we should go into the captain's office about some small matter. Considering ourselves as fellow officers, we marched in proudly. After the customary salute, we relaxed. We relaxed so completely that my companion casually sat on the corner of the ranking officer's desk. Our superior officer was irritated, and barked in a voice loud and clear, "Attention!" We snapped to instinctively. Our records as officers already had a smear on them.

A few days of furlough followed. I met Dorothy in Oklahoma City, and we caught a commercial plane to Wichita to visit Dad and Mother. When Mother saw me in the new officer's uniform, she was surprised. Looking at me in perfect innocence, and noticing the staff sergeant stripes were missing, she asked, "Son, what happened to the stripes on your sleeves?" I tried to explain that I was no longer an enlisted men, that I'd been promoted to an officer. I'm not sure she ever understood or cared. Either way, she loved me and was proud of my army service.

By this time, twin brothers, Ray and Raymond, had joined the Navy. Jay and Charles were the only ones left at home out of the ten siblings.

After a short leave from duty, I was sent to San Marcus, Texas to fly student navigators cross country to hone their skills. We flew twin-engine planes to various parts of the United States. From San Marcus to El Paso were the wideopen, treeless spaces of West Texas. I was surprised by the barren country that could be seen from the air. On our Ariel maps, for checkpoints, there were marked trees and windmills. These served us well for when we saw one by dead reckoning, we knew where we were.

Dorothy and I begin going to church regularly when possible. Orville Filbeck preached there while working on his doctors degree at the University of Texas. We became friends with him and his wife Marie. Their pre-school son delighted us. When we assembled on Sunday Morning, to take Communion, Orville insisted that I help with the Lord's Supper. Realizing my life style at the time, I felt uncertain, unworthy and that I shouldn't be serving in that way. Nevertheless, I carried through with the assignment.

After only a few weeks at the San Marcus Air Base, I was ordered to report to the Air Base near Alexandria, La. where my B-17 crew was formed for training and future duty in the European Theater of Operation. After only six months flight training in much smaller planes, we were given the task of learning to fly the four-motor B-17 bomber that played such a large part in winning the war against the Axis.

Dorothy and I rode to Alexandria with Lt. Gidcom and his wife, who owned a car. In our new officer uniforms decorated with shining insignias that were plainly visible for all to see, we were eager to begin training in one of the largest planes that ruled the air

The wives were eager to get settled. Where? They did not know. By this time, they were experienced in finding a place to stay in those crowded times and didn't seemed concerned.

Our crew of ten men was brought together by higherups in the army who had studied our temperaments, our abilities to work as a team and to make sure each member of the crew could do his assigned job under the stress of combat. We were to train as a unit, learn to respect and depend on one another Like any team, whether preparing to participate in sports or in combat, we had to learn to trust every man to occupy his station and do a creditable job. Each man had to learn his particular work and be efficient in it when the chips were down. We were to train together, often eat together, sleep in the same barracks and practically live together for the next few mouths.

Our crew was made up of the following men:

Our pilot was Robert W. Kaub from Los Angeles, California. Bob was 21, a serious young man who smiled frequently, never seemed to loose his cool, seemed cut out to lead men. He joined in the fun but never got loud like the rest of us were prone to do. Before long, he got the hang of the big bomber. He soon became an excellent pilot that we always trusted to do the right thing while in the air. Bob was single and concentrated completely on the job of flying. I was married and had other things to think about. I readily conceded that Bob was the better pilot.

I was co-pilot of the crew: Leslie Eugene Fooks, from Oklahoma City, whose adopted hometown was Ponca City, Oklahoma. Gene, as I like to be called, was trying to find himself; making a transition from a serious, independent youth to a loud mouth whose language was an item he would never want his Mother to hear. His job was backup to Robert and to do a hundred little things our pilot didn't have time to do. With all his faults, I think our very efficient leader trusted his judgments

Our navigator was Thomas F. Cavanagh from Staten Island, New York. Tom was 21, full of life but somewhat subdued. He used oneliners to make us laugh and was always eager to enter in on the jolly times.

Our bombardier was Charles S. Grover from Alton, Ill. Charles was 20, and if a party were in progress, he put life into it. He was a jolly guy that every one liked and desired his company. He and Cavanagh became friends, and were often together when off duty.

The four-crew members mentioned above were commissioned officer. The six that follow were non-coms or enlisted men.

Our engineer was Richard O. Wright from Detroit, Michigan. As I recall, Richard was 23 or 24. He was quiet and seemed to be forever studying the mechanics of our plane even when he was relaxing. He was very good at his job. He proved worthy of our trust many times.

Our radio operator was Frank Howell from Michigan. Frank was a friendly man in his mid twenties but, from my point of view, he was hard to really know. He knew his job and was able to send and receive messages on that dit-dot-dit-dot contraption as well as the next fellow. He kept our radios in top-notch condition as long as we had electricity.

Our armament man was Cecil Raley from Enid, Oklahoma. Cecil was overweight and in his mid-twenties. He was very knowledgeable about all armaments on the plane. He saw that our bombs were loaded properly. Our twenty 50 mm guns were always clean, polished and ready to fire at the enemy when challenged.

The gunner on our plane was Roscoe L. Overton from Indiana. He was slender and taller than most of us and I think in his late twenties. Working closely in conjunction with Raley, they made a good team. I got the idea that sometime he wondered about the foolishness of some of the younger members of our crew. Nevertheless, he fit in very well.

Another slender member of our team was Robert M. Lee, the tail gunner, from Delco, N. C. Robert was also older than most of us. He was quiet and seemed to tolerate some of the antics of his younger associates. He was trained to wiggle his slender body through a narrow passage to the tail gun, lying flat on his belly in cramped quarters to guard against enemy planes attempting to creep up on our tail and destroy us. He was a good man.

Last and least in size was Roy. G. Munooy from Tennessee. I think Roy was only 18 and was a little over five feet tall weighing around 110. His magnetic smile on his boyish face drew all of us to him. His small body fit comfortably into the ball turret where he manned two guns to keep the German fighters from coming up from beneath and eliminating us. He was well adapted for the position.

Though it has been over sixty years since I have seen any of these airmen, I can still see their smiles, hear they voices, listen to their jokes and read each of their characteristics when we were off duty. I remember their serious dedication when in the air ready to meet the enemy with guns blazing. You can't forget, and don't want to forget, men in whom you trust your life, and they protect you by exposing themselves to grave danger and all this with uncommon valor and undaunted courage.

It should be remembered these airmen, these men, along with millions of other service men and women, were sons and daughters of the unparalleled Great Depression. It was during this time these service personnel were growing up. Citizens were losing fortunes over night, families illegally hitched rides on freight trains crossing this nation looking for work. Proud men in expensive suits, who once owned profitable companies, were reduced to poverty, sought any help that was offered to feed, clothe and house their families It was certainly hard times.

Yet, despite all the hardships of youth, these men and women heeded the call of a beleaguered nation when their homland was threatened. They went forth in time of peril, with minimal training and defeated, against all odds, two enemies far from the shores of their native land, on opposites sides of the world. These young citizens offered their very lives, and many paid the ultimate price, to preserve a way of life, the Four Freedoms, the free enterprise system that had not been so kind to them.

Why? Because they trusted the democratic way and had hopes, believing, if given time, the system could work for the benefit of all

It was around 1 August 1944, and we were near the end of our training in the B-17. On a night flight over Louisiana, we flew into a thunderstorm. Bolts of lightening were flashing all around us, hitting the plane causing St. Elmo's fire to flash across our windshield. The updrafts and downdrafts tossed our plane, with ten men and all the armament aboard, around like a ping-pong ball. As we flew at about 30,000 feet a downdraft would sling us down to 28,000, then an updraft would fling us up to 32,000 feet. We thought we were goners a time or two. This experience was profitable for us, for we learned the durability of the plane assigned to us. She could take much more punishment than we realized. That was the flight that we gained much more confidence in the B-17.

It had been one year since I begin flying the plywood, single engine PT-19 without a canopy near Stamford, Texas. Now with all flight training behind us, and as members of a trusted crew, we received written orders to report to Lincoln, Nebraska. There we would receive orders to fly across the Atlantic prepared for combat missions over Europe.

Dorothy went back to Oklahoma City to be near her sisters while I was overseas. Traveling to Lincoln, my mind went back, a little more than eight years, to the rented farm in the pocket of perpetual poverty. I pictured myself as a barefoot boy running wild over the prairie, the escarpment and going to the one room school learning to read, write, add and subtract under the tutelage of Mrs. White. I saw Dad struggling, trying to make a living for his growing family during those awful Dust Bowl days. I reviewed in my mind the children at school I played marbles with, the farm families, the ranchers and the cowboys they employed.

A motion picture of the action appeared on the screen if my mind. I saw clearly the sad day when we loaded the old used furniture into Mr Kerr's truck with Joooio and five of us boys crowded into the bed of the truck with the furniture. As we drove down the lane, with dust boiling all around us, I continued to wave goodbye to my big black dog, Towser that had been my constant companion for many years in my childhood.

However, enough, enough of reminiscing. It was time for a disciplined mind to look forward to the adventures that lay ahead.

AFTER A DELAY, WE HEADED FOR WAR IN EUROPE

"We've got to fly out of here early in the morning," our flight commander roared as he slammed his fist down on the doctor's desk.

"That co-pilot on the Kaub crew is not going anywhere until we check him out. He's a sick man, and it will take at least three days," the doctor responded with equal determination.

The Colonel stood straight and tall, stating emphatically as he clenched his teeth, "Orders from General Hap Arnold have already been cut and sent down to me. The flight I'm in charge of is taking off for England tomorrow morning come hell or high water."

The Doctor responded, "Lt. Leslie E. Fooks is in the hospital right now. He's not going anywhere until we make sure he's okay to fly. You can take the rest of your flight and go without this man. He's not leaving until I say so."

It is assumed the Colonel phoned the General and got permission to take the flight eastward with nine instead of ten B-17s crews the next morning before sunrise. I was stuck in a hospital bed with a high fever and energy level far below par. When Lt. Kaub and the rest of our crew came to see me, I apologized to them for I knew all of us were disappointed because of the delay. Each of the crew said, "That's okay. We'll fly when you get well."

Three days later the Doctor came in my room to say, "You were just exhausted from over work and heavy responsibilities.

I'm releasing you to fly, but I want you to take it easy until you regain your strength."

New orders were cut for us. When all the Army paper work was finished, each member of our crew, wearing full flight gear, took his station in a brand new B-17. I was especially proud because I kept thinking of my Dad who helped build this plane. Lt. Kaub reved the four motors making sure they were warmed up and ready for flight. Taxing out to the runway, he talked to the tower making sure all was clear for takeoff. Lined up with the runway, he pushed the four throttles forward with his right hand. We were on our way to do our part in the hot war in Europe we had read so much about. As we accelerated down the runway faster and faster, I was busy hitting toggle switches making sure everything was ready for the long flight ahead. I yelled out air speed above the roar of the powerful motors: 25 miles per hour, 30, 40, 50, 60, and 70. By this time the whole crew was getting tense, for it was our first time to fly such a beautiful, clean, smooth operating lady. I continued giving Lt. Kaub the air speed. When we reached 95 miles per hour he pulled back on the steering column and she took to the air like a soaring eagle.

We climbed into the cool morning air with the bright and glorious sun shining down on her silver wings. When we reached our assigned altitude, we relaxed a little, keeping a sharp eye on the instruments and scanning the surroundings for other planes that might be in our air space. Slicing through the early August elements at 160 miles per hour, it took several hours to reach our destination. When we neared Bangor, Lt. Kaub radioed the airport near Bangor, Maine for landing instructions. We landed in the cool atmosphere, without mishap, to refuel and for an over night rest.

The next morning we bid good-bye to the army personnel that had met our needs, and took off for the next leg of our journey. In a few hours, we landed in snow-covered

Newfoundland where all the airmen were wearing parkas and hanging out close to Quonset huts. Other "fly boys" welcomed us, and showed us quarters where we would live until orders came down from above.

Since we were a lone crew, not traveling in a flight, special orders had to be cut for us and it took time. While we waited for the days to pass, we played cards, went to the bar and got acquainted with the GIs stationed there.

Finally, sealed orders came down. We couldn't open them until we had flown for an hour eastward over the icy Atlantic. Everybody understood the familiar slogan in those days, "Careless lips sink ships." The caution was necessary lest some careless person would reveal a military secret unintentionally.

By this time we had grown pretty familiar with our new B-17. On the day the higher-ups told us to fly, we went through the back door of one of the largest planes that flew in those days and took our stations. It was dark when we passed the southern tip of Greenland, and we saw electric lights shining from the army camps in the frozen wasteland.

After opening our orders, we learned they called for us to land in Iceland to refuel and rest. I was still weak after the stay in the hospital, and there is no denying it, I slept much of that leg of our journey leaving the entire flying to our Pilot. Lt. Canvanaugh, our navigator, was busy with his sextant plotting the stars to keep us on course. His job was necessary, for we had been warned by intelligence officers to be careful for the German submarines had our radio frequency. These sly German sailors would lurk fifty to one hundred miles off our course, posing as United States army officers, sending us a radio message that we were off course and that we should make false correction in their direction. If we fell for this enemy trick, we might wander around over the ocean, run out of gas and go down into the drink

We couldn't depend on radio messages. That was no problem, for Lt. Cavanaugh kept us on the straight and narrow course by reading the stars with his sextant.

I awoke the next morning to see the beautiful orange sun creep slowly above the horizon flooding the clouds with colorful light. Nothing but water was below us and a gentle breeze kicked up waves on the salty ocean surface. I thought this must have been the scene in primeval times when the earth was created. At thirty thousand feet, we could see only the sun, the clouds and the water far below. A sight I've never forgotten.

Lt. Kaub lifted his arms to stretch his body for he had been sitting in a cramped position all night piloting the plane. "I'm tired," he yelled above the roar of the four motors. "Would you mind flying this baby and let me take a nap."

Sitting in the right seat of the cockpit, I took control of the B-17 with all motors purring like a house cat. Within an hour, our commander was awake ready to take control of the beautiful aluminum bird glistening in the early morning light. Alone in the heavens, we flew until we saw a dot in the middle of a great big body of water. Our map told us that it had to be Iceland, a place we had only read about. Kaub radioed the tower at the airfield near Reykjavik for landing instruction. The airport personnel knew we were coming so when we identified our plane they invited us to land clearing the airspace and runway for us.

Again, Robert Kaub kept his eyes clued on the concrete runway landing the big bird with the perfection of a seasoned pilot. Neither of us noticed the unusual topography on the island nation until the plane was safe on the ground. When we came to a stop, we sat for a long moment in the cockpit, looking out the windows from a high vantage point amazed at what we saw. The glaciers were brilliant in the bright sunlight and the steam coming up from the boiling pits added to thoughts of the morning of creation.

When we got out of the plane, the Icelandic personnel met us with kindness and respect. They fed us well and housed us in comfortable quarters. It was an unforgetable short visit.

The next morning we flew to Wales where we landed and showed the American commander our orders. We saw a sight for real that we had seen only in pictures. Scottish officers, stationed in Wales wore kilt uniforms. It amazed our crew, but to them it was standard fare. Grown men carrying out their duties dressed in skirts made us snicker, and we made funny remarks when they were out of earshot.

Here American officers took our pretty silver bird away form us and sent us to billet in London to await orders to fly into combat. While in this enormous, strange city for about a week, the four officers stayed in one place and the six non-coms stayed in another The only duty required of officers was that we check with headquarters each day for assignment. Beyond that, we were free to visit historical sights and enjoy nightspots. In wartime, this really wasn't as enjoyable as it may seem. We saw very large balloons, tethered to mother earth by thin wires, flying thousands of feet above the city. Londoners hoped these balloons, attached to wires, would deter German pilots from venturing over the metropolitan area to bomb the city. At night, powerful lights switched back and forth across the sky to spot enemy aircraft that got too close. If so, they could be shot them down by antiaircraft fire.

By this time, the Englishmen were familiar with the German V-2 rockets that could be heard coming from miles away before they exploded in the city, or flew by to land in the vacant countryside. During the day when Air Raid Wardens and others rushed about the streets doing their patriotic chores, the Englishmen kept about their work seemingly oblivious of the incoming missiles. Many had a philosophy that stated: "If the bomb has your name on it, it'll get you, otherwise don't worry about it."

But many of us Americans, including me, didn't subscribe to that philosophy. When we heard the unmistakable sound of an incoming V-2 rocket, we started looking for a basement or any hole we could find to shield us from the expected storm.

Our crew fully believed we would take a Flying Fortress loaded with bombs from England over occupied Low Lands, France and Germany, to face a determined enemy, and drop the load of destruction. The enemy forces changed our orders.

The change came about because the Germans had destroyed so many of our planes and crews stationed in Italy. When Americans bombed the Concordia Vega Oil Refinery near Ploesti, Romania, the B-17 and B-24 crews flew very low over the target to escape detection by the brand new contraption called Radar. It was reported that these planes flew fifty feet above the refinery, dropped their bombs, gave the motors full power and shot up as fast as they could. For some, it wasn't fast enough, for several crews blew themselves out of the air. A large number of airmen were killed on these raids. This Vega Oil Refinery was top priority, for it was the source of much of the enemy's oil and gasoline supply for their planes, tanks and other war machines.

After so many crews were killed or wounded on these raids, several crews were sent from England to the 15th Air Force stationed in Italy. Orders were issued in late August 1944 for our crew to be transferred to fill the gap. In wartime, we got use to rapid change of plans. The Robert Kaub crew boarded a B-24, which had been converted to haul passengers, and headed for the 15th Air Force, 463rd Bomb Group, 773rd Bomb Squadron stationed near Foggia, Italy.

The B-24 pilot took a course straight south from England swinging far out over the Atlantic, missing Spain completely. This maneuver was necessary so the German fighter planes would not be tempted to attack an unarmed plane carrying passengers. Our crew spent the time in flight playing cards on the makeshift floor of the B-24. By this time in the war, the Allied forces had defeated General Rummel and his army in North Africa sending them back to the "Father Land" to face Hitler's wrath.

We flew over Morocco, Algeria landing in Tripali, Libya where we stayed for three days in the sweltering heat and strange atmosphere. Strange, because it was so different from anything we'd ever seen. In the city, the streets were filthy and children seemed weak and unresponsive, half naked with flies crawling over their bodies and around their eyes. The women wore veils that covered their faces except their eyes.

After three days, we were flown to Foggia where another world opened up for us. We'd seen the devastation German bombs caused in London where the courageous citizens of that city were busy adjusting to war time condition by keeping the streets as clean as possible and caring for their children. In Italy, where bombs pulverized towns and hand-to-hand battles occurred in the streets, it seemed the attitude of people was different. Food supply for the Italians had diminished considerably, many homes and businesses were in a shambles, children were roaming the streets in U. S. Army clothes, or rags they had found. They begged GIs for candy, chewing gum, and nickels and dimes to buy food.

I got the impression in those days, and it remains with me, the adults had to work so hard for meager food and the absolute necessities of life, they had little time left for anything else. Despite their deplorable condition, we found the people friendly and helpful to the army personnel.

We soon were settled in the 773rd Bomb Squadron on a very rocky piece of ground where officers were separated from the enlisted men. An olive drab tent was assigned to us officers with four folding cots. Each man was given a couple of blankets: one to sleep on and the other served as cover. Some of the men who had been on the airbase for a while made their area around their tents look much like home. They used the stones close by to build a kneehigh rock fence around their tent, and from oil barrels, they made stoves to dispel the cold at night. Inside the fence, they planted small trees and a few flowers. These amenities made being in a war torn country feel more like home in America.

When these men finished their missions and ready to return home on rotation, they sold their tent, fence and all to the highest bidder.

While waiting in the chow line just as the sun was sinking into the Mediterranean Sea, in the land far from the New Mexico farm where I grew up, a GI reporter gave us the latest copy of *The Stars and Strips*. Our crew had not yet been assigned a plane for our first mission over enemy territory. In the centerfold of this issue of the Newspaper were pictures of historical planes that had been roughed-up in battle. Most of them had been shot down in combat over Ploesti or some other enemy venue, but a few remained to fly another day - but just barely.

Pictures of pretty, scantily dressed girls were painted on the nose of the planes that had been given feminine names. One plane that stood out from all the rest for the picture on the nose was much different, as was the name. This picture caught the attention of us four officers who stood in the chowline. While Lt. Kaub held the spread open, the rest of us gathered 'round with eyes focused on this one plane.

Instead of a painting of a girl on the nose, the plane that captured our attention had a picture of a man painted on it. This man was dressed in a black suit with his collar turned backwards, a black derby hat on his head, a bomb in one hand and a Bible in the other. In large distinctive letters, the artist had painted **Holey Joe** as the name of the plane.

We talked and laughed as our commander read the caption beneath the picture. We learned the name was given because **Holey Joe** had 96 bullet and dissension holes in it from bow to stern. Several airmen had been killed within her walls while manning their stations on missions, and more had been wounded. This ship was one of the few that returned to home base after raids on the oil fields and refinery near Ploesti, Romania.

After supper, our crew, along with other crews, went to our tents and bedded down for the night anxious to learn what the next day might bring. The first night in Foggia, after an extra hot August afternoons, we learned two blankets were not sufficient to keep the chill from our bodies. The cool winds blowing inland from the Adriatic Sea made us uncomfortable.

Before the sun rose the next morning, we were awakened by the sound of the bugle. We ate a quick breakfast and rushed to the conference room for the briefing that day. After a short talk by a couple of superior officers, a sergeant stood before us and called off the new crews and the B-17 airplane each was assigned to do battle over southern Germany, Yugoslavia, Romania and surrounding countries. These countries had been occupied by Hitler's forces. Since northern Italy was still occupied by enemy forces, we may be ordered to strike German and Italian strongholds in those mountains to assist Allied combatants.

The sergeant began calling out each commander and plane assigned to each crew. After several commanders names and the matching plane number were called off, he called out 2nd. Lt. Robert W. Kaub and his crew are assigned to B-17G Flying Fortress Number 231834.

When our flight commander dismissed us, all the new crews left the briefing on the run to the ramp where the planes were standing. Each crew was excited to learn the name of their plane and to inspect it. Our crew finally found 231834 in the long line. Our excitement was subdued when we found Number 231834 and saw the "holy man" painted on the nose and its name **Holey Joe** painted in large letters. Next, we noticed the

96 aluminum patches that covered the holes on the fuselage. It reminded me of a Roman gladiator patched up with bandaids after a battle in the Coliseum.

Our spirits took a nose dive while gazing at this old worn out battle-scared, piece of junk that should have been salvaged or put on exhibit in a museum instead of sent back into combat. Lt. Kaub said, "Men this is the draw we got, so let's make the best of it." Mumbling among us followed. We thought we would be flying new a plane into combat like the one we flew from the States.

Lt. Kaub, our commander continued, "We're soldiers, and we've learned to take what the army gives us. It stands to reason that the pilots and crews that have flown many mission against the enemy, and are still around, should get the new planes and we new guys should take the old ones."

With this said, with sober minds and doubts showing on all our faces, the huddle broke up, and each crewmember slowly went to his station in the plane to check it out. I kicked the tires and gave the plane the once-over that is required before any flight. Our commander went to the cockpit to make sure it met his satisfaction. Cavanaugh, our navigator, went to play around with the sextant and other equipment. Grover checked out the Norden Bomb Sight, a new toy used by bombardiers for dropping bombs more accurately. The enlisted men went to their respective stations to make sure they were in working order.

With several orientation meetings the following days, the bugler called us from our bunks at four in the morning. We knew full well what was up - our first combat mission.

Nervously we dressed in jump suits and headed for the briefing room to learn of our mission and what to expect. The briefing officer told us that our mission was to knock out bridges around Munich, Germany. He warned us that the Germans had increased their anti-aircraft power since many of their planes had been downed by Allied forces. So we needed to be careful when we approached the target for ack-ack would be bursting all around us. So make sure we practiced the maneuvers in such a situation that we'd practiced in training.

When the briefing was over at 5:30, the officer in charge told us to hurry, eat breakfast and dress for the flight. "You'll be flying at an altitude of 32,000. You don't have much time for we start warming engines at 6:09."

With a skimpy breakfast finished, we rushed to our tent to dress. Over our jump suit, we each put on a belt with holster and in it a Colt 45. (In case we were shot down, we had protection and a weapon to protect ourselves if we wished to use it.) We put on our fleece-lined pants, jacket, helmet and boots for warmth for the old B-17s didn't have air conditioning and it can be freezing at the altitude we would be flying. Over all this, each strapped on a parachute.

With all this gear on, we waddled to the ramp to find **Holey Joe** waiting to be awakened from deep sleep. Could the old warhorse make one more flight into combat to battle the enemy forces that awaited us? We hoped so.

By 6:10 that morning powerful motors, all up and down the flight line, were humming being checked out for flight into the hostile blue. When each crewmember was at his stations, our commander, hit the buttons and engines 1, 2 and 4 came alive clattering and roaring. However, engine number 3 was still tired and drowsy. It just didn't want to kick off until Sergeant Wright, our flight engineer, was called. With his prompting, the engine coughed a few times, sputtered and joined the other motors in unison. The pilot and I had straps with sensitive buttons around our necks for radio communication. With motors running smoothly, Lt. Kaub pressed the buttons firmly against his vocal cords and called the tower for instructions.

When it was our turn to taxi into position, our commander pushed the four throttles forward and we began to move. I was busy studying the panel instruments and calling out their readings over the roar of the engines. With four 1,000 pound bombs, equipment, twenty 50 caliber guns and long strips of bullets for each gun, full equipment and ten men aboard, at the signal from the tower, **Holey Joe** began to roll toward the dirt runway covered with perforated metal strips from one end to the other.

With clearance, Lt. Kaub gave plane number 231834 full throttle and the old, tired lady strained, giving it her best, as she rolled down the runway. We heard the rattle of the runway's metal rattling above the roar of the engines. As the battle weary lady struggled to pick up momentum, I called out the accelerating speed. At 95 miles-per-hour, Robert pulled the steering column back, and the dear old lady, which should have been in a nursing home, gave every ounce of power she had and lifted us above the barbed wire fence at the end of the runway.

We sailed alone following the planes that took off before us. More and more planes followed behind us all gaining altitude to get into flight formation to go on the bombing raid. Higher and higher, we ascended. At about 10,000 feet our 773 Bomb Squadron began to form with the 463 Bomb Group. As we climbed to higher altitude other bomb groups stationed in different air fields around Italy joined us until by the time we gained 20,000 feet about 100 hundred B-17s were in formation, headed north, leaving con trails in our wake. We were soon on the enemy's turf, and he had home field advantage.

By the time, we reached our assigned altitude of 32,000 feet all planes were in formation ready to do battle with a seasoned protagonist. In addition to our own firepower, red tailed P-51 fighters planes, flown by Black Airmen, protected us from German fighter planes until just before they reached the point of no return. Their limited range forced them to turn back. It was always a welcome sight when they buzzed around us looking after our welfare.

As we approached the target near Munich, nervous chatter over the intercom from men in the bowels of **Holey Joe** intensified. Lieutenants Grover and Cavanaugh tried to keep all of as relaxed as possible. Without warning ack-ack began to burst all around us. Deadly black clouds form exploding antiaircraft fire below began popping 200 feet below us and 200 feet above us. The Nazis figured that our maneuvering within this range would be useless. The closer to our target the heavier the ach-ach became. Lt. Grover bent over his bombsight, twisting knobs and punching buttons, making ready to drop our bombs at the appropriate time. Flying in formation, Lt. Kaub, with nerves unshaken, kept a steady course along side the other planes.

Suddenly the B-17 on our left wing was hit in the bomb bay by a shell from the ground. The bombs exploded, and the plane with ten men was blown to smithereens. I saw pieces of the plane and pieces of men float slowly toward mother earth. Our commander didn't bat an eye. Just kept piloting the plane on our deadly mission.

Back at our home base in Foggia, we viewed the pictures of the damage and lack of damage we did to the bridges we wished to knock out. We failed to take them out completely. A few days later, our flight commander led us back to finish the job.

On the second mission, our crew congratulated ourselves prematurely for making the bomb run. We thought **Holey Joe** was in as good shape as when we first flew the old plane. After landing at the Foggia Air Base, we inspected the old warhorse. To our surprise, we found a rip the full length of the underside of the right wing. We figured that a sharp piece of flak, traveling a tremendous speed, ripped the skin on the wing without damaging its structure. Lt. Kaub said, "Somebody must have been looking after us." The crew members said, "Boy, weren't we lucky."

(With the war over, in 1953 a German citizen, Gottfried Reichel, a young man who had been converted to Christianity, was visiting America on a Lecture tour. I attended the auditorium where he spoke, visited with him afterwards, and invited him to spend the night with my family and me. During the course of our conversation, I learned he was in the Hitler Youth Camp outside Munich. I told him that our B-17 wing of the 15th Air Force made a raid on the bridges around his hometown in September 1944.

"Yes," he said, "I remember it well."

"What did you 14 and 15 year-olds do?" I asked.

"We were very angry with you," he answered. "We thrust our fist in the air at you and cursed you with everything we had.")

The next few days while **Holey Joe's** right wing was being repaired, our crew had some time off. We went to the Adriatic Sea shore, rented a rowboat, paddled off from land and swam in the salty sea. We dove off the boat as deep as we dared. That was our first encounter with Jellyfish. We were warned their sting could be very harmful

While our crew was waiting for **Holey Joe** to be patched up, I watched the planes taking off in early morning on a bombing mission. I visualized what the pilots and co-pilots were doing during their warm-up and taking off. As another old warhorse of a plane was gathering speed down the runway, I watched with intensity, wondering if he would be able to lift himself, with the heavy load of bombs and ten men, off the runway and over the barbed wire fence. In my mind, I saw the pilot pull back on the steering column to lift the plane up over the fence. I sighed relief. They got about fifty feet off the ground. The old boy, tired since he had so many encounters in battle, just couldn't make it further into the air. He plummeted to earth, as a boxer in the ring after an opponent, with great force, hit his glass chin. The bombs in her belly exploded. Another plane was gone forever, blown to smithereens, and ten men were unceremoniously delivered to kingdom come.

Before our crew's eighth mission, every officer in the 463 Bomb Group was called out to stand at attention while one of our commanding officer lectured us. He put the fear of court martial into our hearts by stating emphatically, 'Men, our Group is getting a bad reputation in the 15th Air Force because some of you are bringing your plane back early before you finish your missions. You 'fraidy cats, scared to challenge the enemy on his own grounds. You have some minor thing go wrong with your airplane and you turn tail and run back home. As of this meeting, we're putting a stop to that nonsense. NO MORE COMING BACK EARLY! Have you got that? Any crew bringing their plane back before the mission is completed is subject to court martial. If you don't think I mean what I say, just try me. I'd rather you ditch your plane in the Adriatic than bring it back early. That's all. FALL OUT!"

Remembering the dilapidated condition of **Holey Joe**, and wondering, each time we flew, if he was able to get off the ground. I visualized our crew spending the rest of our lives in Fort Leavenworth if we couldn't finish a bomb run By the light of a lantern, in the tent that night, the four officers in our crew talked and worried about the commanders statement. When we finally hit the sack, sleep was hard to come by.

Weary and sleepy after spending much of the night rolling and tossing, we answered the call for the 4 AM briefing the next morning. Unknown to us, we prepared for our last mission, and **Holey Joe's** last flight for the old warhorse was never to return

THE LAST FLIGHT OF HOLEY JOE

The ominous threat from our ground commander, the day before, was still swirling in our heads as our crew left the briefing filled with apprehension and doubts. Since we had been assigned to *Holey Joe*, concerns flooded our hearts. Could the old battle-scared warhorse possibly make another successful bomb run while wading through black clouds of exploding ack-ack? Could the weakened plane bring us home again after another challenge of German fighter planes bent on our destruction?

We ate breakfast in silence, each airman just wondering what was in store for us. After eating, each man strapped on a forty-five over his flight suit, put on fleece-lined outer garments that covered us from head to foot. The last to go on was a parachute. We officers met our enlisted crewmembers that waited for us under the patched wings of our plane. While Lt. Kaub and the rest of the crew crawled into the plane to take their stations, I remained on the ground to inspect the outside of *Holey Joe* for flight worthiness.

I entered the back door of the plane. As I passed by each airman at his station, I patted each on the back and tried to say anything to release the tension that had built up in our hearts. They were subdued, and gave little response. I stepped on the eight inch catwalk with two 1000 pound bombs on either side, entered the cockpit and strapped myself in the co-pilot seat and gave our flight commander the thumbs up indicating that the outside of the plane was ready for takeoff, and he could start the engines.

Lt. Kaub hit all four-starter buttons and engines 1, 2 and 4 coughed a few times but soon came to life with a roar. Engine number three refused to awake from deep sleep. Flight Engineer Richard Wright was called to help. There was nothing he could do, from inside the plane, to start the engine. Kaub called the tower to send the ground engineer to help. When the ground chief arrived, he got on his ladder, took off the cowling that housed the motor, tinkered with a few wires, checked the carburetor, replaced the cowling, pushed the ladder away and gave our pilot the thumbs up indicating for him to try starting the number three engine again.

Lt. Kaub hit the started button, and as if by magic, the old tired motor belched once and came to life purring in unison with the her three sisters. It was my job to read off the checklist before every flight, so I began shouting over the roar of the engines each item and our commander checked them all.

With the tower's permission, we taxied to the end of the runway and waited for the all- clear so we could take off and join the other B-17s in formation. With permission granted, our pilot gradually pushed the four throttles forward, and we began with accelerating speed to move down the strip. Since he had his hands full, I began to call off the speed until we reached 95 mph. It was at that point, he lifted **Holey Joe**, with four thousand pounds of bombs, over the fence, and we were airborne. At fifty feet, we began a shallow turning climb to the left, careful not to turn too sharp lest we stall into the ground.

At two hundred feet, Lt. Kaub leveled the wings and began to ascend to ten thousand where the other planes were circling for us to join them in flight. When all the planes were in proper formation, the led plane took the heading north ordered in the briefing earlier in the day.

In formation, I could relax a little while Robert flew the plane. Nevertheless I kept a roving eye on what was going on about us and on the instruments for I never knew when the flight commander might ask me to take the controls. I noticed the beauty of the morning at 8 AM. The Sun was shining bright, glistening off the silver planes. There wasn't a cloud in the sky, and the P-51s, with their red tails, flown by black patriotic pilots trained in Tuscaloosa, Alabama, protected us from German fighter planes stationed in Yugoslavia. We always welcomed the sight of P-51s buzzing around our much bigger planes.

Onward we went, climbing higher and higher toward our selected target, the Synthetic Oil Production Plant in Brut, Czechoslovakia, for that day's bombing. Flying over the top of the Italian boot, which was still occupied by German troops, number three engine just conked out; its life was gone. The old motor, tired and worn, had served its useful life in combat, and it was now time for it to rest. The thing refused to come to life, despite all the expertise learned in training we put into the effort to get it started. At more than 20,000, we couldn't park it and work on the motor. It was impossible for us to keep up with the formation. Our speed was reduced, and we were forced to drop behind the great armada of warships. We watched the mighty group of around 100 planes of war, armed to the hilt, slowly pull away from us, leaving **Holey Joe** alone in an empty sky, and his forlorn crew wondering what steps to take next.

Remembering the warning if we returned early, Lt. Kaub and I decided to continue on our mission hoping to drop our bombs on the target if at all possible. With great apprehension, we watched the formation grow smaller and smaller from our vantage point until it was completely out of sight.

Robert ordered me to feather engine number three, for it was only windmilling causing drag and making the other three motors work harder.

As we passed over a battery of antiaircraft guns far below us, suddenly all hell broke loose for we found ourselves in the midst of devilish, dreaded black clouds. Ack-ack was exploding all around us. Lt. Grover, our bombardier, was ordered to open the bombay doors and drop our bombs hoping to knock out the nest of vipers on the ground. After bombs away, I tried to use the intercom to communicate with Grover, but learned all our electricity had been knocked out. I stuck my head into the nose of the plane where he sat over his bombsite and yelled at the top of my voice, "Did you hit anything when you dropped the bombs?"

Our twenty-year-old bombardier, never at a loss for a good on-liner, even in a life and death situation, shouted back, "It's one o'clock. I figured Hitler was eating his noonday bowl of soup. So I dropped the bombs in his bowl."

After we passed beyond the range of the enemy below, we assessed the damage to *Holey Joe*. The electricity had been knocked out, the bombay doors would not close by pushing the button. There was a long wormscrew near by that we could crank them to close the doors. The thing had been broken by flak. Our gyrocompass was out of whack, forcing us to rely on the directional compass that bounced around in a bath of clear oil. Two motors had been damaged, leaving them with only half power. We limped through the air with only one good motor.

Holey Joe had acquired more holes making him more holey than before. Among the holes discovered, while in the air, was one about the size of a silver dollar directly behind of my seat. If that hole had been six or eight inches forward, I would not be writing this account. The fuselage of our plane resembled a sieve, but not a man was hit. Just a little shook up. The ack-ack had also destroyed our oxygen supply.

With one motor feathered, two drawing only half power and one operating at full capacity, and with no oxygen, we could not retain our altitude. It was time to start descending to a lower level and jettison all equipment we could in order to stay airborne.

As we glided **Holey Joe** to a lower altitude in order breathe, the men in the back threw all guns and other heavy equipment out vie the open bombay doors. Lt. Cavanaugh, eager to do his part to lighten the load and perhaps a little nervous, threw out the large bag containing aerial maps, sextant and other supplies leaving us with no navigation equipment The last heavy object to be jettisoned was the ball turret that was secured in the belly of the plane by four large bolts. When these bolts were removed, it was "bombs-away" for the enclosure that eighteen-year-old gunner Roy Munsey of Tennessee had occupied on all our missions.

The tenseness of the situation and the hard labor that ensued, during our descent, caused all of us to be short of breath for lack of oxygen. As we sought a lower altitude where we could breathe better, I noticed Lt. Kaub slump over the steering column exhausted. I took the controls giving him a chance to relax and regain his strength. It wasn't long before I passed out for lack of oxygen. By that time, Robert had awakened enough to take over the controls. This on again off again between us continued until we reached an altitude we could breathe normally.

We hobbled along at about 14,000 feet. I kept my eyes peeled for German fighter planes. I saw two enemy planes coming straight at us from two o'clock high, at more the 300 miles per hour. I touched the pilot's right shoulder. He looked at me and I pointed to the fighters barreling down on us. One thought filled our minds: we were absolute defenseless and had no way to fight back. A decision had to be made in the next few seconds.

Commander Kaub yelled to me over the roar of the motors and the swishing of the wind coming through the open bombay doors and the hole left when the ball turret was dropped, "What do you suggest we do?"

I pointed to a bank of clouds to our left. Screaming as loud as I could, "Hide in those clouds. They'll never find us there."

Robert banked the plane to the left, and before the German fighters could make a kill, we were safely hid in the clouds. Secure from the enemy for the time, I began to laugh almost uncontrollably.

"This is not a funny situation," My commander wailed. "Why are you laughing?"

I couldn't tell him, and didn't think he really wanted to know. But running like a scared rabbit and hiding from gun fire reminded me of my life as a boy on the patch of earth I like to think of as *the pocket of perpetual poverty*. Back in those long-ago days, I often went rabbit hunting with my .22 single shot rifle with the slightly bent barrel. I'd spot a rabbit nibbling on grass, raise my gun to shoot, but before I could, pull the trigger, the little defenseless animal would high-tail it to the nearest clump of mesquite brush and hide. Our action in the B-17 reminded me of the rabbit. Crazy minds with vivid imaginations, forgetting the moment of great danger, think that way and burst out in laughter. Laughter may have come from nervous tension,

In the mean time, since all the tools of war had been thrown from the plane, our navigator, bombardier and the enlisted men were suffering in the back separated from the pilot and me. They had to endure the strong, cold winds that whistled in through the open bombay doors and the hole where the ball turret had been. They had no idea what was going on and the decisions that had to be made in the cockpit.

The deeper we got into the clouds, the thicker they became until the wing tips of **Holey Joe** were hardly visible. We had escaped the deadly firepower of the German fighters, but another enemy just as deadly confronted us. Since our oxygen was all knocked out, we had to fly below the peaks of the Alps. We dared not return to the clear skies for fear the German fighters were waiting to rid the "Father Land' of another plane that had wrought so much destruction on their factories and cities.

Under the circumstances, we decided to fly a straight course hoping to break out into the clear. But that was not to be, for the heavy cloud layer covered the entire range of the Alps. Whether we were flying over German, French or Swiss Alps, we had no way of knowing.

We had been flying for over seven hours, and we knew ***Holey Joe*** was getting thirsty. The gages on our instrument panel could not tell us, but simple reason told us our gasoline was nearly depleted. We couldn't see the ground, thick clouds turned bright sunshine into darkness. Our plane was winging its feeble way below the snow capped mountain peaks. Radio communications was cut off and the lives of ten men were at stake. So what could we do?

It was possible and probable that we would crash into a mountaintop if we continued on the straight course. If that happened, we may be buried in deep snow, never to be heard of again.

Above the howling wind and the roaring motors, one of the best pilots in the 15th Air Force, screamed to me, "What do you think we should do?"

I'd been thinking for some time about the question, so without hesitation, I shot back in a loud voice, "I suggest, we start right here spiraling downward. If we run out of gas before we see daylight, we all bail out. If we come out beneath the cloud cover, we land this baby if we can." If we can, was the deciding factor!

Lt. Kaub accepted my suggestion and began a shallow spiral toward the earth hoping for a miracle. With uncertain compass readings, maps tossed out in the navigators bags, we didn't know where we were. The only thing we knew for certain was that we were in a tough spot and wanted desperately to get out of it.

Slowly and downward we spiraled. Occasionally, in our circular track, we hit a hole in the clouds about the size of the okay sign when one puts thumb and forefinger together. The hole, often missed as we went around, gave us hope that we might get out of this situation alive for it went all the way to the ground. After sweating it out for an undetermined time, we broke beneath the heavy cloud cover at about 500 feet above the ground. It was dark at three o'clock in the afternoon, rain was pouring down so heavily, from the clouds we had been flying in, that we could not see a flag anywhere telling what country lay beneath us.

When we broke out of the clouds, a small one-seater airplane, with a stubby nose, came up to meet us. The pilot began tailing us for some unknown reason. Lt. Kaub and I could see the pesky little aircraft, but the airmen huddled in the rear could not see it from their vantage position. We had never seen a plane like it, and could not read its markings, so it gave us no indication where we were. One of the men in the belly of **Holey Joe** saw a 2 x 4, that had not been jettisoned before, and threw the timber out the open bombay door. If the little plane behind us had not maneuvered quickly, it would have been knocked out of the air by a flying 2 x 4. The first and only aircraft in WW II downed in such a manner.

Since our intercom was no longer working, it was necessary for me to walk the narrow catwalk between the open bombay doors. I needed to remind the men in back how to protect themselves from possible harm for we thought our landing was going to be a rough one. Looking down 500 feet though the huge holes in the floor, with the wind gushing in, I walked very, very gingerly. I told the men, "Open your parachutes, wrap the silk around your bodies and heads for padding because this plane may bounce all over the place upon landing."

Our commander spotted an airport. While he positioned our flight for landing, I retraced my steps through the narrow passageway and reclaimed my co-pilot seat. With only one good motor functioning, two drawing half power and one feathered, there was no such thing as a second try for landing. The first approach had to be *it!* With the precision of the best pilot in the Army Air Corps, Lt. Robert W. Kaub trimmed the tabs and kept a steady hand on the controls positioning the plane ready to land.

While he was fully concentrating on his job, I was busy calling out air speed for we certainly didn't want to stall and crash so near the end of a hectic flight. While the rain was still peppering down, Lt. Kaub lined *Holey Joe* up with a long, inviting runway, but we feared to land on the concrete strip. With the bombay doors open and the wheels up, knowing we had to make a belly landing, sparks caused from metal scraping along concrete might ignite the remaining gasoline. We opted to land on the wet, knee-high grass along side the runway. Beside calling out air speed, I was taking every precaution to keep the plane from blowing up, killing all men on board, by turning off toggle switches and prepared to take the controls if necessary.

As we touched down, ever so lightly, on the wet, tall grass, the bombay doors, hanging below the belly of the plane, crushed like eggshells, and the propellers bent back over the cowling of each motor. Kaub killed each engine, and we began the long slide until the plane stopped about ten yards from the door of a large hanger.

It was September 23, 1944 when we completed our eighth combat mission, and *Holey Joe* was never to fly again. *Holey Joe* was one of 163 American aircraft that crashed in the small nation. The old plane just couldn't take it any more. He had died never to be resurrected. He had fought his share of battles for the war effort. He was ready to be cut up into little pieces, melted down and made into another useful machine.

When our plane ceased skidding on the wet grass, men in green uniforms, holding long rifles with bayonets attached, surrounded it. Lt. Kaub and I walked back on the narrow walkway as the men shed their silk cocoons that kept them from being injured. The ten of us stepped out the back door of the plane, on to the soggy ground, one by one, only to face soldiers with hard faces and determined looks. They made upward motions with their rifles for us to hold our hands high. We did as they directed. Their speech sounded German to us.

We stood before them with hands held high for what seemed like an eternity. Did the solders intended to shoot us or take us prisoners? We did not know, for we believed we had landed in Germany.

Finally, the pilot in the small plane landed, walked up to us and announced in perfect English, "You men are all right. You are in Switzerland." With this good news, we lowered our hands and the soldiers, with their intimidating rifles, left the scene.

The American Attache was called. After he assured us that it was his job to take care of downed American airmen, the tenseness in our bodies relaxed a little. The Attache called for a MD to check us for wounds and each man's vital signs. The doctor pronounced all a-okay, no wounds and everything else normal except all of us were a little shook up from our ordeal.

Next, the ten members of the crew of **Holey Joe** took our places around a long table, and we were served the best food Switzerland had to offer during wartime. This was in a large hall, I can't remember if it were a hanger or some other. There were other flyers from America, Spain and England, who had experienced a similar fate as we, only a few days earlier, sitting at tables some distance from us. Now those men had been on the solid earth long enough for the trauma of their unfortunate missions to ware off.

It was nearing 4 PM and our crew had not eaten since 5 AM. Despite our extreme hunger, all of us sat at the table spread with food, with blank faces, not touching the food nor making any indication that we wished to eat.

The American, Spanish and English airmen who sat at tables some distance from us had been smoking cigarettes, playing cards, telling jokes and laughing up a storm. Suddenly they were quiet as church mice. They looked at us, with strange looks in their eyes with mouths hanging open, as we sat motionless around a table filled with food and not eating.

Finally, Lt. Robert W. Kaub, the commander of our ship, said in solemn tones, "Men, I think we should pray thanking God for this food and bringing us down safely from a perilous flight." We all nodded in agreement. Then the captain of our plane led us in prayer. It was only after the prayer that members of our crew picked up the sliver ware and began to eat. The downed flyers from the three nations, at the far tables, continued their activities in a relaxed manner.

Another author writing about all the problems we had on the last flight of *Holey Joe*, reported that we were lucky that we landed at Dubendorf, and that not one crewmember was injured in the crash landing. This author would have had a difficult time convincing members of our crew that we were lucky. For it was while we ate that each man confessed he prayed for God's help for a safe landing. However, our crew was probably as raunchy and any flight crew in the United States Army Air Corps, some admitted they had not prayed since their mother's encouraged them to pray beside their beds when they were little boys.

The day after we landed, the Swiss officials at the airport invited us to see *Holey Joe* for the last time. All the clouds were cleared away and the sky was a deep blue. The snow-covered mountains, pointing toward heaven, stood majestically against the clear blue sky. *Holey Joe* was a sad sight. They had lifted his carcass off the water-soaked sod by propping him up on 4 x 4 timbers. His four propellers were bent back over the cowlings, and his bombay doors were crushed like great wads of tinfoil. The old warhorse had made his last flight. He was headed for the B-17 graveyard after doing his part that led to victory over a very stubborn adversary.

One of the officials said to us as he pointed, "See that mountain. We were watching you on radar. If you continued in the straight line you had been traveling, in three or four more minutes you would have ran into that mountain. That would have been the end of you and your plane. But when you began to spiral downward, we figured you had a chance."

Each in our crew sighed, thinking about such a close call.

The official continued, "Know how much gasoline you had left?"

"No Sir."

"Well, you had less than forty gallons in all your tanks. That could keep a big bird like yours in the air for only a few more minutes."

One of our enlisted men said, "That's scary!"

Another official standing by remarked in language that reminded us of home, "You men must have had help from the Man upstairs."

"Yeah."

At a time of Swiss choosing, the four officers in our crew were escorted on a train by armed soldiers to the eastern village of Davos close to the German, Austrian and Northern Italian borders. These three countries were occupied by the Nazi war machine. It was hard for us to understand, if we were guests as they claimed, that it was necessary to have armed guards accompany us. Later we learned why the military went along. The vast majority of the Swiss people were for America, hoping that we would win the war. The Swiss government was cheerleaders for Germany, probably because Switzerland made precision instruments and sold them to Germany. It was this sort of equipment of war, which kept our archenemy fighting.

The Swiss government permitted German trains to haul soldiers and supplies through their nation to furnish enemy troops with guns and ammunitions to kill Americans in the battle for the mountains in Northern Italy. Switzerland was noted for its mighty streams and water falls. These were sources of vast amounts of hydroelectric power for German factories. Americans whispered that Swiss bankers were laundering money for the Nazi war machine. Many of us believed the Swiss shipped unlimited amounts of sophisticated and intricate machine parts to Germany. Without these parts, the Third Reich's juggernaut would have rolled to a dead stop.

(For more information on Switzerland's part in the war, see Don Waters book *Hitler's Secret Ally, Switzerland*, ISBN 0-9640011-7-9.)

We arrived in Devos, with Swiss soldiers guarding us-each packing a gun. The military men escorted us to a hotel where there was no heat or hot water because they conserved everything possible. It was a hotel for tourists, but since tourism was non-existent during World War II, the hotels were used to house internees from Nazi Germany and the occupied countries, France, Spain, England and Italy

To me, Davos was in a lovely sitting having one long street with homes and hotels lined on either side. Towering mountains, with tops covered with snow, stood behind each row of dwellings. Robert and I were assigned to a room, with two beds, in a hotel dug into the side of a mountain and the ground came up to the first-story windowsill. Uncle Sam paid the Swiss government for our lodging. Each American was advanced $150 a month from his pay to spend while interned. Switzerland had no tourist dollars coming in during the war, so the citizens of our host country were pleased with this arrangement for we spent most of the money on trinkets, meals and recreation that helped their economy.

The hotel across the street, formerly occupied by German internees, was vacant. The reason, we were told, the Germans flew the swastika through the night in front of their hotel. One night about midnight, American airmen took down the Nazi flag while the Germans slept, tromped in the snow and urinated on it. Before the Germans awoke the next morning, the Swiss guards learned about the incident, hustled the Germans out of bed and hauled them out of town before daylight for fear a riot would begin if the Nazis remained in town.

The Giddens had left a King James Verson of the Bible in our room. In my spare time, of which there was plenty, I attempted to read the Scriptures hoping to gain knowledge and receive encouragement from the ordeal in captivity. I received neither. The Old English was confusing to me with its "thees and thous" and the ancient way the truth was phrased. If I had been taught the difference from the Old and New Testaments in that little shotgun church house on Fifth Street in Ponca City, I had long since forgot the difference. I struggled to read the Bible, but since I didn't make sense to me, I eventually tossed it aside and didn't pick it up again.

One night Pilot Robert Kaub and I were listening to recorded music of popular American songs. We heard a tapping at the back window at ground level. We pulled back the curtain and two women, in their twenties, motioned for us to let them in. Both of us figured why they had made an appearance by coming in the back way instead interring through the lobby. They were seeking to get a part of our $150 by our engaging with them in their type of party. After hints from the women, we both said "no deal, but if you want to dance, we can do that." We danced a couple numbers and they left as that came in.

The American internees spent much of the daylight hours in Snyder's cafe a short walk down the street. There we ate delicious pastries and played chess to while the time away. Time was a commodity, heavy to bear and we had plenty of it. This life pace was a great contrast from the times past we spent in training and flying combat. It was a monotonous way to live and some airmen tried to escape through the line of 400

Swiss soldiers that surrounded Davos. These uniformed men stood guard to keep internees of all strips hemmed in so they couldn't escape to fly combat missions again. Some did escape, a few got back to their air base, but many Americans were caught and either shot or sent to prison located in central Switzerland at Wauwilermoos and Hunenburg. The everyday rigors of these filthy, rat-infested prisons were more than any human should have to experience. We witnessed happy-go-luck Americans, who attempted to leave Switzerland, were caught and put in prison to do forced labor. They return to Davos after their sentence of six months, with sores all over their bodies, and with all the laughter drained from their souls.

Despite what we had witnessed, Lt. Frank Hoch, a B-24 pilot, and I began to plot our escape from this guarded environment. Two months of such confinement were more than we wanted. We chose to take our chances flying in combat, helping our comrades defeat a ruthless enemy, so we all could return home to families and friends.

Neither Frank nor I remember how we met. It may have been while playing chess in Snyder's cafe. After we did meet, we began to secretly plot how we could escape out of the small nation and get back to our home bases in Italy. When we gathered to eat pastries and drink coffee, we heard our comrades talk in whispered tones about the discrimination the Swiss officials directed against the Americans. The talk was fueled by first hand accounts of U S airmen who had been abused. Such rumors flew faster the snowflakes among the Alps. Gossip piled higher than the mountain snows.

Lt. Frank Hoch was raised in Buffalo, New York where his German grandparents settled. They spoke their native language at home. Though rusty, he could converse in the speech of his ancestors. This 21 year old, B-24 pilot had a slight build, with blond hair looking every bit like a fair complexioned native German, but an American to the very depth of his soul.

Frank was an intelligent, decent sort of fellow that I felt I could trust completely. It was he, I believe, who first met the underground fellow, I'll call Johnny Q, because I don't remember his name. For a handsome price, Johnny promised to do all he could to help us escape. The two of us began a clandestine association with this guy. For fear of leaks, I told none of the officers in our crew what was going on. Didn't even tell Robert Kaub with whom I roomed.

This was all new to Frank and me. We knew the Swiss detectives could easily spot the American plotting to out smart them. From the advice of our underground contact, we enrolled in piano lessons, dancing class and skiing. We hoped this would indicate to our guards and the Swiss officials that we intended to stay under their thumbs for the duration of the war. Some of the American downed flyers made the choice to stay cooped up under the control of Hitler's ally. That was all right with us, for each man had the right to make the choice.

After a couple of weeks of secret planning sessions, Johnny Q bought three train tickets, one for himself and one each for Frank and me, to travel to Bern on the night express. At the proper time for our departure, our guide told us to be at the railroad station in our raunchy Red Cross issued uniforms. When we got there, he would be waiting for us and give us a sign to enter a certain vacant room. Make sure to lock your room, we were told.

In the room waiting for us were two complete sets of civilian clothes. Frank and I stripped off our old uniforms throwing them in a corner. We donned the white shirt, tie, pants and coat. Johnny Q had purchased a green stylish hat for me to wear, for he reasoned my light brown, wavy hair didn't look much kike a German or Swiss. I must wear the hat at all times.

We were wearing civilian clothes for the first time in many months, and it made us feel good. We unlocked the door, stepped out among the civilian crowd feeling like a silkworm larva that had just crawled from its cocoon. We spotted our underground guide, and followed him through the gates onto the train. As we followed, I pulled the brim of my hat, with a red feather in the outer band, down over my eyes hoping none would recognize me as an American.

So far, so good. We had not been caught, yet. This was the beginning of the first leg of a clandestine journey, the details of which remain in my memory after more than sixty years.

SIX DAYS OF SUSPENSE

"Keep your damn mouth shut!" Johnny Q whispered to me in such a stern voice I knew he meant it. "You want us to get caught just as we're beginning this escape!"

I was excited and asked a question in English with normal volume, while all the people about us were speaking in French, German or some other. Standing out like a sore thumb, my speech was a dead give away especially with the American sound. Our underground guide didn't want me to spill the beans, for he would be punished, as well as Frank and me, if the Swiss authorities knew he were helping us vamoose from confinement of the little country.

Afterwards my lips were sealed. Nevertheless occasionally an English phrase would slip out, and I'd get a sharp punch in the side with an elbow coupled by a strong reprimand followed by a look of disdain.

The towheaded, freckled face kid who ran wild, free and barefoot over the caprock hills in New Mexico, dodging mesquite bushes, beargrass spears, chasing jackrabbits and prairie dogs, killing rattlesnakes and trapping quail was about to embark on an adventure he had never even dreamed about.

Johnny Q led as we worked our way through the crowd at the railroad station. It was a real test if I could keep my mouth shut. I wanted to say, "Excuse me," several times as I bumped into someone. And say "Thank you," when I was ushered through the train door. But fear of another elbow kept reminding me.

On the train, we were shown seats facing each other with a table between. I was pushed into the seat next to the window

287

and forbidden to say a word. "Act like you're deaf and dumb," I was told. When the porter asked what we wanted, Johnny Q ordered for me.

Some one produced a deck of cards and we began to play. It was difficult to play cards and not talk. It was especially difficult when it came my turn to shuffle and deal the cards. I was excited and became all thumbs. Johnny played it cool by scolding me, in no uncertain terms, and making motions to show me how to play the game.

We traveled on the electric train through the night until we got to Zurich. There we disembarked into another crowd. Our guide gave instructions how and where we could meet our next contact that could put us on the next leg of our perilous journey. Johnny Q. was about to leave us for good when I blurted out something in English. He rammed me with another elbow and whispered sternly, "If you don't keep your damned mouth shut, you're going to end up in prison at Wauwilermoos!"

Alone, Frank and I followed Johnny's instructions to the letter. He read the German names of streets while I counted the blocks. Well after midnight, we shivered in the cold November darkness slipping and sliding on the snow-covered sidewalks. Eventually we came to the big house with a large yard and huge evergreen trees. This appeared like the dwelling that had been described to us by Johnny Q. A dim porch light was shining. As we were told, we pitched pebbles onto the porch until a tall man dressed in housecoat and slippers came to the door. We watched from behind a tree.

The man in the doorway surveyed his yard for a few minutes. In the crisp, cold air, goose bumps covered our bodies from head to foot making us very anxious to get inside where it was warm. Still the man in the doorway waited making sure everything was foolproof before he invited men, whom he had never seen, into his house. Finally, the man, dressed comfortably in the dim light, gave a prearranged signal. Watching from behind a large evergreen, we recognized the gesture. It was then Frank pronounced the password soft and low. Our new friend turned and went back into his house leaving the door open. That we read as an invitation to come in. We ran upon the porch, stomping the snow from our shoes, and entered the mansion closing the door behind us.

We received a warm welcome from the American official and his wife. After warming before the fireplace, they served us coffee and light refreshments. Soon we were escorted upstairs to a room with two beds, each fluffed high and soft by a mattress filled with feathers. It was covered with a colorful bedspread.

There wasn't much time for socializing, for our host knew we must leave about the time the sun made its appearance over the snow-covered mountains.

An underground network of American officials and friendly Swiss and been formed to assist U. S. fliers to escape the guards stationed all over the country. As long as we didn't make a misstep or show ourselves to the wrong party, we were safe. One mistake would land us in the rat-infested, disease-ridden hoosegow to work at slave labor until our captors wanted to release us.

Nobody ever told us how we would get out of Switzerland or if we would get out at all. Each contact along the way simply told the identity of the next person we should follow. It was left up to us to use our own wits and follow their instructions.

After about three hours of wonderful sleep on the feather beds, our host in the mansion served us breakfast. By this time, there was a car with official markings waiting for us at the curb. The tall man, still in his robe, instructed us to get in the car and the driver would take us to our next stop and tell us what to do when we left his car.

On a beautiful morning with the bright sun shining from a very blue sky, we left the mansion and entered the car having no idea where the driver would take us. Trust the other fellow was the nature of the business in which we were engaged at the time. As we sped toward an unknown destination, the snow was melting and sloshing upon other cars we passed. Since we rode in an "official" car, the police didn't stop us.

Our driver, with a large handle bar mustache, stopped at several places, leaving us to sweat long periods while he took care of business. It was almost midnight when he let us out on the nearly deserted streets of Bern, Switzerland. Unlike Italy where every town and city was littered with signs of war, and every place was blacked out at night, this small "neutral" country had no fear of bombs hitting it. Bern was awash with streetlights and every store window was well lit.

Before we left the car, the driver told us to walk the street making ourselves visible at all times. At the proper time, our next contact man would find us and signal us to follow him.

We played the game of windowshopping growing tired, weary and nervous with each passing minute. Occasionally we passed another human being in the early hours of morning and Frank greeted them in German, and I acted the part of a dummy. An hour passed and nobody had showed up and time continued to move forward. Could any one ever find us in this large city? We walked and walked some more. Our bodies began to tire, and we began to wonder if escaping was such a good idea.

Another hour dragged by. Still our next contact had not showed up. Our patience was growing thin. We struck out on a sidewalk beside a park. A snappily dressed man, with the tail of his overcoat flapping in the breeze, came walking toward us. He was about a block away when we first saw him. He took a cigarette out of its pack and lit it. We noticed he handled the smoke between his middle and index fingers like an American. When he got with in ten yards of us, he flipped the cigarette to the ground, with some force, instead of dropping it to the ground and stepping on it like most Europeans did.

When the stranger got within a few feet of us, without saying a word, he made an about face and began walking briskly toward a hotel. Being sure in wartime was impossible. Nevertheless, we followed him into the hotel, into the elevator and finally into a room. Still not sure whom we followed, the stranger closed the door and asked, "Are you American flyers?"

I pulled off the Swiss hat with its feather stuck in the band. My hair, which had been slicked down with water to make it straight, had dried and the wave had returned.

I tried to explain in my Southwest dialect. Before I finished, the stranger stopped me and said, "Yep. You're the guys I'm looking for."

It was past two in the morning. Frank and I were worn out from the long, exhausting day behind us. The stranger followed up with these instructions: "You men will stay here for the rest of the night. At seven o'clock in the morning there will be a car, with official Swiss markings on it, waiting for you at the curb. When you get into the car, the driver will take you to your destination and tell you what to do next. If you sleep late and miss the driver at the curb, you will probably foil your entire escape plan." With his work completed, the stranger left the room without giving his name or business, and we never saw him again.

After a restless three hours of sleep, Frank and I dressed. I didn't forget to put the green hat with the red feather on my head. As I pulled the brim of the hat down over my eyes, we took our leave from the room, entered the elevator, and walked through the lobby, acting superior to all the guests, left the hotel and entered the marked car.

The driver evidently knew who we were, for when we were seated, he drove off without saying a word.

The fake markings on the automobile were necessary for most vehicles were banned from the streets and highways because of the severe shortage of gasoline. Most Swiss citizens had to use public transportation.

It had been three days since we left Davos, and we were tired physically and emotionally, yet we stayed alert enough to listen to instructions and follow them to the letter. After we left the city, our driver speaking in broken English, told us to be prepared for we would be stopped at roadblocks along our route. The Swiss officials were very suspicious during the war wanting to check every vehicle that looked suspect.

Our drive asked, "You got passports?"

Our passports were crude, looking like they had been fashioned by some elementary student. The pictures were out of focus and the print was barely legible. Frank and I answered in unison, "Yes. Such as they are."

As we traveling down a paved highway, the driver spotted a roadblock in the distance. "This is it," he said. "Get ready to show your passports." When we got closer, he said, "Wait a minute. I think I know those guards. If they ask who you are, just turn your heads in a superior manner and refuse to answer. I'll tell them you are German officials on assignment for your Government."

At the checkpoint, our car came to a gradual halt. Frank and I played the drama as planned. After our driver had a short chat with the guards, he received the motion to proceed.

We had to trust each stranger that helped us. Sometimes he was Swiss and sometimes American. Anyone of which could have turned us in to the authorities. In that case, we would have spent months under the commandant who justly earned the nickname "The villain of Wauwilermoos." He was known as "a tough sob," that hated Americans more than he hated the rats that infested his prison.

After traveling for many miles through a beautiful valley on the bright day in November with the snow-covered Alps towering above us on either side, our driver pulled off the road where a forest surrounded us. "This is the place I am to let you out," he said matter-of-factly. "You are to stay here. You must go one hundred meters to the left of the road, hide among the trees and wait. Sometime this afternoon a large truck hauling furniture will stop in this very place. The driver of the truck will get out and take a leak, as you Americans say. Then he will kick the back tires. That will be your signal to come out from hiding and introduce yourselves. Now, if a truck stops and the driver does not go through the procedure, stay hid, for he will be an impostor."

The truck sped away and was quickly out of sight, as Frank and I stood trying to imprint on our memories the details of the instructions. For none were ever written down. We scampered to our hiding place to watch for the furniture truck.

It was the middle of the afternoon, and the sun was shining bright through the tall trees that surrounded us. The birds provided music for us and the squirrels put on a show by chasing one another over the ground and up and down trees. Each creature, in its own way, went about merrily doing what it was programmed to do since the beginning. They lived happily one day at a time oblivious of the deadly war taking place only a few miles away. Frank and I were very aware of the war for we could hear the boom of Howitzers in the battle for northern France.

As the sun sank lower and lower in the western sky and the shadow of the trees grew longer, the chill in the air became more pronounced. Aware that it would soon be dark in these woods all alone in late November, we began to wonder if our next contact had forgotten to pick us up. If the driver of the furniture truck failed to show, could we survive the night in the midst of mountains covered with snow? Our furry and feathered friends were not concerned about such things for their Creator had provided for them.

This beautiful setting, with nightfall approaching, reminded me of the late afternoons spent in the Rocky Mountains back home. There it was different, for friends and I knew our location and had transportation to leave any time we wished. But, here in the Alps for the first time, it was different. We knew nothing about the place. By circumstances, we were forced to rely on an unknown stranger for a way out. This was becoming of great concern.

As time dragged by, we waited and waited, looking out from behind the trees, hoping, hoping. Then, when the sun was about to disappear behind the mountains, we saw a truck coming around a curve. I held my breath. The driver stopped, got out, relieved himself and kicked the back tires. We ran toward him. Frank identified us in the German language. With minimum conversation, the man raised the back door of the truck. We hustled in and settled down on cushioned furniture for the next leg of our escape route.

The truck driver proved to be trustworthy. It was well after dark when he drove into some unknown city and parked in front of an office building. He opened the back door of the truck, and Frank and I crawled out only to find guards patrolling the area. To throw the watchmen off, we helped the driver unload the furniture. When the last piece was unloaded, while we stood inside out of earshot of the guards, the driver whispered, "You men will stay in this building until daylight. Go up three flights of stairs and you will find room 310. Go in that office and spend the night. Make sure you leave by the back window before the office workers arrive in the morning."

Frank and I felt our way up the dark stairway, and in the dim light found the designated room. When we opened the door, to our surprise and amazement, we found two American airmen waiting for us. These men had instructions for the coming day.

All were tense and tired from the uncertainty of our escape and desired rest and sleep. We lay on the hard wooden floor and desktops. Rest and sleep was hard to come by. What would tomorrow bring? Would we make good our escape attempt, or would we end up in prison? We couldn't rule out the possibility of getting shot. These thoughts roamed through my mind interfering with sleep that was difficult, even without the worry

Long before sunup as the first light began to peek through the office window, the four of us stretched and yawned hoping we had enough strength to face all the strain of the new day. When we got awake, we tidied up the office as best we could. The two men (Sorry, I don't remember their names) informed Frank and me of the instructions received from their last contact.

This office building, like the hotel in Davos, was built in the side of a hill. When we opened the window to make our exit, we stepped out on solid earth. Outside the window there was a small garden surrounded by a rock fence about waist high. On top of the fence, there were large pieces of broken glass embedded in hard concrete. In the semidarkness we had to crawl over the fence being careful not to cut ourselves too severely lest it be necessary to see a doctor to stop the bleeding.

On the fifth day of our odyssey, instructions were for the four of us to walk the streets of the city until a limousine stopped to pick us up. First we had to slip and slide down the hillside to the street without being spotted be early commuters. We wore civilian clothes. I still had the brim of my green hat with the red feather pulled down before my eyes. The four of us reached the street unharmed and began to walk. We didn't stop for breakfast for fear we would miss our ride. Also, we feared being spotted as escapees.

We walked, and walked and walked, bowing to the ladies, nodding to the gentlemen and doing a lot of window-shopping. It wasn't until afternoon that an old 1930s limousine stopped at the curb, and the driver tooted the horn. We hesitated to answer until he called out in broken English, "Looking for four men." After Frank, who could speak his lingo, talked to him, we all jumped in the back of the vehicle.

The American ground forces had liberated southern France up past Lyon. It was our goal to cross the Swiss border into France hoping to catch an Army Air Corps plane back to our home base in Foggia, Italy.

The man up front drove around until dark making us sweat for a few hours. It began to snow making the snow in the country even deeper. Well into the late November night, we stopped at a tavern, and the driver went in without telling us now long he would be. The four of us sat in the back of the limousine for a couple of hours with the shades pulled and no heat. With our light suits our only cover, we got cold. We talked exchanging notes about our lives. With nervous tension building up, we argued. One of us swung his hand in the air and flipped a switch on the side of the automobile flooding the inside with light. The other three whispered in unison, "Turn that thing off. You want some body to see us and turn us in!"

The driver stayed in the tavern far to long for our comfort. The longer he stayed the more impatient and nervous we got. We whispered constantly, wondering what would happen to us next. Finally, about midnight, the driver with another man walked slowly though the heavy snow toward the limousine laughing and talking. We saw nothing to laugh about for we were cold, hungry and past ready to move on.

As we traveled from the populated area westward toward France, the falling snow continued to pile up. The men continued to talk and laugh among themselves while we shivered. It got more difficult to drive on the country road as the snow continued to fall.

Our driver stopped the vehicle and told us he had gone as far as he dared, and the man beside him would walk with us to the border between Switzerland and France. After that, we were on our own. Before the driver left, he asked, "Do you men know the Allies had moved into southern France and were pushing their way to Paris?" Yes, we had heard about it via radio. We would have to walk the last couple of miles to the border. He gave assurance he had placed us with a trustworthy friend. His friend had led other airmen across the rugged terrain.

After a day of long rides and waiting that tried our patience, we stepped from the limousine into the bright moonlight. The heavy, dark clouds drifted overhead. The ground was covered with knee-deep snow. The beautiful, fluffy stuff glistened from the light of the bright November moon. The white Alps in the background showed up as ghostly silhouettes.

As the driver pulled away to return, our guide whispered, "Okay, you men follow me." We had no other choice. He told us it was a difficult walk to the border; we would have to stick together and walk briskly.

It was the early hours of the sixth day since Frank and I left Davos. The temperature was hovering around 32 degrees. We were cold, hungry and full of hope knowing freedom was not far away. The twinkling stars smiled down on us. A few farmhouses still had lights shining through windows. We heard dogs barking from all sides as we trudged through the deep snow. The barking and excitement of the many dogs was a serious concern to us. Would they alert the Swiss farmers that something strange was going on? In that case, would the farmers tell the Swiss authorities? Would we be caught and sent to prison when freedom was so close?

In the wee hours of the morning, we came to a small river that separated France from Switzerland. We no longer heard the dogs. All was quiet except the rippling sound of rushing water. The moon and the clouds were playing hide and seek, for sometime we could see the bright moon and sometime it hid behind the clouds.

As we watched chunks of ice floating on the river, our guide told us this is as far as he could go with us. He informed us the flowing stream was about chest deep. Unless we wanted to wear wet clothes that would probably freeze when we came out on the other side of the river, we'd better strip to the bare skin, tie the clothes in a bundle and hold them on top of our heads as we waded across.

After we stripped, standing in the snow, he gave another warning: beyond the stream was a swamp that extended about half a mile. The swamp was filled with cypress stumps. When we waded through all that, coming safely on the French side, we could put our clothes back on. As if an after thought struck him, he said, "Beyond the swamp, you'll see a light in a farm house to your left. They've been notified by radio that you are coming."

The four of us airmen, thanked him, paid his fee, and stepped reluctantly into the swift flowing stream. There we were, four once proud members of the United States Army Air Corps, naked as the day we were born, humbled by circumstances, each holding a bundle of clothes on his head. Shivering and numb from the cold, but thankful, we waded through the freezing stream, as chunks of ice hit us around the chest and shoulders.

By the time we reached the bank on the other side, the moon was completely hidden from view. Walking across the swamp in the darkness, each of us in turn, stubbed a toe against a cypress knees and let out a yell that corresponded to the hurt.

Nearly paralyzed from the cold, with the skin over each entire body swiveled like a dried prune, we emerged from the swamp. Still naked, we thrust our hands high into the air and cried out in the darkness, "Long live France, and God bless the USA!"

After dressing, we searched for the light in the farmhouse to our left. We had been told that a farmer and his wife would be waiting for us. By this time a stiff wind was blowing at a rapid clip kicking up snow so thick we could see only a short distance. We walked facing a bitter wind, hoping the light in the farmhouse would appear.

While we walked laboriously through the blowing snow, we searched for the tiny light that was our beacon to guide us to safety from the elements that engulfed us. Our bodies grew colder with each advancing step. We dared not stop to rest believing, we may freeze to death.

Suddenly one of our number cried out, "Look! I see it!" In the distance, the light shined ever so dimly. We kept trudging onward. After a while, we could see the very faint outline of a farmhouse where a light shined from the upstairs window. Soon the sound of cowbells was heard and the cows began to bawl. Being the only farm boy in our foursome, I assured the others that was a good sign for the day was about to break and the farmer would soon be milking the cows and doing the outside chores.

Weak and trembling from the cold, we stumbled upon the porch of the farmhouse and one of us knocked, with an icy fist, on the door. A heavy woman dressed in a faded dress came to answer. When she opened the door, she asked, "Who are you?" She saw our pitiful condition, but before we could answer, she called her husband who approached slowly dress in overalls ready to do his early morning chores.

"Who are you?" he asked. Through lips numb and purple from the freezing cold, Frank answered, "We are American airmen."

"Where did you come from?" In war time the gentleman had learned to be extra cautious.

"We have just escaped from Switzerland."

"Where were you interned?"

"Two of us were interned in Davos."

The couple seemed satisfied and welcomed us into their country home. This part of their beloved country had recently been liberated from the Nazi horde, and they welcomed us with characteristic French enthusiasm. We observed their humble manner, as they prepared to care for us until Americans came from Lyon to pick us in a Jeep.

The man left to milk the cows and do the other farm chores, and the lady busied herself preparing breakfast for four very hungry Americans. It had been more than twenty-four hours since we ate, but the coffee made from grounds that had been boiled several times, and the thin potato soup with a glass of whole milk tasted delicious. We expressed our profound gratitude to her. For she had prepared the best breakfast, she could, so soon after the Nazi occupation.

After we ate, the lady showed us rooms up stairs where feather beds awaited us. It was the sixth day since Frank and I left Davos. We, with the other two airmen, fell into beds exhausted and slept for hours.

When we awoke, the farmer and his wife informed us they had contacted the United States Army at Lyon, via radio, that we had arrived as planned. The Army assured them a Jeep would be sent as soon as possible to take us to the Air Base near Lyon.

After a couple of days with the farmer and his wife, who treated us like conquering heroes, the Jeep arrived and hauled us to the Air Base that had been bombed by both American and German forces. The base was in shambles and was in great need of reconstruction.

Frank and I were examined by an Army medic. I learned I had lost twenty-five pounds since we brought **Holey Joe** down last September. At 135, that was the least I'd weighed since graduating from high school four years earlier. The best meal since we left the States, cooked on a real stove, not cold from a can, was set before us We filled our GI issue tin plates heaping full, but soon learned our stomachs had shrank so much we had to leave most of the food.

After we ate our fill, we mingled with fresh troops from America, the French underground, and escapees from Holland, Germany, Spain and many survivors of Nazi atrocities. Each had an interesting and exciting story to tell.

Since the Air Field was still in the reconstruction stage, rooms for service men were nonexisting. I spent one night with air control men in the tower. A young French boy, wearing a GI uniform that hung loosely on this thin body, also spent the night with us. The U. S. service men shared their k-rations with the boy. I was still hungry and craved some of the food that, under ordinary circumstances, I wouldn't eat on a bet. None was offered me, and none was asked for. I spent the restless night with my stomach growling.

Frank and I told the story of our escape to the de-briefing officer who warned us not to relate the details to anyone lest other internees making the attempt would be jeopardized. We waited around the Lyon Air Field for a military plane, which had room for us, to take us on the next leg of our journey. Finally, the authorities notified us we would leave for Naples, Italy early the next day.

On the morning, they scheduled us to leave on a C-47 to Marseilles and on to Naples, the entire field was socked in by heavy fog. No planes could take off. Even the birds were walking. The Army was experimenting with such conditions to see if man's methods would cause the fog to lift. We had a saying in those days: "The difficult we do immediately, the impossible takes a little time."

Barrels filled with used oil were placed on various spots around the Field and set afire hoping the heat from the burning oil would cause the fog to rise so planes could take off. The impossible took more than a little time. The fact was, the experiment did not work. Planes were left on the ground until the sun burned the fog away.

After the fog dissipated about noon, we boarded the C-47 and flew to the city on the southern coast of France. We landed at Marooilloo, took care of business, and flew across a sliver of the Mediterranean landing at Naples Airport. There we hitched a ride on an Army truck to the hotel.

Red Cross uniforms, complete with high top marching shoes, were given us at Lyon. Our dress had a remote resemblance to the US military, but very remote. The uniforms and the crude passports we carried made us highly suspect to any MP who checked us out.

The 10th Mountain Division of the American Army was still fighting the German Army in the rugged mountains of Northern Italy. The German Army was supplied with fighting men and implements of war by trains that rolled through the heart of Switzerland. The cargo these trains carried kept the Nazis fighting much longer and killing many more Americans.

While Frank and I waited in Naples for a military plane to fly us across the boot to Foggia, we spent much of our time sightseeing in and around the city. This was a welcome respite from flying bombers over enemy strongholds and the uncertainty of escape.

One day we visited the city of Pompeii that was buried in 79 AD by the ash from the eruption of Mt. Vesuvius. This city was one of the choice vacation spots for the ancient Romans for here they could engage in every immoral act their flesh desired. Our Italian guide showed us and explained the decadent life style of the Romans of the first century. He made a comment that lingers with me to this day: "These people became so corrupt that God destroyed their city."

Since the German Luftwaffe, were still roaming the Italian skies and dropping bombs on cities, Naples was blacked out every night. One evening a group of us took a walk in the darkness around our hotel. Our flashlights shining on the ground guided us. A lone young woman approached us insisting that she would show us a "good time" in her room for $5. The question was raised among us: "What do you think?" I had kept silent. Then someone asked me, "Well, how about it." Not wanting any of the men to get involved, I replied, "She's probably got a venereal disease." Immediately she retorted in broken English, "Me no got no disease," and raised her dress to prove her point. All flashlights focused on her. She went on her way without any takers.

After a few days of waiting for transportation to our home bases, the busy Military Police in this large city hauled us in to headquarters thinking we were AWOL. Our sloppy uniforms, our amateurish looking passports and everything about us caused them to think we were deserters. All our explanation could not make them change their minds. They took us to the guardhouse and were about to slam the door on us for a lengthy stay and possible Court Marshall. Frank saved our hides by producing a letter from General Carl Spaats stating that we had escaped from Switzerland.

This letter put a different light on our situation. MPs and their commander were not satisfied. In wartime, all possibilities must be checked and rechecked. They wired across the Italian boot to our bases for conformation of our stories. When the authorities learned our stories were true, they loaned us money and ordered us to go to the Post Exchange and buy new uniforms. We did as told and came forth feeling 100% better and looking like proud Second Lieutenants of the United States Army Air Corps.

I began to think about the contrast between the countries of Switzerland and Italy and France. Switzerland had escaped the ravages of war, while Italy and France had experienced the madness of Adolph Hitler. In these later nations, homes, businesses and public buildings had been bombed, leaving them in shambles. The economies were in ruins. Mothers and fathers cried openly because their families were separated or killed or lost in the maze of evil. Children in their rag-tag dress roamed the streets in droves pleading, begging for candy bars, or a few pennies to buy food. They tried to sell pornographic pictures or symbols to GIs for a few cents. Pretty teenagers and young women sold themselves for an hour or overnight for a five-dollar bill. It reminded me of some of the ancient cities of Israel when they turned from their God who delivered them from Egyptian bondage.

Granted, I knew little about the details of the Biblical stories. Down deep in the recesses of my heart, I believed God is all-powerful and good. A few verses were still lodged in my memory form Sunday School during my boyhood. Admittedly, my life style did not demonstrate this admission.

Surely, it was because many people had left God out of their lives and followed evil instead of the good. Somebody had committed a terrible sin, and as a result, catastrophe was brought upon an entire generation. I kept quiet about it, but back in my mind, I wanted very much to do something so it would not occur a second time.

These thoughts roamed about in my innermost being. I didn't even tell Frank about these thoughts. I wanted nobody to know about my thinking lest they get the impression that I was developing a superficial conviction about the Lord. Christianity, as I understood it, was all right in the Army Air Corps as long as one didn't take it too seriously. If that occurred, it was taboo.

Passage was secured for Frank and me to return to our respective bases on the Adriatic coast of Italy. Seventy two days had past since my crew lifted **Holey Joe** off the 463rd Bomb Group Air Field September 23, 1944. All the other nine members of my crew were still in Switzerland.

I fully expected to fly more missions when I got back to my home base. But I was told, because of some regulation in the Geneva Conference, pilots who had been gone as long as I had could not fly in combat again. Apparently, Frank was given the same information. Being persuaded this was a fact, I began immediately to make arrangements to go home in the States. If possible, I wanted to go home as a First Lieutenant. Attempting to make this a reality, I caught a ride to Berea, Italy where the headquarters of the 15th Air Corps was located. While waiting for the time of my appointment in a top office to arrive, I studied carefully the arguments I'd make to the officer in charge of promotions. When the time arrived, I walked into the office loaded with reasons I should get a higher rank. I saluted and was invited to sit down. I presented the officer the orders to return to the States. "What brings you here to see me?" he asked.

"Sir, I've been a Second Lieutenant for some time," I stated, "and I've flown missions in combat, my plane went down and I escaped from internment."

"So you think you should be promoted," the officer spoke with a little laugh.

I began to use some logic, "Sir, you are well aware that many of your First lieutenants and Captains have either been killed or else they are no longer able to fly because of wounds"

"Yes, I know that."

"In that case, it leaves many officer ranks open. I am hoping to get one of those slots."

"But there will be other men coming in to take those positions."

"Yes, Sir, I'm aware of that. I have orders to leave the 15th Air force pretty quick and the slot will still be open for new officers."

"You make a good case." the officer said. "You may go now. I'll see what I can do for you."

In a few days, I had papers stating that I was promoted to First Lieutenant.

One of the first things I did upon returning to the Foggia Base was to write a letter to my bride of a little more than a year. The Army had notified Dorothy that I was missing in action.

That is all she knew. We were forbidden to write while in internment. She didn't know if I were dead or alive, and if alive what condition I was in. At this point in time, all letters were subject to be censored. If an airman wrote something home that was forbidden, he could be in trouble. This was the later part of November and radios all over the western world were playing Bing Crosby's song *White Christmas.* I wrote in the letter *I'm Dreaming of a White Christmas* hoping such popular sentence would escape the censors black pencil, and that Dorothy would pick up on my hope to see her during the coming holiday.

My footlocker was given to me all packed with my personal belongings ready to be sent to my wife if I were confirmed dead. Cold chills ran through my body when I opened it up to find my formal uniform, a stack of letters received from home, my war medals, ribbons, battle stars and other stuff. A strange feeling enveloped me as I kept thinking this is what my wife would have received had I not survived.

It was time to complete preparation to board the Liberty Ship I was assigned to for passage back to the United States of America. There was no way I could be prepared for the events that lay ahead.

HOMEWARD BOUND

Weighted down with an olive drab duffel bag stuffed full and a heavy footlocker, I managed to carry them up the plank into the ocean going vessel named Brazil. All the while, I looked for Frank Hoch. Men, who experienced what we had, grow very close in a short time.

More than a thousand men, loaded down with their possessions, were bumping into one another eager to settled in assigned bunks. Some were hollering, others laughing while some cursed Hitler and his gang. The boys that had left home to join one of the services one, two, three years ago were now seasoned men hardened by the rigors of war. Many had killed enemy service men and had seen friends killed in the awful war. They were no longer the eager young men who left jobs, school and home to fight a war they knew so little about. Now they knew and hated what they had seen and learned.

I kept looking for Frank. *Where was he? Did he board this ship, or was he going back to America some other way?*

When the ship was fully loaded, and orders were given, we weighed anchor and sailed form Naples Harbor into the wide Mediterranean headed for Strait of Gibraltar. Passing through the Strait, we broke out into the Atlantic sailing for "home sweet home". There is absolutely no place like it. Every combatant was anxious to get back to step on American soil and see folks left behind.

After we had been under way for about a day and a half, I ran into Frank. With the excitement of being together again subsided, we reviewed events that transpired since last we met. There was much to talk about.

Frank was a D-24 pilot assigned to a different United States Air Base along the Adriatic coast of Italy. I don't remember how it came about that we were fortunate enough to get passage on the same ship. Strange things happen in the Army, and we gladly accepted being together.

The compartment I was assigned to had bunks stacked four and five deep from the floor to the ceiling. These bunks were so close that men had to walk sideways to pass one another as they made their way down the aisle. Since most of the men were not use to the rolling ship on the high seas, some vomited on their bunks or the floor before reaching the head. The place was already dirty - perhaps filthy better described the place. With the sweaty bodies of great numbers of men crammed together in such a tight place in hot quarters without air conditioning, the place had the odor of a pigpen. I just couldn't stand the quarters for long. The U. S. Coast Guard ran the ship, and my concept of this branch of the service was just about zero.

Later I began to realize these service men were short handed. So many men who had served their time in the European Theater were so anxious to leave the war zone and go home, the Coast Guard was over burdened with the great numbers. Though the accommodations were atrocious, every man aboard was thankful to be aboard going home.

Sometime I just had to get away from the suffocating atmosphere in our quarters and the large number of sweaty men. Often I went alone to the deck of the ship, walked to the bow and breathed the fresh air as I watched the mighty ocean waves driven by high winds play with the ship as if it were a toy.

Navigating into the stiff southwest wind on the rough North Atlantic seas, the bow of the ship rose to highs and dipped to lows. It was scary. Standing on the bow was like riding a roller coaster. One instant the front of the ship would be twenty feet above the surface, and the next instant it would be below the surface with salt water washing over the deck. Not accustom to such, the experience was a little frightening yet pleasant at the same time. I wondered if the bouncing vessel would break apart.

I'd look across the vast expanse of waves on the endless ocean, and wonder that perhaps there were German submarines lurking out there in the deep waiting for the correct time to send a torpedo into our ship blowing us to smithereens. What could I do about it? Nothing! If such a catastrophe occurred, I was as safe on deck as in quarters. So why worry?

Most of December 1944 had slipped into the past and a shipload of weary United States service men were only a few days from America's shores. Every man on ship was glued to the broadcast on the radio. "THE GERMAN ARMY HAS OPENED UP A LAST DESPART EFFORT TO DRIVE THE ALLIED FORCES BACK INTO THE SEA. THIS LAST DITCH MANEUVER IS CALLED, 'THE BATTLE OF THE BULGE.'"

A chorus went up from the embattled men from every quarter on the Brazil: "LET'S TURN AROUND; GO BACK AND HELP WHIP THOSE DAMNED KRAUTS!" I'm not sure all of us meant it. Nevertheless, the shouting continued as we thrust our fist into the air. One thing was for sure: The more we heard of the slaughter of fellow Americans, the madder we got.

Despite the emotions displayed aboard the ship, the card games continued day and night. Porker took priority over all the other games. I knew its rules and played the game. It didn't take much prodding to get me involved since I was "flush" with money. Uncle Sam had given us back pay after being interned. Between periods of vomiting and riding the ups and downs on the deck, I sat at the poker tables attempting to take from my fellow veterans their hard-earned money saved to start a new life after their discharge. Since they were willing to take the chance to win my money, I figured it was fair to take theirs if I could.

Some of the guys who sat across the table from me had fought more battles than I, been in combat much longer and the looks in their faces and in their eyes were hardened as a result. Many men were older and more experienced at the card table than I was. My face always had a youthful look, and I must have looked like an innocent schoolboy to them. The tough and seasoned men seemed pleased to see me sitting at the same table with them.

Before I sat down to play the game, I'd find a hiding place and take from my concealed money belt all the cash needed. Then return to the table looking innocent as possible. Sometime I thought I saw a smirk on the opponents' faces that led me to believe they expected to take me to the cleaners. All that was well and good, for I had learned to have confidence in my poker-playing ability.

Each time the cards were dealt, I checked them shyly with a worried look. The men sitting at the table would smile, and I imagined they were licking their chops expecting to line their pockets with my money. It didn't work out that way. By the time we reached New York, I had stuffed ($600) six hundred dollars in my money belt. That was enough to buy a new Ford automobile when I joined the Army Air Corps back in February of 1941.

When the Brazil eased into New York Harbor, every man was on deck screaming, yelling, crying and praying in thanksgiving. It was the morning of December 22, 1944. Early in the day, clouds hovered over the great City and a light fog made the towers in lower Manhattan appear as ghosts. When that beautiful Lady, the Statue of Liberty, came into view, the screaming veterans of that terrible war became silent. With tears in most every eye, we gazed respectfully upon the majestic symbol of America's freedom, justice and hope that we had fought to preserve.

Time was rapidly slipping by, and every man was eager to prepare to disembark from the ship. Each hastened to retrieve his belongings to take his station, walk down the plank and take that first step on American soil after an absence of so long. We hoped to forget the awfulness of war. Our desire was to be in the warm, welcome arms of family and friends who loved us.

After leaving the ship, hundreds of men lined up in sloppy formation with our luggage sitting on the ground beside us. We noticed a multitude of Army vehicles lined up ready to take us to Fort Dix. An Army Captain mounted a truck to instruct us as to the procedure we should follow. Before he dismissed the formation, he called out the names of six men who had escaped from somewhere in Europe. Franks name and my name were among the six.

The six of us stepped forward We were hustled into a plush automobile designed to transport high ranking brass. As we sped off, we watched hundreds of men left behind scrambling with their luggage to get into waiting trucks.

In the speeding vehicle, we were told the investigating officer wanted to debrief each of us hoping to learn how we escaped from our respective places of confinement. The information we gave may possibly help other Allied prisoners of war to escape.

At Fort Dix the six of us were taken to a vacant officers home where we were to live during our stay at the camp. In addition, a car and driver was assigned to us for transportation to places we needed to go.

As we traveled to our destination, an Army Major riding with us, asked, "Just how did you men escape form detention?" We six escapees, of much lower rank, had been taught since the day we enlisted, to obey officers who out ranked us. All of us had been warned not to divulge any secrets to absolutely nobody except investigating officers whose duty it was to debrief us.

While the vehicle sped toward Fort Dix, we sat in complete silence. The Major said, "Well, aren't you guys going to tell me how you got out?" Still silence. Upon the Major's insistence, a young 1st. Lieutenant, a P-47 pilot, who had escaped from Franco's Spain replied, "Major, we ain't telling you nothin'." I doubt if I could have spoken to a superior officer as the young pilot did. We sat in silence waiting for the Major's response.

Finally, the Major said, "If anyone of you had told me how you escaped without permission, you would have been subject to Court Martial." His statement was followed by our nervous laughter.

After we settled into officers quarters, our driver took us to the place for debriefing. He also drove us to the mess hall where we could stuff our faces with delicious food until we were satisfied. I was anxious to eat Army chow prepared by some of the best cooks in all the armed services for men who were home from combat. These cooks made sure the food was the very best they could produce.

Standing in the chow line, my mouth began to water in anticipation. When it came my turn, I picked up a steel tray, knife, fork and spoon with plenty of napkins. Passing down the cafeteria line, I chose an inch-thick, juicy stake about the size of my hand that the private behind the food line put on my tray. I grabbed a quart of milk that was sitting in ice, ask for fruit and vegetables to round out the tray, grabbed a fist full of cookies and, for good measure, I took a large piece of chocolate cake on a saucer.

Found a completely vacant table, without saying a word to anybody, I sat down and began cutting the steak into bite sizes. While cutting the meat, I ate cookies and drank half the milk. After gorging on steak, vegetables and fruit, I began to gag. Before long, my innards began to growl, and I began to feel like chucking all I'd eaten. Not wanting to nauseate the rest of the returned veterans by exposing to them, in an unwholesome manner, what I'd eaten, I pushed to the center of the table more than half the food on my tray and rushed out of the mess hall to get fresh air. Breathing deep to settle my stomach, I came to realize it had shrunk during the months I existed on an insufficient diet. I remembered my Mother saying to me as a farm boy, "Your eyes are bigger than your stomach," when I took more corn on the cob, fried chicken, mashed potatoes, corn bread and milk than I would get down.

By late afternoon December 24, the interrogation officer had finished with us. Knowing we were anxious to get home, he had orders cut for us to go be with our families on R & R. Frank caught a train to his home in Buffalo, New York. The quick witted P-47 pilot and I were going west. Our army driver took us to the airport.

We struggled to get our luggage inside only to find the huge lobby was nearly vacant at the late hour. No ticket people were behind the counter. As my pilot companion and I talked, the sound of our voices sounded ghost-like bouncing off the cavernous walls. We saw a single light shining in an office far down a long hall. Dragging our footlockers and duffel bags, we made our way to the light. When the lady behind the desk first saw us, dressed in our new First Lieutenant uniforms, she exclaimed with slight fear in her voice, "O, I didn't know anybody was near. What can I do for you young men?"

We told her we wanted to buy plane tickets going west.

She laughed as she said jokingly, "Perhaps you didn't know there's a war going on."

My comrade replied, "Yes. We know. We've been there."

Hoping to clarify her statement, she said, "I was only joking."

"That's okay. We understand," I said.

"I'm sorry," she said, "every seat on all the planes is booked for at least thirty days in advance. We simply don't have any at this time."

313

My companion asked, as he stood with four flat boxes in his hands, "Is there someone else we can talk to?"

I wondered what he had in the boxes that caused him to hold them so tight.

Pointing to an office in the back, the lady replied, "My boss is in her office. But I'm sure she will tell you the same thing."

After getting permission to leave our luggage in the office, we trekked to the bosses office. When we appeared in the doorway, the lady in charge invited us to, "Come in."

"May I help you?" She asked in a cool, professional manner.

"We're here to buy plane tickets going out west," I responded.

"Everything is booked. I can put your names down. It'll be at least thirty days before any seats are available. If you'll give me your names and telephone numbers, I call you as soon as I can book you."

The P-47 pilot said, "But you don't understand. We just came in on a ship from Europe where we flew combat missions. We're anxious to get home, and our families are waiting for us."

"Sorry, but rules are rules. You men should know that, particularly in wartime. I can't possibly help you. You'll have to wait your turn."

My comrade, (whose name I've forgotten), holding the boxes before the boss-lady, said with a smile, "You may be interested in what these boxes contain."

"No. I can't possible be interested."

He opened the top box and twelve pairs of shiny silk lady's stockings were exposed.

The lady behind the desk dropped her professionalism, with a giddy, high pitched voice exclaimed, "Where did you get those. I haven't seen silk hose since the war started!"

"You know some of the South American countries aren't fighting in this war." He indicated their origin. "How do you like them?" My friend asked.

With eyes brighter than the overhead electric light, the lady rose from her cushioned chair, and ran her right hand over the smooth surface of the contents in the box. "They are absolutely beautiful."

The savvy pilot egged the lady on by saying, "I've got four boxes. Each box contains twelve pairs of hose."

The lady became as giddy as a schoolgirl about to open presents on Christmas morning. She exclaimed, "What I'd give for those hose!"

The sharp P-47 fighter pilot said, "There are all yours,....." He stopped short, watching her strong professional demeanor change to weakness. He added, "If."

"We came here to buy plane tickets going west. That's what we want. You want these beautiful hose. There are forty-eight pairs and all yours, if you'll sell us tickets on the next flight going west." My companion bargained.

With uncertainty in her voice, she whispered with a whimper to herself. "I don't know." After a pause, she braced herself and said, "If you were generals instead of lieutenant, I would arrange to sell you tickets without hesitation. Why should you combat men be treated any differently." There followed a longer pause. She then exclaimed, "Okay, I'll do it!"

He placed the four boxes carefully on her desk. The lady got busy scratching out names on her list and adding ours. With tickets in our hands, we thanked her and left to wait until after midnight when the next flight took off for Wichita, Kansas where my family was waiting.

After flying through the night, our plane landed at the airport in Wichita where I got off leaving the feisty P-47 combat pilot on board to complete the last leg of his homeward journey. It was about noon when I de-planed into a beautiful Christmas morning with warm sunshine flooding the city. Since none of my family had an automobile, I hurriedly hailed a cab, stuffed my luggage in its trunk, and we sped to my sister's Etta's home on Water Street. My dream of a White Christmas had become a reality without a snowflake in sight.

After hugs and kisses with the family and tears of joy with thanksgiving for my safe return, I spent time with Dorothy behind a closed door.

Returning to my family, minus our three brothers who were still in a war in the Pacific zone, I reached for my wallet. It wasn't to be found. For the first time in my life, I remembered the number of the cab and the name of the driver that was posted on the sunvisor above the cabby's head.

Without wasting time, I phoned the cab company and reported my loss. They dispatched the same cab driver to deliver by wallet. After examining the billfold, I found nothing missing. The moneybelt was concealed, for I didn't want to explain how I got all that cash.

Dad was still working at Boeing Aircraft. While I was in Wichita, he wanted me to go with him where he worked on the assembly line. He wanted to show me off to the men he worked with as he had his navy sons when they were on leave. I was dressed in my uniform with ribbons and medals, and the sloppy officers hat with Air Corps wings attached. We marched down the assembly line as Dad proudly introduced me to each of his fellow workers saying, "This is my son I've told you about that flies these planes we make here."

I was greeted by all the workers with respect. One of them, however, didn't seem so happy to meet me. When I was introduced to this one fellow, he said, "Yeah, Mack, all your boys look just alike. Everyone of them have a nose right in the middle of his face." With this remark, he turned his back on us and walked away.

After spending a few days in Wichita visiting the family, Dorothy and I flew on a civilian plane down to Oklahoma City to visit her brothers and sisters. In a few days, I was notified by the Army Air Corps that my wife and I could continue our R &

R in a Miami, Florida hotel with all expenses paid. We caught a bus to Miami where we stayed in a reserved room enjoying luxury that we'd never experienced before. Since I was so busy and money scarce when we married a little over a year ago, we called this our honeymoon.

Beside having quality, free time with my wife, two highlights stick out in my mind. Some of us rented a boat for deep sea fishing. I caught a baby shark about two feet long.

In order to draw flying pay in addition to our base army salary, pilots had to fly at least four hours a month. Arrangement was made with an Army Air Base in Florida, for me to fly on a night mission as an observer to get in my time for extra pay. It was a beautiful star-lit night, and I observed the brilliant lights along the east coast of the Sunshine State.

When we returned to Oklahoma City, I had orders to report to the Air Base near San Marcus, Texas for a second time to fly Navigation cadets around the country in order to sharpen their skills.

Not much had changed since I was there before going over seas to fly in combat. Orvil Filbeck still preached at the small church I attended. By this time, he had received his doctor's degree in Psychology from the University of Texas. Doctor Filback had his thesis put in book form with a hard back. He gave one of the books to me. Orvil continued to use me in the church services, and I continued my wayward ways.

On a day when central Texas was socked in with heavy, dark clouds and the rain was coming down in sheets, all planes were grounded. A group of us flyers met at the officers club to drink and tell jokes that we would not dare tell if women were present. Before we left, many of us bought a fifth of whiskey to take with home. Leaving the club, we ran through the downpour to our cars. I got in the little Nash automobile I had purchased recently, revved the motor and headed for home through the rain.

Within a stones throw of the club, at an intersection of streets, a big G I truck plowed into the left side of my car. The police were called, and they decided it was the truck driver's fault and the Army should pay for damages. I was not hurt, but my pride was damaged.

While getting soaked in the rain, others fliers stopped to check on my condition. I was concerned about the loss of my car, for I knew in wartime it would take months to repair it for all parts and labor went into the effort to defeat our enemies.

Torrents of rain were still coming down, the streets were flooding, and the water was now ankle deep. I stood bent over trying to explain to the police how it all happened so they could fill out their report. A fellow officer stopped his car to yell above the storm, "How you doin'?

I shouted back, "I'm okay. Since they are going to haul my car to a garage, I would like a ride home."

"That's all right. I'll wait for you."

After the police completed their work, I crawled into my friend's car and was silent as he drove through the storm to our apartment where Dorothy waited for me.

As a small boy, I've believed that God worked in my life. While we traveled slowly this very wet early afternoon, my mind was flooded with thoughts such as: *Of all the men at the club, who did the same things I did, why was my car damaged severely without me getting hurt. Was the Lord telling me something?*

When the friend stopped at the curb, where water was running over it, I gave him the fifth of whiskey telling him I didn't want it. He thanked me as I jumped from his car and rushed through the weather into our apartment. In drenched clothes, I had to tell Dorothy about the wreck, but I didn't tell her about the alcohol. Her dad was an alcoholic, and she hated the stuff.

My Nash was hauled to a garage in San Antonio for repair. The months rolled by. I listened more closely to what was taught at church. My interest in flying was waning. My thoughts and desires were shifting to other things.

By April 1945, the military could see the light at the end of the long tunnel of engagement with our determined enemies. From all indications, the Allies would soon win the most damaging war in history, and the Axis would soon capitulate by signing "Unconditional Surrender."

It was the 12th of April, while my little Nash was still in the garage, I stood on a street in San Marcus waiting for a bus. Dressed in military officer's uniform, I was enjoying the sunshine beaming down from above, observing the lovely venue and watching the shapely girls pass by. My joy was brought to abrupt close when a passerby asked tearfully, "Have you heard the news on the radio?"

"No. What happened?"

She announced, "President Roosevelt died today in Hot Springs Georgia."

My spirits wilted. Looking in the faces of others waiting for the bus, I saw sadness and tears flowing down the cheeks of both young and old. Many dabbed salty tears from their eyes. All was quiet except for sniffles.

President Roosevelt, in his fourth term as president, was the only Commander in Chief most could remember. We had grown up under his leadership. We had watched him lead us through the worst Depression America had ever experienced. He was constantly in the headlines and the newsreels at the movies, showing his stewardship of the Great War and of the home front. This enormous loss was devastating to most citizens of the time.

The American people knew nothing about the Atomic Bomb, but the military was hastily making every preparation to use it if necessary. The Army Air Corps had more pilots than needed and was preparing to release all who wanted to leave. A point system was prepared and posted on bulletin boards on all airbases. After calculating my number of points, I knew I was near the top and would soon be release from my obligation to the Army.

The first wave of airmen with the most accumulated points was released from active service. I was not in that group. My points added up for me to be released in the second wave on July 7, 1945. Since I had two months furlough time built up, I was sent home in early May to await formal release in July.

I was very anxious to get out and be on my own. Dorothy and I settled in Wichita, Kansas because my parents had lived there since Dad started working for Boeing.

I received an order dated 4 July 1945 from commander Brigadier General Acheson stating that I would be "released from active duty at Fort Leavenworth on 11 jul 45 not by reason of physical disability. Tem AUS apmt of 1st Lieutenant Fooks will continue in force during period of present emergence and for six (6) mon, thereafter unless sooner terminated by DP"

My sister Jessie, whose husband was still serving in the South Pacific, went with me to Fort Leavenworth, to receive my "MILITARY RECORD AND REPORT OF SEPARATION CERTIFICATE OF SERVICE dated 11 July 45. First Lieutenant Leslie Eugene Fooks, Army Serial No. 0 711 ••• has been relieved from active duty with the United States Army Air Corps."

A letter followed from General Henry (Hap) Arnold: "1st. Lt. Leslie E. Fooks; 0-711 •••, I cannot meet you personally to thank you for a job well done; nor can I put into words the hope I have for you in future life. Together we built the striking force that swept the Luftwaffe from the skies and broke the German power to resist. Although you no longer play an active military part, the contribution you made to the Air Force was essential in making us the greatest team in the world.

"The ties that bound us under stress of combat must not be broken in peacetime. Together we share the responsibility for guarding our country in the air. We who stay will never forget the part you played while in uniform. We know you will continue to play a comparable part as a civilian. As we part, let me wish you God speed and the best of luck on your road in life. Our gratitude and respect go with you."

Signed: H. H. Arnold

Commanding General

Army Air Force.

Complete adjustment to a new life began.

TOUGH ADJUSTMENTS TO A NEW LIFE

I had recently turned nineteen, a visionary boy, not long out of high school, when I joined the Army Air Corps in February 17, 1941. In the summer of 1945, with four-and-a-half years of wartime military service, a life time of experiences behind me, and a few months short of twenty-four, there were unimaginable adjustments to be made. Instead of dreamy visions, followed by years of taking orders from higher-ups, it was time to face cold realities of life with a wife and a baby on the way.

I had to find a job, pay bills, buy groceries, get health insurance and a dozen other things to do, most of which was furnished by the Army. To pay for these, money was deducted form my pay while with Uncle Sam, and I never had to be concerned about them. Dorothy's parents were dead, and my parents were barely getting by so there was none to help us financially. Our livelihood depended solely on me. Yet, I was better off then many discharged veterans, for I had some severance pay and the six hundred dollars secretly hidden in my money belt.

Everything was changing for us. Not only that, but America and the whole world were changing. With millions of veterans coming home from the wars anxious to try our new ideas having strong determinations, we were ready to make the sacrifices necessary to make better a world for our children and all mankind.

Women had sacrificed their former way of life to work in factories building machines so their men could defeat a ruthless enemy and return to them. Couples, joined in holy wedlock, were eager to start a family, build schools, start businesses and rebuild the infrastructure of America that had long been neglected. While never forgetting our comrades lying silently in cemeteries on foreign soil, Americans were willing to work hard to avoid another Great Depression and another World War.

Remembering the disastrous plight of multiplied millions around the globe, including our wartime enemies, we looked beyond our own shores to give a helping hand to the former Axis powers that formerly attempted to destroy us and our Allies. One era was rapidly coming to a close. A new epoch was taking shape. We didn't know or understand what lay ahead, but with confidence in ourselves and faith in our God, we trusted the future would be better than the days of our youth.

Since so many service men were being discharge and war-time-factories were closing down, jobs were scarce I was better off them most of the vets, for I had a little money, had gone through photo school and knew something about that work, and I was a certified pilot and could fly airplanes. My interest in photography and flying had waned considerably. Outside of officers training, formal education ended with a high school diploma. I needed a college education.

While waiting to enroll in the University of Wichita, paid for by the G I Bill, I took a job in a chemical warehouse to pay bills and get the family settled. With the help our government gave all returning veterans, we bought a three-bedroom house on Madison Street for a little more than $5,000.

All the time, inside my head was churning images of the destruction I saw in Europe, and the little children, in ragged clothes, begging for food, gum, candy and pennies form the American personnel. Knowing little about the God of heaven, still I was fully convinced He loved the people He created in his own image, and He had a better plan for us than war where we killed one another, destroyed much of His creation and the works of our own hands.

Dorothy and I began attending the Cleveland Avenue Church of Christ where Malcolm Hinckley preached. This is the same church where we worshipped in Ponca City, Oklahoma. Dad was the janitor there, and I helped him on Saturdays. That is where I was baptized. This church operated the Children's Home in Tipton, Oklahoma where Dorothy and her siblings lived during the Great Depression.

This church had a completely different atmosphere than the officers clubs I had frequented in the army. There were no dirty jokes, no cursing and no alcohol. All seemed perfect on the surface. It was something of which I wanted to be a part. Malcolm Hinckley, the highly educated minister, was a striking figure as he mounted the pulpit each Sunday morning and evening to deliver his sermon in a quiet voice, using perfect English.

I thought: *Can I do what he does. Not without a lot more education.* On second thought: *With my background,* I felt unworthy to even think such things.

We met Mr. and Mrs. Charles Love at the congregation. They were a retired business couple who were advancing toward eighties years of age. I often sought council from them. They were forthright and honest in their kind, compassionate way. This loving couple apparently thought I had potential, and they encouraged me in every way.

Mrs. Love, a great lady, was Poet Laureate of Kansas. Through her influence, I began to understand poetry and its beauty. I have kept one of her poems for the sixty years that followed. I'd like to share the poem that has meant so much to me:

> *I saw the master paintings*
> *Hanging in hall of fame;*
> *I saw emblazoned on a wall*
> *An honored soldier's name;*
> *I heard the famous symphonies*

> *Played before noble's seat,*
> *But, yet, I saw Christ's teachings*
> *Trampled 'neath careless feet.*

At their age, Mr. and Mrs. Love weren't fond of driving their Plymouth that was manufactured before the war. So I walked about a mile to their house, drove them back to our place, picked up Dorothy and together the four of us went to church. While driving, I listened attentively to their spoken wisdom.

In the midst of this serenity came the mighty blast that sent shock waves around the world. In the Great Chihuahuan Desert, in an isolated place called White Sands Missile Range, near Alamogordo, New Mexico, USA, the first Atomic Bomb was detonated July 16.1945. That was only five days after I was released from military duty. The world will never be the same. A new weapon was born. The most deadly weapon ever devised, that could kill thousands of people with a single drop, was added to the arsenals of nations facing one another.

The all out race by nations to acquire this devastating weapon began. Espionage, lying, stealing of secrets took place. Men and women turning against their native countries for a price became all too common. The methods of war changed for the worst. Leaders of mighty nations were frightened. Innocent school children would soon be hiding under desks.

I reiterate: The world will <u>NEVER</u> be the same. THE PRE-ATOMIC AGE had come to an end. The most dangerous weapon ever devised, hangs precariously over every nation on earth, ready to be dropped, killing millions, motivated by the evil aspirations of any mad ruler who possesses it.

Printed in the United States
By Bookmasters